The Care and Feeding of Your Brain

How Diet and Environment Affect What You Think and Feel

By
Kenneth Giuffre, M.D.
with Theresa Foy DiGeronimo, M. Ed.

CAREER PRESS

Franklin Lakes, NJ

THE CARE AND FEEDING OF YOUR BRAIN
Cover design by Rossman Design
Printed in the U.S.A. by Book-mart Press

To order this title, please call toll-free 1-800-CAREER-1 (NJ and
Canada: 201-848-0310) to order using VISA or MasterCard, or for
further information on books from Career Press.

The Career Press, Inc., 3 Tice Road, PO Box 687, Franklin Lakes, NJ 07417

Library of Congress Cataloging-in-Publication Data

Giuffre, Kenneth.
    The care and feeding of your brain : how diet and environment
affect what you think and feel / by Kenneth Giuffre, with Theresa
Foy DiGeronimo.
      p.   cm.
    Includes index.
    ISBN 1-56414-380-5 (pbk.)
    1. Neuropsychology. 2. Nutrition. 3. Brain--Effect of drugs on.
4. Human ecology. 5. Intellect -- Physiological aspects.
I. DiGeronimo, Theresa Foy. II. Title.
QP360.G58   1999
613--dc21   98-48721

Dedication

To Lori

Acknowledgements

This book is my attempt to give you good advice on choosing what to do for your brain, based on the scientific work of some brilliant individuals working in a variety of areas, from medical neuroscience to traditional Chinese medicine. In doing this, I have attempted to synthesize a palatable and understandable core of concepts from a wide, diverse, and often contradictory collection of schools of thought, scientific studies, and essays from the fields of neuroscience, allopathic medicine, alternative medicine (now termed, more appropriately, "integrative medicine"), psychology, psychobiology, physics, and philosophy. The result is an abbreviated summary that owes a great deal of credit to those luminaries whose level of intense focus, example, and devotion have created a rich body of knowledge from which I was able to draw to help construct a set of recommendations to influence the "weather patterns" in your brain. My deepest thanks go out to all of those people who, in some way or another, directly influenced me, provided opportunity for exploration, and/or helped fuel my relentless obsession with the brain, mind, and consciousness.

In the area of medical neurophysiology, biology, and medicine:

Henry Seidel, Solomon and Elaine Snyder, Richard Traytsman, Rob Udelsman, George Chrousos, Lynn Loriaux, Ellen Henderson, Sanjay Datta, Dan Carr, Ted Stanley, Roger Wilson, Richard Kitz, Jeff Cooper, Larry Alessi, Tom Pollard, Jerome Torsney, Tom Sofianidas, Bob Widows, Mark Schlesinger, Arthur Lacher, Peter Migel, and Julianne Zenn.

In the areas of integrative medicine:

Joe Helms and the American Academy of Medical Acupuncture, Arnold Cianculi, Larry Jackson, Kris Tom, Larry Burk, Mietek Wirkus, Melinda Connor, Jim Laukes and the people from the University of Arizona involved in Tucson III, and all my acupuncture patients whose responses to this powerful method of healing continue to amaze and exceed my expectations.

In the areas of philosophy, religion, music, and art:

Eugene Geinzer, Harvey Rich, Frank LoBianco, Mike Rotondo, Tai Hee Kim, William Sneck, Nella Barkley, J.D. Hughes, and Armand Quinto.

In the areas of computer science, artificial intelligence, and chaos theory:

Steve Ward and Marge Sherald of Ward Systems Group, Fred DeBros and Jimmy Thompson at Mass General Hospital/MIT, Dave and Terry Anzano at Machinery Control Systems, Dr. Frank Moss, Eileen Ronca, "Big Doug" Craft, and the Trilobot Institute of Applied Research.

Furthermore, my thanks go out to those great individuals whose contributions I have admired from afar—many of whose ideas I borrowed and hopefully have done some justice to in this guide, including:

Douglas Hofstadter, Robert Sapolsky, Vernon Mountcastle, Albert Ellis, Aaron Beck, Victor Frankl, Paul and Patricia Churchland, Terry Sejnowski, Roger Penrose, Stuart Hameroff, Marilyln Schlitz, J. Allan Hobson, Marvin Minsky, Rupert Sheldrake, Larry Dossey, Andrew Weil, Herbert Benson, Matt Ridley, Simon LeVay, Rodolfo Llinas, Martin Seligman, Eric Kandel, James Schwartz, David Ruelle, Richard Feynman, Albert Einstein, Neils Bohr, David Bohm, Basil Hiley, Thomas Jessel, Thomas Merton, Ramon y Cajal, Caroline Myss, James Gleick, Benoit Mandelbrot, Ilya Prigogine, Phillip Gold, Michael Cousins, Phillip Bridenbaugh, Candace Pert, and Hans Selye.

I give special thanks to Michael Scully for his friendship and his role in helping initiate this work by introducing me to Theresa DiGeronimo.

I would also like to acknowledge many of the various clinicians, colleagues, and patients who have recently and in the past inspired me by opening up and sharing their own personal philosophies and experiences in dealing with the complex weather patterns of their own minds.

Thanks to our agent, Jeff Herman; our editors Sue Gruber, Stacey A. Farkas, and Betsy Sheldon; and our publisher, Ron Fry.

Finally, I am deeply indebted to my wife, Lori, and to my children Jacqueline, Aaron, and Jennifer, for allowing me to complete this at home and for tolerating my carting around a separate suitcase full of books, papers, and laptop computer equipment wherever we went in the Summer of 1998. And to my parents, Rita and Carmelo Giuffré, for taking the kids to their "duck house" when I went into overdrive in completing the manuscript with my wonderful and exceedingly patient co-author, Theresa.

Disclaimer

This book was written to provide accurate and authoritative information about the topics covered. In writing this, the Author is not rendering any medical or other professional service, nor does he intend this to be used as a substitute or in lieu of the reader's personal physician or any other licensed health professional.

Before utilizing this book, the reader is expected to be familiar with his or her medical history, including allergies. All treatments, descriptions, and combinations discussed in this book should be discussed in advance with your physician or health professional, who should be contacted immediately in the event of any allergic or other unexpected reaction.

The Publisher assumes no liability with respect to the efficacy or the possible side effects of the treatments and methodologies presented in this work, and all views expressed herein are strictly those of the Author.

In no event may the names or trademarks of the Author or Publisher be used in connection with the marketing or distribution of any of the combinations or derivatives described in this book.

Contents

Introduction

It is not a secret: What you put into your mouth affects your health. We have been bombarded over the past decade with nutritional advice on how to build stronger muscles, leaner bodies, healthier hearts, and cancer-resistant immune systems. We have also learned that our feelings and emotions are all part of the healthy-body package. When we feel up and happy, our bodies are stronger and healthier. When we're stressed, we're open to illness, fatigue, and depression. So what's new?

The Care and Feeding of Your Brain puts into place the last piece of the big picture—the physical health of the mind. The holistic view of mind/body health has too long ignored the fact that "mind" doesn't mean just thoughts and feelings. It means the brain—the billions of nerve cells connected by trillions of fibers, all leading to a network of brain systems that reach out and regulate every aspect of physical health. The health of these systems will determine how well you remember things, how attentive and awake you feel, how well you sleep, how you react to stress, how you perceive pain, how likely you are to fall into depression, how a woman reacts to the hormonal changes during menstruation, childbirth, and menopause, and even how sexy you feel. These things cannot be left out of the whole-body health formula. This book completes the puzzle of human well-being. Caring for your brain is an important part of caring for your health.

Perhaps the reason that the brain is the last piece of holistic health to be explored is that until recently, the functional anatomy of the human brain has been poorly understood. Obviously, invasive experiments in humans are unacceptable because of ethical reasons. But the new imaging techniques, such as positron emission tomography (PET) and single photon emission computed tomography, have made it possible now to study the neurophysiology of living humans. We can see where foods and chemicals go in the brain. We can track the effects of behavior (such as exercising or napping) on brain function. We can see what happens in the brain when certain drugs are ingested. We can scientifically answer questions such as, "Why do hot dogs zap sex drive?" "Why does marijuana ease pain?" "Why does salt aggravate the symptoms of PMS?" This is all fascinating science—and what you'll find in the pages of this book.

As you pursue a healthy mind, however, I must warn you that you cannot separate brain health from body health. In fact, it's difficult to delineate where the brain begins and the body ends. You can define neurons as part of the brain, but neurons end up on organs. The whole gastrointestinal (GI) tract, for example, has its own built-in nervous system. You can get stomach pains when you're nervous. Furthermore, certain anxious personalities are prone to certain GI disorders. There is a whole system of information transfer throughout the body that does not end at the neurons coming out of the spinal cord. It's not as though the brain and neurons can be pulled out by the roots. The brain and the body are not two separate things. They work in concert.

Although I will focus on the brain and its reaction to drugs, foods, supplements, herbs, and lifestyle choices, always keep in mind that these things affect the body as well. If this were a book about golf, we would talk about your swing, putting, driving, fairway shots, chip shots, and the clubs to use. However, the ultimate goal would be to put all the information together to win games. If you decide to work only on your putting, you'll fall short of your goal because you haven't learned how to swing on the fairway or in a sand trap. Each aspect affects that final outcome.

The way the brain and the body function together is similar. I can isolate the working pieces, but to attain the goal of total body and brain health, these pieces must all be brought together. For example, if you're diabetic because you're grossly overweight (not because of juvenile diabetes or a genetic propensity), you can expect to experience complications in blood flow to the brain that will weaken brain function. All the herbs and supplements in the world will not give you better brain function until you lose weight. In the same way, you can take gingko biloba to enhance short-term memory and prevent memory loss, but if you're out getting drunk every night, drinking a lot of coffee, and smoking cigarettes all day, you can't expect one herb to cancel out the memory-zapping effects of a negative lifestyle. There is no magic pill here.

The mind, body, and spirit are one entity called *you*. This book will show you how to feed and care for the mind. Combine this fascinating information with a healthy lifestyle that is good to your body and spirit, and you will have it all: a long, healthy, and life-affirming existence.

An Invitation

While writing this book, I found myself reminded of the introduction to Kurt Vonnegut's *Breakfast of Champions*. Vonnegut proposed the very belief that has been the driving force behind my own work:

"I tend to think of human beings as huge rubbery test tubes with chemical reactions seething inside....So it is a big temptation to me when I create a character for a novel to say that he is what he is because of faulty wiring or because of microscopic amounts of chemicals which he ate or failed to eat on that particular day."

Eerily, Vonnegut describes us all. We are what we are because of the way our brains are wired and because of the things we eat or don't eat each day. I have based my own telling of this phenomenal tale not on science fiction, but on scientific studies. However, I am well aware that what is fact today may be myth tomorrow. I encourage you to send me your comments or any supportive or contradictory literature on the subject of "brain feeding." This information will be invaluable to me in future editions of this book or in other works I will pursue on the care and feeding of the brain. You can contact me at the following address:

Kenneth Giuffre, MD
Trilobot Institute for Applied Cognitive Research
637 Wyckoff Ave., Suite 235
Wyckoff, N.J. 07481
Kenbrain@neurostuff.com

Chapter 1

The Big Picture: From Nerve Cells to Brain Function

I remember back in my neuroscience class in medical school when, in amazement, I held a preserved brain in my hands for the first time. I didn't know whose brain it was. Maybe it belonged to a former graduate who donated his or her body to the school, or a World War I flying ace, or a mother who died during childbirth. I remember thinking that it was so astonishingly small for all of its complexity and capability—for all it had done for this deceased person, whoever he or she might have been. Although difficult to describe, this was the most beautiful creation of nature I had ever seen.

Inside the brain are hundreds of billions of nerve cells connected by trillions of fibers called axons and dendrites. The activity between them controls your thoughts, feelings, drives, aspirations, and personality. This control center of all that you do, think, and feel is very vulnerable to its environment as it floats in a bath of cerebrospinal fluid—much like a fish in a tank. A fish will passively absorb whatever you put in its tank. I was fascinated by this fact even as a little kid. My friends and I used to sneak into the pet store and drop a sugar cube into one of the fish tanks. After about 15 minutes, the fish, especially the small ones, would dart around as if someone had turned on a switch. In many ways, the brain is similar in the way it reacts to foods, drugs, herbs, bodily activities, and lifestyles.

The Millions of Things That Affect the Brain

In this book I will explain how certain things you eat and do affect conditions in the brain in either a "boosting" or a "zapping" way.

Choosing the topics to include was not easy. My first goal was to provide recommendations based on scientific knowledge currently available. Most of what I have included, particularly in the way of herbal treatments, foods, lifestyles, and supplements, is based on scientific data. (If not, I have indicated so.) I also indicate where I think a lot of hoopla is being made over nothing.

I admit that the recommendations you'll find in the coming chapters are not all-inclusive. There are literally millions of things we do and eat that affect brain function. Obviously, I had to be selective. There are, for example, thousands of plants and other derivatives from nature alone, which are discussed in the Traditional Chinese and Indian Ayurvedic literature on healing. Each of these is a complex science in itself and would require volumes to describe. Also, many of the ingredients for a complete regimen are either unavailable in the United States or are very hard to find (and when they are found, their purity, cleanliness, and authenticity are frequently questionable).

Most of the treatments, herbs, and supplements described in this book are readily available at your local drug or health food store. Most are from industry standard preparations, and their safety and purity is generally more uniform than some of the more obscure and rarer remedies. The recommendations are at least partially supported by scientific data, or are popular enough to require some comment because of their prevalence in either the culture, news media, or in general use. I have tried to include some rationale as to the degree in which I favor or oppose each remedy and its effect on the mind.

A Butterfly Flapping in the Brain

One thing that is not debatable is the fact that the brain is complex and chaotic, because of all of the hundreds of different types of molecules that influence it and all the cross-connecting neurons that conduct impulses through it. In addition, every one of these hundreds of billions of interconnected neurons has a fine network within it that is made up of pathways called microtubules. These may carry information as well, and their interconnections within a single one of these neurons may each be as complicated as a "minibrain" in itself.

In this complex brain system, no single neurotransmitter, neural pathway, or brain region works alone. Just as a symphonic masterpiece is the result of many individual instruments working together in harmony and balance, brain function is the end result of all the neural elements working together in concert.

Traditional neuroscience doesn't always acknowledge the extreme interdependency of each neurotransmitter. In contrast, older theories, such as traditional Chinese medicine, acupuncture, and bio-energetic models, and newer theories, such as chaos theory, fractal geometry, and even quantum mechanics, all seem to accept this concept of brain function as a symphony of interdependent activities resulting in the whole that we refer to as a person.

In relation to chaos theory, for example, Benoit Mandelbrot, the "father" of fractal geometry, devised the now-famous and often-quoted "butterfly concept" that states that even a minor air disturbance from a butterfly flapping its wings in China will eventually affect weather patterns everywhere. In the same way, the sum total concert of brain function involves individual interactions between billions of neurons representing trillions of separate yet interdependent simultaneous activities, each one affecting the whole in some significant way.

This is the reason it is inaccurate to compare the brain to a computer, imagining an instantaneous booting-up process that occurs the same way every time, by the flip of a single switch. A more accurate picture would be a comparison to the Earth's complex and chaotic weather patterns, which are always changing, often unpredictable, and influenced by many factors. For instance, just as weather varies with such factors as barometric pressure, the Earth's rotation, temperature, time of year, moon position, and so on, the state of the brain is affected by varying levels of neurotransmitters, such as dopamine, norepinephrine, serotonin, and histamine, as well as the predominant emotional state, the time of day, lifestyle choices, and the intake of certain foods, drugs, and supplements. As I discuss each of these things in this book, you must keep in mind that nothing works independently; all substances and effects we discuss work together.

Keeping It Simple

To explain why a food, drug, supplement, herb, or lifestyle choice will boost or zap conditions in the brain, it is necessary to understand a certain amount of basic anatomy and biology. In the name of clarity, you'll find that I have occasionally simplified the process of brain function in cases where I felt it would not be misleading. For instance, there are many types of receptors on neurons that respond to molecules such as opiates, serotonin, gamma-aminobutyric acid (GABA), and others. However, I generally only mention them as if there were a single type of responsive receptor, or molecule type. If I were to include every detail of brain interaction and function, this would read like a rather boring medical text and would not inform or enlighten you. If you find an area of interest that you would like to know more about, check the section at the end of this book for further, more detailed resources.

Brain Power 101

To fully understand why a cup of coffee and a cigarette can zap your memory, you'll need to know how the brain works. What makes it strong and healthy? What makes it weak and vulnerable? The answers lie in the facts of brain anatomy. The following quick tour through the central nervous system will give you some background to take with you into the upcoming chapters.

The Central Nervous System

The brain and spinal cord make up what is called the central nervous system. These structures are comprised of neurons and different types of support cells that are thought to help keep up with the high maintenance and metabolic (glucose and oxygen) demands of the specialized nerve cells.

The central nervous system has two general classes of material—gray and white matter. When you look at a brain slice without using a microscope, the outside has a gray hue and much of the inner region, a whiter hue. The opposite occurs in the spinal cord, which is mostly white. The white color is from the myelin insulation. It is where long tracts of fibers run—like the main communication trunks on a phone system. The switching areas, where nerve cells or neurons synapse with other neurons and where cell bodies exist, are grayish. Most of the brain structures I will talk about are made up mainly of gray matter. This is where all the action occurs.

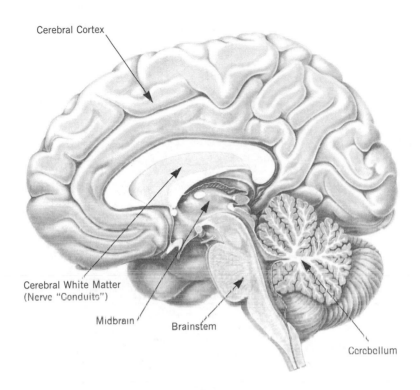

Cerebral Cortex

Cerebral White Matter
(Nerve "Conduits")

Midbrain

Brainstem

Cerebellum

FIGURE 1A

The Brain

The brain is subdivided into four major areas. (See Figure 1A.) From the top down, you'll find: 1) the *cerebral cortex,* which I refer to throughout most of the book as the cortex; 2) the *midbrain,* which contains a lot of the switching areas where nerves that pass up from below go to and from the cortex; 3) the *brainstem,* where much of the basic nervous system controls sit (coma occurs when this malfunctions, and death occurs when it is severed); and 4) the *cerebellum,* which sits behind the upper part of the brainstem and has traditionally been thought to regulate coordination of complex movements.

Before jumping into a chapter on a specific aspect of life regulated by the brain, take a minute to stop here and learn the basics of these four parts of the brain that will be referred to throughout the book.

The Cerebral Cortex

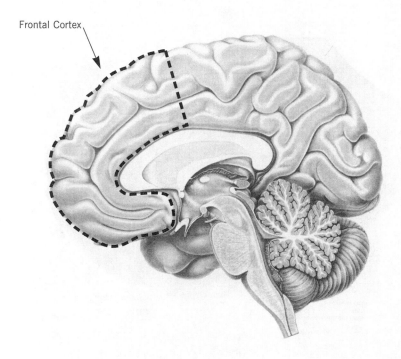

Frontal Cortex

FIGURE 1B

The cerebral cortex is the most newly evolved region of the brain and it is the part that separates humans from all the other mammals, especially the area in the front, appropriately named the *frontal cortex*. (See Figure 1B.) This area acts as a bridge between the sensory and motor circuits of the rest of the cortex and the older, deeper structures of the limbic system, which regulate drive and emotion. The frontal cortex is probably where much of our complex and abstract thoughts occur. It is probably where we put today in context with yesterday and tomorrow. When the frontal lobe is damaged, we become either more reactive and hypersexual like wild animals (without the step of logic in between to stop us) or very docile and unconcerned.

Behind the frontal cortex are the sensory and motor regions of the cortex, each divided up to correspond with specific areas on the opposite side of the body. Along the side are two protruding horns of cortex called the *temporal lobes*. Here, much of the processing of sound and verbal information occurs. Inside sits a deeper part of the limbic system called the *hippocampus*. The hippocampus acts like a way-station that coordinates the placement of information as it moves from sensory input to other areas of the brain. (You'll learn more details about the hippocampus in Chapter 3.)

In the back is the *occipital cortex*, where much of the processing of visual information occurs. The remaining areas along the side above the temporal horns form the *parietal cortex*. These areas are thought to be where a lot of cross-connection between the different sensory structures occurs. When the right side of the parietal cortex is damaged, very bizarre perceptions and reactions occur, such as ignoring one side of your body because you think it is a stranger.

The limbic system consists of the hippocampus, the rim of cortex on the inside of the halves around the corpus callosum called the *cingulate cortex*, and two almond shaped heads near the frontal region, each one called the *amygdala*. This set of structures is the closest thing to what Freud referred to as the id, the seat of emotion and animal drive. It is the older region of the cortex in terms of evolution, and is also involved in memory. I will discuss its important roles in the sexual response, the stress response, sleep, and depression.

Strange things can happen when the cortex is damaged. (A great book on this subject is *The Man Who Mistook His Wife for a Hat*, by Dr. Oliver Sacks.) I find this particularly fascinating because it means that who you are as a person in terms of identity and interaction with other people depends completely on the complex and precise interaction of all these neural areas. It suggests that your identity depends on your neurology and not merely on a spirit living in your body.

The Midbrain

The midbrain is made up of three parts: 1) the *thalamus*, which is the main switching area of the sensory system; 2) the *hypothalamus*, which is an important but tiny area controlling body temperature and organ function; and 3) the *pituitary gland* (connected to the hypothalamus), which sends many hormones into the bloodstream to control the body stress response, the sexual response, the menstrual cycles, and growth and development. (See Figure 1C.)

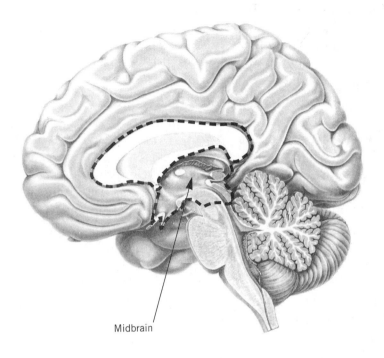

Midbrain

FIGURE 1C

The Brainstem

The brainstem is where the upper brain connects with the spinal cord. (See Figure 1D.) This area controls the autonomic nervous system. This is also where the *reticular activating system* originates from. (If the reticular activating system is damaged, unconsciousness and coma result.) The brainstem is like the light switch of the cortex. It sends axons of nerve cells that make the stimulant amine neurotransmitters norepinephrine, serotonin, dopamine, and histamine. These are essential to the alert conscious state, and when depleted, result in everything from narcolepsy (uncontrollably falling asleep) to depression. They are major players in many of the brain responses described throughout this book.

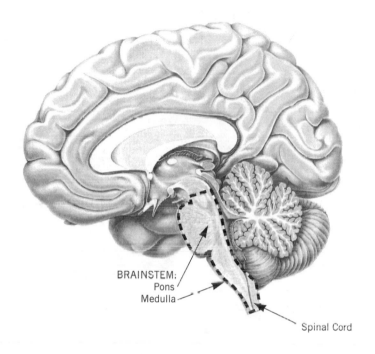

BRAINSTEM:
Pons
Medulla

Spinal Cord

FIGURE 1D

Also located in the brainstem are the control areas for eye movement, the switching areas for hearing and balance, and the motor and sensory connection areas for the face, nose, and mouth. All of the spinal cord nerves to and from the cortex pass through here, along with those to and from the cerebellum.

The Cerebellum

The cerebellum sits behind the brainstem and consists of a regular, repeating pattern of nerve cells. (See Figure 1E.) The wiring between them seems to control and remember complex sequences of movement and balance control. It has recently been discovered that the cerebellum is involved in rapidly processing incoming sensory information to produce automatic responses (such as when you show excitement at a good poker hand before you realize it). You'll learn more about its role in processing pain and stress in later chapters.

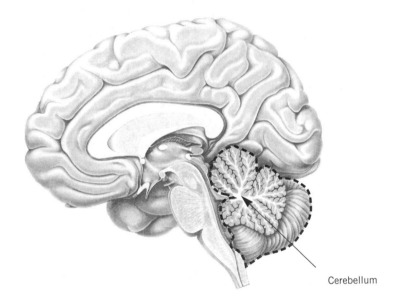

Cerebellum

FIGURE 1E

The Spinal Cord

In addition to carrying information from sensory nerves in skin, muscle, bone, and other tissue, the spinal cord sends motor impulses to muscles to make individual areas of muscle contract in a coordinated fashion. Each motor nerve is an axon that synapses on a small unit of muscle, releasing acetylcholine, the neurotransmitter of muscle contraction. These motor and sensory fibers leave the spinal cord as nerve roots at every level of bone segment or vertebra. Nerve roots branch out to form the nerves that travel throughout the rest of the body.

The spinal cord also has its own complex control circuits, including the reflexes, where an incoming impulse causes a motor output to muscle before it reaches the brain. This is what causes your bicep muscle to rapidly contract and pull your arm away from a hot stove before you feel it. These circuits are described in greater detail in Chapter 7.

The Autonomic Nervous System

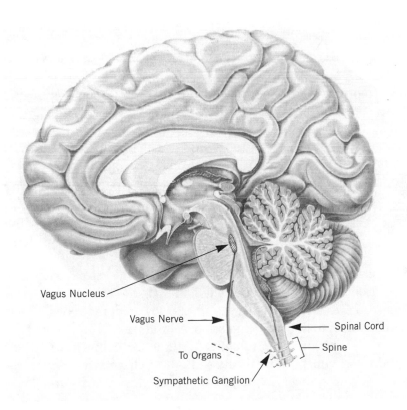

Vagus Nucleus

Vagus Nerve

To Organs

Sympathetic Ganglion

Spinal Cord

Spine

FIGURE 1F

The Care and Feeding of Your Brain

The nerves that travel from the spinal cord throughout the body are regulated by the *autonomic nervous system.* (See Figure 1F.) This system controls organs that you don't voluntarily control, such as your heart, your digestive tract, blood vessels, blood pressure, bladder, and sexual organs. It is divided into the *sympathetic* and *parasympathetic nervous systems.*

Each starts with its control centers in the hypothalamus and the brainstem. They respond to stress messages sent either from the spinal cord, the cerebellum, or the limbic system. Generally, in adults, stress activates the sympathetic system—known as fight-or-flight—and it deactivates the parasympathetic system—known as the relaxation response. (You'll see how this system is affected by the things we feed the brain in many chapters, especially Chapter 6.)

The sympathetic system consists of ganglia, or bead-like collections of cell bodies, that sit along the spine, receiving spinal branches all the way down. In response to stress, each "bead" or ganglion sends out a branch to major organs, such as the heart (speeding it up and increasing its force of contraction), the lungs (causing opening of the bronchial tubules), salivary glands (causing dry mouth), pupils (causing dilation), and other organs, the most important of which is the adrenal glands on the top of the kidneys. Here, the sympathetic nervous system stimulates the glands to release epinephrine (adrenaline) into the bloodstream, exaggerating the stress effects. The main neurotransmitter in these sympathetic nerve fibers to the organs is norepinephrine, the same activating amine that projects from the brainstem to the cortex for alert focus, also needed during fight-or-flight.

The parasympathetic system, or relaxation system, sends fibers from an area in the brainstem called the *vagus nucleus* that becomes the *vagus nerve,* and from nerves in the lower spinal cord. This system causes heart slowing, digestive stimulation, pupil constriction, salivation, relaxation of sphincters to allow for urination and defecation, and other effects to be discussed later. The main neurotransmitter to the organs is acetylcholine (remember this word—you'll see it a lot in the upcoming chapters).

Together, the brain and spinal cord function 24 hours a day, 365 days a year, nonstop from conception to death. The quality and health of life is profoundly affected by the way you feed and care for these complex pieces of anatomy.

Chapter 2

Alertness: Getting the Brain Ready to Think

The brain never shuts down completely, but it is not always alert or working at full capacity. You've probably noticed that there are times when your mind is alert and focused—you follow even the most complex directions and explanations with ease; you are able to concentrate and think clearly without effort; you're right on the ball. But then there are other times when your mind wanders and you lose track of even a simple conversation; you read basic information and come up blank; it takes great effort to stay focused on your work. Have you ever wondered why this happens? The reasons are not as random or uncontrollable as you might think. Common drugs, foods, lifestyle choices, and supplements have a profound effect on when and to what degree your mind can "boot up" to full capacity. In this chapter we will take a look at the internal and external factors that keep your thinking sharp and focused or make it muddled and scattered.

The Holistic Brain

There are several small areas near the brainstem that send projections all over the cortex (as if the cortex were a parachute and the projections its cords). These projections begin in the reticular activating system (where the upper brainstem meets the midbrain), and each type sends a different brain chemical (neurotransmitter) via these projections, which spread out to cover wide areas of the brain. There are several thousand neurons at the base of each "cord." Although this sounds like a lot, it's a relative drop in the bucket if you consider that each cord from these brainstem nuclei sends projections and its specific neurotransmitter substance to literally billions of neurons all over the brain. When you realize that each of these billions of neurons has some small effect on wakefulness, attention, and ability to focus, you begin to get a general idea of how impressive the holistic functioning of a brain truly is!

Blood Flow and Brain Power

Positron emission tomography (PET) scanning has shed new light on the workings of the living human brain, including insight into what happens when we pay attention. Patients undergoing a PET scan are first given a radioactive form of glucose, which is taken up by active brain cells and sensed by the scanner. The resulting scan reveals a detailed view of the brain showing where cells are most active. Brain cells that are more active use more glucose and hence, active areas show up on the image as bright areas. Through mechanisms still under study, active brain regions also draw blood flow toward them. Brain cell regions not active at any given moment have limited glucose metabolism and blood flow and do not "light up." For example, when someone is awake but not focused on a particular thought or object, the PET scan will show generalized activity and blood flow everywhere. But when that person focuses intensely on something, you'll see the blood flow directed to very specific areas of the brain. If, for example, the person focuses on a picture, you'll see increased blood flow in the areas involved in optical processing. If the person concentrates on music or speech, the areas involved in deciphering complex sound patterns light up. A focused brain shows blood flow to very specific areas. This same process explains what happens when you lose the ability to concentrate. The blood flow is robbed from the areas where it is needed most and spread over the entire brain in a very nonspecific and "unfocused" way.

How Experience Affects Intense Concentration

Experience will affect the brain's ability to concentrate. This is proven by comparing the PET scans of someone learning a new skill to someone well-experienced in the skill. A person learning to drive a stick-shift car, for example, is thinking of many things at once: right foot pressing gently on the gas pedal, left foot easing up on the clutch, right hand putting the car into gear, left hand steering, eyes watching the road, and so on. That person is focused intensely on the job at hand while paying little mind to the radio, conversation, or a cellular phone. Even though a great deal of focus is being attempted, a PET scan of this inexperienced driver would show generalized blood flow all over the brain (an indication of lack of focus). In contrast, a scan of an experienced stick-shift driver would be quite different. You would not see blood flowing to each brain region responsible for visual input, memory retrieval, or motor control of the right foot, left foot, hands, eyes, and so on. Instead, the blood flow would be efficiently concentrated to a few specific areas needed to drive safely and reach a given destination without paying particular attention to the task at hand. In this brain state, you can drive, listen to the radio, and talk on the cellular phone at the same time without giving much attention to each shift of the gears. Clearly, focus involves the ability to filter out distractions in lieu of concentrating on a single object, goal, or purpose. In this definition of a focused state, the driver is still alert enough to notice when a distraction suddenly becomes important, such as when the row of telephone poles on the side of the road gets too close to the car.

> *Children with attention deficit disorder (ADD) live in a state of "hyperfocus." Unlike other children who, on demand, can focus their attention on one task or input (thus bringing the blood supply into specific areas of need), ADD children continuously concentrate and focus on the newest distraction to present itself. This rapidly changing mode of hyperfocus is seen as a generalized blood flow all over the brain, preventing organized attention to any one thing. The brain of an ADD child is like a warship on which the entire crew is working furiously and constantly merely to keep the ship afloat. When something out of the ordinary happens, the already-fragile system fails to adapt, and chaos takes over. There is no captain to direct crew members to the area of the ship in greatest need of attention. The brain of a child without ADD functions more like an organized ship, where everyone does his or her job according to a master plan without frantic effort and where emergencies are planned for and handled in a coordinated fashion.*

Alertness Boosters and Zappers

The awake brain is called to attention thousands of times each day. Although we expect it always to be in a state of readiness to help us concentrate and focus when we need to, there are different degrees of wakefulness. Sometimes the brain responds with quick, sharp thinking. Other times it responds with slow, disorganized, fuzzy thinking. The level of alertness or fatigue has a lot to do with the way the brain is fed and cared for. Sometimes it receives what it needs to boot up efficiently; sometimes it doesn't. The rest of this chapter will explain how we can influence our level of alertness and readiness by recognizing the effect of neurotransmitters, drugs, foods, lifestyle choices, and supplements.

Boosters and Zappers in Your Own Body

Adequate and balanced supplies of certain brain chemicals (called neurotransmitters) are necessary for booting up the brain to an alert state. Projections of nerve cells that release the neurotransmitters acetylcholine, dopamine, histamine, norepinephrine, and serotonin act together to stimulate the higher cortex and produce a sharp and attentive state. An imbalance in the production and/or distribution of any of these chemicals will zap the brain's ability to act alertly.

Booster: *Acetylcholine*

Unlike the other neurotransmitters produced in specific brain-stem nuclei, acetylcholine is produced and used all over the brain. It is found in the cerebral cortex, the hippocampus (involved in memory), the basal ganglia (involved in motor function), and the cerebellum (involved in vocal and motor coordination). This essential and versatile brain chemical has many vital functions—one of which is the ability to affect awareness and wakefulness. In fact, patients recovering from the effects of anesthesia are often given a drug called physostiginine, which raises brain levels of acetylcholine to help make them more aware and able to focus.

A deficiency of acetylcholine causes memory loss and eventually impairs all cognitive brain functions. Without adequate supplies of this chemical, you'll find your memory slipping (see Chapter 3), and over time, you'll notice a global decline in brain function that makes it difficult if not impossible to concentrate and pay attention. The ability to boot up the mind is lost when the levels of acetylcholine are low.

Booster: *Dopamine*

Dopamine is essential for alert awareness and seems to be involved in the excitement you feel from novel stimuli, such as a new love or a foreign adventure. In new, exciting situations, your state of awareness and focus is called to attention. On the darker side, dopamine is also probably the neurotransmitter most responsible for the initial excitement that comes with drugs such as alcohol, cocaine, and amphetamines, and may be responsible for certain addictive behaviors.

Dopamine is produced in nuclei near the reticular activating system. The most notable place where dopamine neurons begin is in the *substantia nigra*, a region essential for the control of voluntary movement and the prevention of involuntary movement such as tics and tremors. The degeneration of this area and, therefore, the loss of dopamine neurons, is the cause of Parkinson's disease, which results in hand tremors and a loss of cognitive brain function. Over time, the ability to remember, pay attention, and effectively boot up the brain in response to new stimuli is lost.

The drug L-dopa boosts dopamine levels and has had much success in the treatment of Parkinson's and Parkinson's-like conditions.

Booster: *Enzymes*

A brain enzyme called monoamine oxidase breaks down norepinephrine, serotonin, and dopamine after they are deposited at the junctions between brain neurons. This normally prevents overstimulation and exhaustion of these neurons. By another mechanism, called re-uptake, these substances are taken up again into the neurons that released them to be used again when needed. Both processes are absolutely necessary to keep the brain in balance so that it can boot up and focus in a consistent and reliable manner.

Booster & Zapper: *Glutamate*

Glutamate is the primary excitatory transmitter in the brain. It is involved in "exciting," or calling to action, most brain cells in the cortex. This call to attention occurs when excited glutamate receptors allow calcium to enter nerve cells. This immediately makes the cells ready for action. This process is vital to brain cell function and therefore to our ability to think and concentrate.

An inadequate supply of glutamate makes it impossible to think quickly and clearly. On the other hand, overstimulation of glutamate receptors seems to be harmful to brain cells—a state called excitotoxicity. When activated, glutamate receptors cause calcium ions to enter nerve cells, increasing their excitability. Eventually, this process may result in cell death. Hence, a chronically overexcited brain (as occurs in chronic use of stimulants, such as amphetamines and cocaine, and in some mental disorders) literally becomes worn out through gradual cell death. This weakens and eventually destroys the ability to pay attention and concentrate.

Booster: *Histamine*

Histamine projections to the cortex originate near a structure at the base of the brain called the hypothalamus. Histamine increases brain metabolism, making it easier to concentrate. Clearly, drugs that block histamine's actions (like the antihistamine Benadryl) cause sleepiness, making it difficult to focus and stay attentive.

Booster: *Norepinephrine*

Another major set of neuron projections release norepinephrine to most of the cortex. Also involved in producing the conscious state, they originate in a cell grouping or nucleus in the brainstem called the *locus ceruleus*. Norepinephrine is a neurotransmitter related to adrenaline (epinephrine). It causes generalized activation in many areas of the brain and is absolutely vital to the booting-up process. This substance activates cortex neurons into a state of "readiness," while constricting blood flow so that only areas truly active will receive it.

Booster & Zapper: *Serotonin*

A few thousand nerve cells in the brainstem (*raphe nuclei*) send projections into all parts of the brain (especially the higher cortex), releasing serotonin. The direct effect of serotonin is mysterious, even paradoxical. You can't be awake without it and it is absolutely necessary to concentrate, yet too much serotonin makes you fall asleep.

High levels of serotonin result in the opening of brain blood vessels, zapping wakefulness by diminishing the brain's ability to focus blood flow to the most-needed areas and to shut down flow to the less-needed areas. This causes everything from sleepiness to fatigue. Mental fatigue impairs the mind's ability to focus well—and so the mind begins to wander. PET scans reveal diffuse patterns of blood flow all over the brain, instead of focused flow specifically to areas needed most for specific functions (such as the visual cortex when reading the newspaper). High serotonin zaps attention and makes the whole brain sleepy and unfocused. (In contrast, low brain serotonin is seen in states of anger, anxiety, depression, and aggression.)

Boosters and Zappers in Drugs

Seven classes of the most habitually used drugs initially stimulate and may even help focus the mind. But they eventually impair this ability, and over time, many cause cell death. These seven classes are:

1. Alcohol.
2. Caffeine.
3. Marijuana.
4. Nicotine.
5. Psychedelics (such as LSD, ketamine, and PCP).
6. Sedatives (such as barbiturates and Valium-like drugs called benzodiazepines).
7. Stimulants (such as amphetamines and cocaine).

Initially, these drugs boot up the mind by causing a sudden increase in dopamine levels and by stimulating certain neurons. With chronic or high-dose usage, they shut down the brain's ability to pay attention. This occurs through direct toxicity, as with alcohol, or by excitotoxicity, and can result in cell death. This dual action of focusing and unfocusing occurs via two main mechanisms:

1. Vasoconstriction: Caffeine, nicotine, and amphetamine-type stimulants cause blood vessel constriction and limit the free flow of blood in the cortex. This readies the brain for attention and action by stopping blood from rushing all over the brain in a free-flow, scattered manner (which can cause inattention and lack of focus). As a result, blood can be directed in large amounts to areas that become activated.

Over time, however, this vasoconstrictive effect backfires. All the cells that have been artificially limited from having a full blood supply demand increased blood flow and even become resistant to the drug. Without the drug, you get massive dilation and inability to focus. A coffee drinker who misses that morning dose feels unfocused and often gets a terrible headache from this increased blood flow.

2. Excitatory reaction: Caffeine, nicotine, psychedelics, direct stimulants (cocaine, amphetamines), sedatives, alcohol, and marijuana are all excitatory drugs. Like the natural neurotransmitter glutamate previously discussed, these drugs excite brain cells toward activation by pushing the glutamate receptors open and allowing calcium to enter. The initial reaction is a sharp, clear, attentive mind that is ready to activate specific areas as needed. Over time, these cells that are artificially forced open to calcium become fatigued and worn and may suffer from excitotoxicity. As they wear out, thinking becomes dull and slow. In extreme cases (as with cocaine and amphetamine abuse), symptoms of severe mental exhaustion, such as paranoia and delusional behavior, can result. Over time, cells die and permanent damage results. (The use of caffeine and of stimulants to treat hyperactivity disorders is probably an exception to this occurrence.)

Booster & Zapper: *Alcohol*

Alcohol is a depressant, so it is not generally included on the list of drugs that boot up the brain. However, initially it does stimulate the same kind of call to action as the stimulants. Alcohol generally depresses neurons in the cerebral cortex. The first neurons to go are the ones that inhibit certain thoughts and actions. With alcohol in the system, we're not as shy about talking loudly, joking boisterously, making new friends, revealing secrets, and so on.

Eventually, over time, pouring alcohol into your system will shut down the brain's ability to function efficiently in two ways: 1) Through a mechanism similar to that used to produce general anesthesia, all cortex function is shut down; and 2) there is a direct toxic effect on brain cells that causes significant cell loss in regular binge drinkers.

Caffeine, nicotine, direct stimulants (such as amphetamines and cocaine), psychedelics (such as LSD, ketamine, and PCP), sedatives (such as barbiturates and Valium-like drugs called benzodiazepines), alcohol, and marijuana all have a withdrawal effect that mimics a deficiency of the booting-up neurotransmitters, particularly dopamine. This happens because, over time, the higher levels of these neurotransmitters (caused by these drugs) become the norm, so that when the drugs are taken away, these levels suddenly fall off causing a withdrawal symptom of fuzzy thinking. This may explain the finding reported in Nature that suggested that smokers who suddenly stop smoking have fewer car accidents after they resume their habit.

Zapper: *Antihistamines*

Histamines are brain chemicals released to excite and arouse brain function. An antihistamine works to inhibit this action—it blocks the histamine receptors that help produce full awareness and wakefulness. That's why antihistamines in over-the-counter medications, such as Benadryl and NyQuil, come with warnings that the medication may make you drowsy. If you need to think and concentrate with great clarity, you should heed this warning. Taking an antihistamine to combat a head cold will leave you feeling sleepy and confused.

Booster & Zapper: *Caffeine*

As all coffee drinkers know, caffeine helps boot up the mind. It may sound like a cliché to say, "I can't think until I've had my morning cup of coffee," but for many people, it's absolutely true!

Caffeine works to focus attention in several ways:

♦ It causes vasoconstriction (as previously explained), which increases the ability to concentrate, because only those areas that really need increased blood flow are strong enough to open up the constricted blood vessels. This cleans up the generalized flow that scatters focus.

♦ As explained, caffeine is an excitatory drug that stimulates the glutamate receptors to open up and accept more calcium. This action excites the brain cells into action.

♦ Caffeine creates a state in the brain that stimulates an overload of acetylcholine—the chemical necessary for clear, focused, cognitive thinking. This results in initial clarity followed by fogginess, especially after several cups of coffee.

So far, caffeine is not known to kill brain cells through excitotoxicity, but excessive use mimics effects of mental exhaustion by impairing focus and even causing nervousness, jumpiness, and actual physical tremors.

Zapper: *Marijuana*

You may have heard users of marijuana claim that the drug helps them reflect and think clearly. Some college students say they smoke pot while they study to help them concentrate. It's understandable how a person might believe that pot improves the ability to focus: Like a sedative, marijuana has the ability to relieve anxiety, which makes it difficult to focus (see "stress" on pages 45 to 46). In fact, the brain's ability to concentrate is wiped out by marijuana.

Although marijuana, like the other stimulants mentioned, initially causes an increase in brain dopamine, it acts through specific receptors called *cannabinoid receptors*. They are found in many areas of the brain (including the cortex and hippocampus) and are activated by the ingredient in marijuana called tetrahydrocannabinol or THC. When activated, the brain's ability to maintain a balanced state of awareness, cognition, and coordination is impaired. Although the "motivational syndrome" associated with marijuana (that claims to rob chronic users of motivational desire and leaves them in a state of perpetual apathy) is unproved, there is some clinical evidence that changes from long-term use affect brain efficiency. Even rats who are given THC have trouble navigating mazes for up to several months after their last dose.

Booster & Zapper: *Nicotine*

Many smokers say that smoking helps them to think clearly. They're right—to a point. Initially, as an excitatory drug, nicotine causes vasoconstriction in the brain (which directs blood flow to the brain cells that need it to focus, as previously explained). It also acts like acetylcholine in the brain by stimulating the brain cells involved in arousal and attention.

However, over time, the zapping effects of nicotine on the brain's ability to function at full speed far exceed the short-term initial benefit in the following ways:

1. Nicotine causes an increase in free radical production that impairs brain function. Free radicals are waste products released when the body burns its fuel for energy. Under ideal conditions, these molecules are kept in check by antioxidants released by cells of the immune system, or by natural antioxidant substances found in the blood stream, certain foods, and the liver. (Antioxidant is a term for substances that absorb or scavenge free radicals). A problem occurs when too many free radicals are generated and overload the body's scavenging mechanism. Free radicals are highly reactive molecular fragments that bond with virtually any biological carbon-based substance with which they come into contact. Free radicals bind to proteins, membranes, DNA, and the protein enzymes that help repair DNA, which weakens the cells, impairs cell function, and shortens cell life. This ultimately causes impaired brain cell function and even cell death.

2. Nicotine promotes plaque formation in the arteries (arteriosclerosis) that can reduce blood flow to the brain and impair the brain's ability to focus.

3. Through chronic overstimulation of the acetylcholine and glutamate receptors, nicotine causes excitotoxicity.

4. Smoking reduces the amount of oxygen and increases the amount of carbon dioxide and carbon monoxide that is delivered to the brain. Reduced oxygen supply has a direct effect on the brain's ability to think clearly. It also promotes free radical formation.

   As explained earlier, nicotine is an excitatory drug and a vasoconstrictor that in the long run weakens and eventually destroys brain cells.

The attention-zapping effects of nicotine can be critical. A recent study by researchers at Erasmus University in the Netherlands found that smokers were at more than double the risk of getting dementia and Alzheimer's dementia, a condition where there is massive brain cell loss and actual changes in brain size.

Booster & Zapper: *Psychedelics*

Another group of brain stimulants is the psychedelics. These include LSD, MPTP (a harmful side product of MDMA or Ecstasy), ketamine (Special K), and PCP. These drugs have an immediate and profound ability to boot up the brain because they enhance both serotonin and dopamine release. Initially, these drugs give a feeling of intense awareness and focus. However, chronic or high-dose usage of psychedelics has been shown to deplete serotonin levels and have a toxic effect on dopamine neurons. When the brain does not get an adequate supply of these two vital neurotransmitters, its ability to think clearly is shut down. That's why "spaced out" is a term that aptly describes "hard" drug users.

Zapper: *Sedatives*

Directly, sedatives depress and "sedate" brain function. All sedatives (including barbiturates and benzodiazepines, which are Valium and Valium-like drugs) inhibit the brain's power to think clearly and focus by enhancing the sensitivity of gamma-aminobutyric acid (GABA) receptors on the brain cells in the cerebral cortex. Just as stimulants enhance the tendency of brain cells to act, GABA receptors decrease or inhibit brain cell action.

Indirectly, in certain cases of chronic stress or anxiety, sedatives can be used to help some people concentrate better. Chronic stress or anxiety interferes with a person's ability to focus and think clearly. By eliminating this anxiety, brain function may initially improve, provided the proper dosage is given. In higher doses or when used for a long time, sedatives cause mental depression and impair the ability to think clearly.

Booster & Zapper: *Stimulants*

As you will remember reading earlier in this chapter, there are five major natural chemicals that call the brain to attention. Direct stimulants like amphetamines and cocaine act on four of them: glutamate, norepinephrine, dopamine, and serotonin.

It's no wonder amphetamines are called stimulants and "uppers." At once, they call to attention four of the five neurotransmitters needed for sharp, clear, focused thinking. They awaken the brain, making it feel alert and ready to go.

Actually, what they create is an artificial state of immediate stress. When first threatened by internal stress (such as sudden fear) or external stress (such as a minor car accident), the brain jumps to an alert state so it can focus clearly on what needs to be done. Amphetamines and cocaine cause the same reaction. But when the stress continues over time, or when amphetamines or cocaine are used repeatedly, the brain can't maintain its high level of alertness and it becomes "stressed out." This results in fatigue, paranoia, and psychotic reactions. Physical effects such as hypertension, cardiac problems, and other bodily illness may result. An initial boost plummets to eventual brain cell destruction.

Boosters and Zappers in Foods

There are few specific foods that can claim to call the mind to attention. Still, the following information will help you see how your caloric intake and a food additive can affect brain power.

Booster: *Low-calorie diet*

A low-calorie diet is not only good for your waistline, it is good for increasing brain awareness. I'm not advocating here that you starve yourself to improve your powers of concentration, but it has been proven that the brain is most alert in a state of starvation. We can assume that this happens because the primitive human needed to be most alert when hunting for food to satisfy hunger. A starving predator is much more aware of his or her surroundings than one with a full belly. Animal studies repeatedly show that alertness and concentration improve when calories are restricted below so-called "normal" levels. This information tells us that if we want to be mentally sharp for a 1 p.m. business meeting, it's not a good idea to eat a heavy lunch at noon.

Zapper: *MSG*

Monosodium glutamate (MSG) is a food additive that dilates the blood vessels in the cortex and excites glutamate receptors, loosening blood flow to the brain and zapping focus and attention.

Glutamate, you may recall, is the neurotransmitter responsible for exciting cells into action. Stimulating specific glutamate receptors will enhance brain function in a specific area of need. But if MSG calls all glutamate receptors into action at once, vasodilation occurs, scattering blood flow all over the brain, and robbing the areas that need concentrated blood flow when called into action.

Not only will MSG muddle thinking, but continuous glutamate excitement and vasodilation can result in excitotoxicity, in which brain cells become fatigued, worn out, and eventually destroyed.

You can avoid this alertness-zapping effect by avoiding foods that contain the MSG additive. This is easier said than done, because MSG is frequently a "hidden" additive that does not appear on food labels. It is commonly called "natural flavors" and is found in most commercial salad dressings, soup bases, and meat stocks, as well as dairy products, sauces, seasoning mixtures, frozen foods, teas, and many convenience foods.

The infamous MSG headache is caused by vasodilation. As the blood vessels all over the cortex open at once, there is increased pressure on the sensitive outer lining of the brain called the meninges.

Boosters and Zappers in Supplements

There are a few supplements on the market that may help your brain kick into action. They include B vitamins, ephedra, and ginseng.

Booster: *B vitamins*

B vitamins, including thiamin, riboflavin, niacin folate, and B12, generally help neural activation, which is the key process in booting up the brain. A proper balance of these vitamins must be maintained, however, to gain maximum benefits from them. A deficiency of B vitamins causes neural collapse, which severely limits brain cell response. An overload of B vitamins can cause an anxious or a hypervigilant state, which opens the gates to generalized blood flow and may even destroy focused thinking.

Vitamin B12, especially, has gained a strong reputation as a brain booster. It has been found to cause a generalized state of arousal and energy when injected into the blood stream. In fact, because the absorption of B12 in the stomach is impaired as we age, many elderly people receive weekly injections of this vitamin for a mental boost. There are also newer tablets that are placed under the tongue and absorbed directly into the bloodstream that are very effective.

The exact reasons B vitamins boost thinking power are unclear, but the need for an adequate and balanced supply is indisputable.

Booster & Zapper: *Ephedra*

Ephedra is a supplement derived from the ephedra plant. It is available as an over-the-counter supplement and is commonly obtained through mail-order catalogs. Although this supplement has been found to boost alertness, it should be used with caution: Ephedra contains two stimulants—ephedrine and khat—that act like amphetamines, releasing norepinephrine and dopamine into the brain. Because of this, regular use may actually be harmful. In fact, ephedra in its purified form is actually used to raise blood pressure in surgical patients, and without close medical supervision, it can cause dangerous elevations in blood pressure.

Booster: *Ginseng*

Although very few studies have been done on the clinical effects of ginseng in humans (most have been done in rats and other rodents), it has become accepted through thousands of years of use in ancient medicines that it improves the booting-up power of the brain and acts as an insulator against the effects of stress on the body and brain. These factors have a positive effect on concentration.

In studies with rats, the results are impressive. Ginseng has been shown to maintain the balance of neurotransmitters during stress, preventing increases in brain cortisol (which can zap concentration) and decreases in brain serotonin and norepinephrine (needed for concentration). In these studies, ginseng has also been seen to decrease anxiety-like behaviors in response to stress (also an alertness booster).

Boosters and Zappers in Lifestyle

The ideal state for enhanced brain activity paradoxically occurs when the brain is most calm. Any strong negative emotion, such as anger, anxiety, or sorrow, causes vasodilation, sending generalized blood flow all over the brain. As we have discussed, this flooding of all brain cells simultaneously makes it impossible for the brain to draw an adequate supply into the areas that need it for concentrated thought. Certain aspects of lifestyle promote calm or chaotic brain states. Knowing the effects of exercise, meditation and relaxation exercises, spirituality, coffee, cigarettes, alcohol, drugs, sleep, and stress and anxiety will help you make life choices that will keep the brain in a calm, organized, and efficient state.

Zapper: *Coffee, cigarettes, alcohol, and drugs*

As explained earlier, caffeine, nicotine, alcohol, and so-called recreational drugs, such as marijuana and cocaine, all have a negative effect on brain function. Each is a short-term booster but a long-term zapper with the ability to destroy brain cells, causing slow, dull, and unfocused thinking patterns.

Booster: *Exercise*

Exercise strengthens the heart, firms muscles, lowers cholesterol levels, opens clogged arteries, trims your waist, boosts your mood, and makes you more resilient to stress. The list of benefits derived from exercise is quite long but incomplete without the addition of its brain-boosting powers. Without a doubt, exercise gives the brain many of the things it needs to boot up efficiently:

1. Exercise is known to raise baseline serotonin levels in the brain. (This alone will decrease depression and improve sleep patterns—automatically improving concentration.)
2. Those who exercise regularly seem to be more resilient to the exhausting effects of stress on the brain.

3. Exercise decreases the amount of hydrocortisone in the brain. (Hydrocortisone is the chemical released during stress, which in excess can cause depression and eventually shrink brain mass through cell death.)

Exercise has been shown to put the brain into an aroused, awake state.

It is obvious, then, that a lack of exercise robs the body of all these benefits. If you need to have a clear, sharp mind, it's time to get out and exercise.

Zapper: *Inadequate sleep*

Anyone who has stayed up all night with a sick child or with a stack of textbooks already knows that lack of sleep makes it tough to call the brain to attention. In fact, studies of sleep-deprived people find that while gross motor skills are not generally affected by lack of sleep, mental skills suffer severely. A high school student who succeeded in breaking the world record of 260 hours (almost 11 days) of sustained wakefulness found that after 230 hours of wakefulness, he was able to compete competitively in 100 games of pinball but unable to recite the alphabet without mistakes. You may not be planning to stay awake for 11 days, but even one night of inadequate sleep can affect your concentration. A 1997 poll by Louis Harris and Associates, Inc., found that when people got less than eight hours of sleep, concentration is only 70 percent of what it is on days when they are well-rested.

This loss of concentration is thought to be caused by the depletion of two neurotransmitters necessary for sharp, clear thinking: norepinephrine and serotonin. This depletion is associated with all of the signs of chronic stress, including loss in ability to focus and concentrate. Extreme stress symptoms seen in sleep deprivation include paranoia, inability to concentrate, loss of memory, and loss of general cognitive function. This chronic stress-like syndrome from sleep deprivation also raises brain cortisol levels, which over time can cause cell death.

The mechanism by which sleep deprivation affects concentration is related to the concept that sleep gives the brain time to do some housekeeping and clean up (through enzyme breakdown or re-uptake) the neurotransmitters norepinephrine and serotonin that are so important to clear, sharp thinking. After a good sleep, these neuron projections are ready to fire up and release a new supply of norepinephrine and serotonin.

Booster: *Meditation and relaxation exercises*

If you want to keep your brain awake and alert, you'll need to calm down. Meditation and relaxation exercises are the antidote to the brain's inability to think clearly when it is stressed, tired, or emotionally distracted. These two brain relaxers create an environment in the brain that allows it to boot up quickly and efficiently and remain at peak performance throughout the day. The effect is so definitive that when people who meditate or practice relaxation exercises (such as deep breathing, progressive muscle relaxation, or positive imagery) are exposed to stressful events during the day, they don't have the same brain-zapped response as someone who has not practiced brain-calming exercises.

The exact mechanism by which this happens is unclear, but it is known that, like physical exercise, meditation and relaxation exercises create a resiliency to stress that is necessary to clear thinking. Both may decrease the levels of brain excitation, which may even lessen the damaging effects of excitotoxicity caused by chronic stress. They also may conserve stress hormones such as norepinephrine and serotonin so that they are available when the brain needs them to concentrate and focus.

Meditation and relaxation exercises are especially good at balancing the "weather pattern" within the brain and in creating a balance that enhances sharp thinking. The possible mechanism by which this happens is caused by enhancing the brain's ability to fire neurons in smooth, coordinated, organized patterns.

Imagine the brain as a rowing team. If each rower is feverishly slapping his or her oars in a chaotic, unorganized, and unsynchronized manner, the result is mass confusion. However, when the rowers move in a slow, coordinated fashion, the sailing is swift and smooth. This is similar to the firing of the cortical neurons in the brain. Chaotic, unorganized, and unsynchronized firing wastes energy and results in confusion and eventual stress shutdown. Meditation and relaxation exercises organize the neurons and train them to fire in a synchronized, more efficient manner, thus using less energy.

The effects of meditation on brain function have been especially well-studied. The results support the use of meditation to improve mental power. Following are mechanisms by which this happens:

1. Meditation has a similar effect to that of the "smart drug" piracetam, which slows brain metabolism. (See Chapter 3 for more details on this drug.) This allows brain neurons to function more efficiently and use up less energy. (Meditation has the advantage over piracetam because it promotes mental power without risking harmful side effects always present in drug use.)

2. Meditation can decrease blood levels of lactate. Excess lactate is known to cause anxiety and insomnia—both definite zappers of brain power.

3. Meditation increases levels of dehydroepiandrosterone (DHEA)—a marker of brain vitality.

4. Meditation is its own stress-management system that decreases blood pressure as well as cholesterol levels. This, of course, may lessen the risk of arteriosclerosis that might otherwise block the arteries and limit the brain blood flow.

Booster: *Spirituality*

People who are spiritual—that is, connected to some inner core of faith and hope—show positive effects on brain power similar to those of people who meditate. In fact, anything that will buffer the effects of stress will reduce the negative effects of chronic neuron excitation and chronic blood vessel dilation in the brain (which zaps brain focus and concentration). Spirituality is definitely useful in boosting brain efficiency.

Zapper: *Stress and anxiety*

The ability to pay attention to even the simplest detail becomes laborious when excessive or chronic stress and/or anxiety distract the brain.

Stress will destroy your ability to concentrate in several ways:

The Care and Feeding of Your Brain

1. Stress causes a release of both norepinephrine and serotonin. Both of these neurotransmitters are necessary for sharp thinking, but prolonged, excessive release depletes their store and eventually leaves the brain without an adequate supply.

2. Stress causes a release of hydrocortisone. Scientists have found that excess hydrocortisone damages the hippocampus, which is the center of learning and remembering. Chronic hydrocortisone release is so damaging that it will actually shrink brain size through cell death.

3. Stress stimulates the glutamate receptors and causes excitotoxicity of the brain cells that are pushed into overtime activity. This condition fatigues brain function and in chronic conditions will eventually also cause cell death.

   Stress interrupts sleep patterns. As explained below, loss of sleep immediately affects one's ability to concentrate.

Anxiety also is an alertness zapper. A PET scan (which shows where brain activity and blood flow occur) taken while a person is having an anxiety attack shows a bright diffusion of blood all over the brain. Everything opens up with no selectivity and leaves the person unable to pay attention to anything. (You'll see this same effect in someone who has been on amphetamines too long.) This is followed by a general "shutdown" of activity. This process reveals how an extremely anxious state can cause complete disruption of brain cell activity, organization, and effectiveness.

Chapter 3

Memory: Helping the Brain to Store and Recall

Can't find your keys? Forgot what time you were supposed to meet with your boss? Do you have a hard time recalling names? It sounds like there's something wrong with one of the three steps of memory:

1. Information must be brought to the brain through the senses.
2. The brain must store that information.
3. The brain must be able to retrieve the information when you need it.

When the keys are lost, it's usually because you weren't looking at what you were doing when you put the keys down (so nothing registered), or because something pulled your attention elsewhere before you had time to store the information.

What about the times when you *do* pay attention? When you say to yourself, "Now remember where you're putting these." Do you still forget? What's going on? The simple truth is: As the cells in your brain gradually diminish in number, your neural circuits have trouble holding onto memories. Some say that it's a natural consequence of aging—but I say it may also be a preventable and reversible product of chronic undernourishment and body pollution.

Memory Under a Microscope

If you pick up a textbook on memory, you'll find detailed discussions on the many different types of memory: visual, auditory, kinesthetic, episodic, semantic, implicit, explicit, procedural, and declarative, to name a few. Each type of memory involves a variety of circuits in and around the cerebral cortex and the cerebellum. (See Figure 3A.) In the interest of simplicity and clarity, and because this is not a text-book, I'm going to generalize this discussion of memory and refer only to the short-term and long-term (so-called "explicit") memory of situations, experiences, and sensory information that is processed through the cerebral cortex. In other words, those memories that make up the explicit events of our lives, our impressions of those events, and the more abstract facts related to those events (like a street name or the workings of a carburetor).

These memories are processed through a seahorse-shaped horn deep inside the cortex called the hippocampus and the egg-shaped structure connected to one end of it called the amygdala. We have one hippocampus and one amygdala in each hemisphere of the brain.

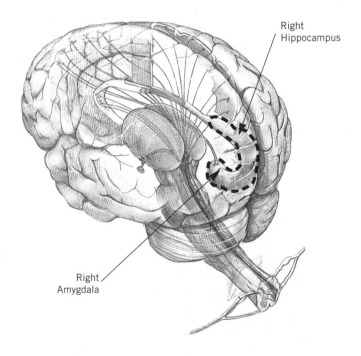

Right
Hippocampus

Right
Amygdala

FIGURE 3A

The hippocampus acts like a way station that coordinates the placement of explicit, situational, or factual information as it moves from sensory input to other areas of the brain for finer processing. It is assisted by the amygdala, which is vital to the rich quality of memories, because its circuits respond to and seem to process emotions. Intense emotional states are remembered more readily than mundane activities such as placing your keys on the bookshelf. That's why frightening, sad, funny, and exciting events dominate the memories of your past.

Many good texts have been written about the role of the hippocampus and amygdala in memory. Unfortunately, because relationships between brain circuits are often complex and even subtle in their nature, much conflicting information exists. A controversial principle involves the mechanism of long-term memory storage. How does it happen?

Some say that the hippocampus stores short-term memory tracks for hours, days, and even weeks and then gradually transfers them to other regions of the brain. I disagree. The hippocampus simply doesn't have enough neurons to hold onto enough pieces of information to create a whole memory. The memory of an apple pie coming out of the oven on Thanksgiving involves sight, smell, bodily sensations of hunger, sounds of the family gathering, sense of the time of day, the lighting in the room, and so on. It is hard to believe that the hippocampus can hold onto all of this input for every moment in a person's life.

More likely, the hippocampus serves as a trigger zone that takes in certain cues, associations, intense senses, and emotions, and then somehow "burns in" the memory of that information on parallel pathways that lead simultaneously to many different areas of the brain. Hence, a single specific memory is probably stored in many different locations and connected via association neurons (nerve fibers running in a seemingly random fashion through the cortex). It is as if memory were an apple pie, in which the individual ingredients are stored in specific areas (apples in the refrigerator, spices in the cabinet, and flour in the pantry) and then brought together when needed to create a whole.

This view of memory production makes it clear that the often-used analogy comparing human memory and computer memory is faulty. Memory storage in the brain is not at all like the process by which a serial computer takes in a string of bits and lines them up on a hard drive. Instead, explicit memory storage occurs by way of a massive system triggered through the hippocampus and amygdala. It involves literally billions of parallel pathways that simultaneously connect sensory traces to areas in and around the cerebral cortex (for example, images to the visual processing areas, sounds to the auditory processing area, and so on).

> *Much of what we know about memory is the result of scientific testing on people who have suffered some sort of brain damage. These studies have helped support the notion that memory is distributed to and stored throughout the entire cortex. Take for example the case in which a stroke victim suffers damage to the part of the cortex responsible for vision. Not only will this person become blind, he or she will also have trouble recalling the visual components of specific memories. When recalling a Thanksgiving meal, he or she will remember the smell of the food and the sound of the voices, but will have much trouble picturing what the food and the people looked like. Because damage to the occipital cortex can wipe out aspects of visual memory while leaving other kinds of memory intact, we know that different parts of memory are processed in different parts of the brain.*

Some of the projections from the hippocampus to other areas of the brain involve special nerve cells called *long-term potentiation (LTP) neurons*. (In fact, the hippocampus has the highest concentration of LTP neurons in the brain.) While other neurons flash quick fire, LTP neurons get stimulated for a specific period of time before they shut off. This specific period of time varies with different LTP neurons. Some stay on for a couple of seconds, some for a few days, and others for months. This is probably why you have trouble getting rid of certain emotional feelings after the circumstance that caused them is over. When you get very angry with someone at work, for instance, why do you so often carry that feeling home with you? It's not because the epinephrine or other stress hormones are still running around in your bloodstream; these are gone in a couple of seconds. It's probably because the LTP neurons have been turned on, creating strong memories of the event. That's probably also why events that are accompanied by strong emotions (that naturally get fired through LTP neurons) are more likely to be burned into the long-term memory and why severe emotional trauma can leave such intense scars and cause post-traumatic stress disorder, flashbacks, night terrors, and depression. The memory is burned in too deeply to be forgotten.

The Long and Short of It

We are familiar with the terms "long-term memory" and "short-term memory." Each, in its own way, is vital to daily functioning. Without a long-term memory, you would live in a permanent amnestic state, without recollection of your name, family, home, or job. Fortunately (unless affected by a disease such as Alzheimer's, or a stroke or head trauma), your long-term memories are quite secure. What you remember now about your name, your family, and even your childhood, you will remember 10 years from now. The weakness of this long-term "memory bank" lies in its sometimes obstinate refusal to give back information we need—especially long-term abstract or factual memories. Faces are solid; we can remember these. Names are abstract; we forget these. In addition to names, other abstract memories include location (for example, we can't find a folder we filed away yesterday) and specific dates (we can't remember important engagements without recording them on our calendar).

We all know that this forgetfulness is worse on some days than on others. Why? Apparently, this happens for two reasons: 1) The fragile retrieval system from long-term memory is susceptible to distractions or emotional states; and 2) it can be influenced by the substances that are feeding the brain at the time.

Isolated, explicit short-term memory (which holds facts for no more than 30 seconds) is even less reliable and even more susceptible to outside influences. Nonetheless, this shaky 30 seconds of memory is vital to everything you do. Your short-term memory reminds you why you picked up the pen, and why you walked to the door, and why you took a dollar from your wallet, and why you're staring into the refrigerator. It's this short-term memory bank that is most sensitive to the health of the brain—and most annoying when it becomes unreliable. Certainly, you have stood at your closet door with some vague sense that you wanted something, but can't recall what. You have listened to directions from the gas station attendant, driven away and immediately forgotten whether to make a right or left turn at the light. You've looked up a phone number in the directory and forgotten it before you got to the phone. How does that information get lost so fast? Why can't you remember things like you used to?

Researchers at London's Institute of Child Health uncovered remarkable information about how different kinds of memory are processed and stored. It has generally been believed that all information and events pass through the hippocampus for processing to long-term memory, and if the hippocampus were damaged, long-term memory could not be processed. There are thousands of cases worldwide in which people suffering hippocampal damage are destined to live in their past because they can't remember anything about the present. While working with three brain-damaged children (who lost hippocampal function because of oxygen deprivation caused by premature birth, convulsions, and respiratory arrest), the researchers found an interesting twist. The children cannot process "episodic" memory, so they don't remember the daily events of their lives. They can't remember what day it is or what TV program they just watched—they have no long-term memory of daily life. Surprisingly, however, they can remember lessons in reading, writing, and spelling. In fact, constant rehearsal and exposure to memory cues resulted in the eventual learning of these facts to equal that of their peers. Apparently, memory of facts, called "semantic" memory, is not processed entirely through the hippocampus, which previously had been thought to serve as a trigger for retrieval of such abstract memories. This is the kind of discovery that reminds us just how fascinating and mysterious the brain really is.

Fueling and Draining the Brain

The hippocampus is complex, intricate, and biologically delicate. It reacts quickly and dramatically to the foods, supplements, and drugs we put into our bodies. These substances are digested and then metabolized into the bloodstream where they are carried immediately and directly to the brain. (The brain has the highest blood flow per tissue weight of any organ in the body.) Some of these substances impair the brain's ability to record or retrieve memory—often, they are the reason we can't find the keys or remember people's names. Other substances we feed the brain give these cells the boost they need to record and retrieve with speed and clarity—they keep us on the ball and make us feel quick and sharp.

Take a close look at the following groups of memory boosters and zappers. Then think about the substances you've ingested today. Are they helping or impairing your memory?

Memory Boosters and Zappers

Memory boosters are substances (natural and synthetic) that help the brain efficiently take in memory, store it, and give it back when we need it. Some memory boosters occur naturally in our bodies; some need to be added to our diets; and some are bolstered through lifestyle choices and supplementation.

Memory zappers are substances that get into the bloodstream and flow up to the brain, where they disrupt the function of neurons in areas responsible for memory. Some zappers have an immediate effect; some have a gradual effect. Some cause temporary memory loss; others cause permanent loss. Combined, they wreak havoc on the fragile brain areas that serve memory storage and retrieval.

Boosters and Zappers in Your Own Body

There are various brain chemicals and functions that are involved in the improvement and the loss of memory.

Zapper: *Depression*

In the state of depression, certain neurons in the hippocampus remain turned on for long periods of time. These neurons produce cortisol, which has the job of moderating activation of other hippocampal neurons during stress. As a result, normal balanced hippocampal function is disrupted and mild to severe memory loss results. In addition, there is a depletion of serotonin and norepinephrin (both needed for full memory function), probably because there is continuous firing of these neurons during stress.

Most drug treatments for depression improve memory function. This is true even with drugs such as tricyclic antidepressants that have their own inherent memory-zapping abilities. Apparently, the effect of relieving depression has more of an influence on memory than the negative effects of the drugs.

On the other hand, electroconvulsive therapy (ECT or "shock therapy"), despite being a very effective cure for severe depression, has a significant and lingering effect on memory. Patients report subtle memory problems for as long as months after this therapy. Some never recover full memory functioning.

Zapper: *Free radicals*

Free radicals are waste products released when the body burns its fuel (food) for energy or when the body breaks down certain toxic substances (a burned steak, for example). Under ideal conditions these molecules are kept in check by antioxidants released by cells of the immune system or by natural antioxidant substances found in the bloodstream, certain foods you eat, and the liver. A problem occurs when too many free radicals are generated and overload the body's scavenging mechanism. Free radicals bind to proteins, to membranes, to DNA, and to the proteins that help repair DNA, weakening the cells and impairing cell function. This degeneration probably occurs as a result of long-term exposure to excessive free radicals and ultimately causes a long list of diseases and ailments—including memory loss.

Some stressors that cause this free radical overload include poor nutrition, physical and emotional stress, and environmental pollution. Once cell function is impaired, nerve cells (in particular) can no longer adequately transport charged particles called ions that are needed in order to function properly. When this happens, brain cell memory functions are among the first to go in a process known as senile degeneration. In fact, The Institute for Brain Aging at the University of California, Irvine, has implicated free radicals as one of the mechanisms by which Alzheimer's disease is hastened.

Booster: *Neurotransmitters*

To have a fully functioning memory, the brain must produce an adequate and balanced supply of acetylcholine, norepinephrin, serotonin, and dopamine. Although these substances are not produced by the body specifically to boost memory, it is known that acetylcholine in the brain is necessary for adequate short-term memory. In addition, depletion of brain serotonin and norepinephrin (as occurs in depression and chronic stress) can have a profound effect on memory. Although none of these substances, when administered to healthy patients, actually boosts memory, it is clear that a brain deficient in these substances (or the neurons that release them) has memory problems. The same is true of dopamine. Dopamine depletion is responsible for Parkinson's disease and the memory-loss states produced in the flu-encephalitis epidemic early in the 20th century. A healthy brain has a sharp, quick memory thanks to an adequate and balanced supply of acetylcholine, serotonin, norepinephrin, and dopamine.

Boosters and Zappers in Drugs

You know that drugs have a clear and profound effect on your physical health and on the way you feel. They can also have this effect on your memory. Drugs known to improve memory include anti-depressants, L-dopa, and ondansetron.

Drugs have also been known to affect the ability to remember where you parked your car and the name of your best friend's first born. The memory-zapping drugs discussed in this section are anti-cholinergic drugs (such as motion-sickness patches and tricyclic anti-depressants), ketamine, marijuana, sedatives, and stimulants.

Booster: *Acetylcholinesterase inhibitors*

Acetylcholinesterase inhibitors is a very long name for the newest class of drugs shown to improve memory in the elderly. There are three drugs available in this class that produce at least moderate improvement in memory in Alzheimer's dementia. These drugs increase acetylcholine in the brain by inhibiting the enzyme that breaks it down. These are tacrine (Cognex), donepezil (Aricept), and metrifonate (this one is now in FDA approval stages). They all require a doctor's prescription.

Zapper: *Anticholinergic drugs*

Scopolamine patches for motion sickness and tricyclic antidepressants are called anticholinergic drugs. Although considered generally safe drugs, they can affect the memory of some people more than others, leaving some with significant memory loss.

Anticholinergic drugs compete with the neurotransmitter acetylcholine in the brain. It is well-known that acetylcholine is absolutely necessary for memory function and that in cases of Alzheimer's dementia and Parkinson's disease (where there is extreme memory deprivation), brain acetylcholine is depleted.

Scopolamine (found most commonly in motion-sickness patches) directly antagonizes brain acetylcholine. Although it is given only in low doses, it has potent antimemory properties. A recent U.S. State Department travelers' warning gives us an idea of just how potent it can be. It has been discovered that in a certain South American country, some taxi drivers inject themselves with a scopolamine antidote and then put scopolamine in their cigarettes. The smoke from these cigarettes makes it impossible for tourists riding in these cabs to remember who robbed and looted them.

Tricyclic antidepressants (such as Elavil, Tofranil, and Pamelor) are used less now that serotonin-based antidepressants with fewer side effects (such as Prozac and Paxil) are more common. Nevertheless, the tricyclic antidepressants are still available, and you should know that they have mild antiacetylcholine (anticholinergic) properties that will affect memory in some individuals. More often, however, depression itself impairs memory more severely, and when treated, memory improves despite the drug's anticholinergic properties.

Booster: *Antidepressants*

Antidepressants are memory enhancers only indirectly. When they relieve the symptoms of depression (over the long term), they also relieve the impaired memory state that often accompanies depression (especially severe depression).

Zapper: *Ketamine*

Ketamine, commonly called Special K, is often abused nowadays. It was originally used as an animal anesthetic, and it also has significant use as a potent, pain-killing, short-acting anesthetic in humans. Because ketamine produces a strange, dissassociative state of unreality, it is open to abuse. The problem is that this action is mediated directly through the neurons in the hippocampus and, therefore, the drug is a very potent amnestic agent. It doesn't just zap memory a bit—it wipes it out completely for most of the "trip."

Warning

Gamma-hydroxybutyrate (GHB) is a very dangerous drug often promoted to improve memory. It is a stimulant also called "Liquid X," "Liquid Ecstasy," and "the date-rape drug." Some popular books on brain drugs claim that the dangers of this drug have been painted in a hysterical light by the FDA. There is some paranoia that the government is trying to squelch the use of a "smart drug" in this country. I have even seen postings on Internet bulletin boards encouraging the use of this drug mixed with alcohol and LSD. Be advised that there is enough scientific and anecdotal documentation outside government sources to establish that this is a dangerous drug. In one hospital in San Francisco, 88 cases were seen and diagnosed, including cases of coma. When mixed with alcohol or LSD, GHB is deadly.

Booster: *L-dopa*

Naturally occurring dopamine is known to enhance memory, but it is not given as a drug to improve memory because it does not cross the blood-brain barrier. This barrier prevents large molecules, such as amines, amino acids, hormones, and proteins, from entering brain tissue. The drug L-dopa, however, does cross this barrier, convert to dopamine, and deliver memory-boosting elements to the brain. L-dopa has had impressive results when given to individuals with memory problems, but it does not enhance memory in brain-healthy individuals.

Zapper: *Marijuana*

Marijuana, specifically its active component THC, works on the hippocampus to jumble memory in much the same way as sedatives: It interferes with the mechanism that burns memory onto neuron pathways to create long-term remembrance.

A 1996 study found that long-term use of marijuana causes a marked disruption of short-term memory and attention skills in older users who had been smoking for an average of 34 years. Studies have also shown that the impairment gets worse with continued use as the years go by.

In 1995, the National Drug and Research Center of the University of New South Wales in Australia conducted a study that set out to answer the question, "Do cognitive impairments caused by marijuana use recover when you stop using the drug?" The results found that even after giving up marijuana, previous users were still partially impaired in their ability to focus and filter out irrelevant information, and there was no improvement with increasing length of abstinence. Because the process of memory demands your attention to make the information stick, and distractions clearly impair the hold your brain has on short-term memory traces, this kind of acquired attention deficit disorder certainly has a negative effect on the ability to remember.

It is also believed that long-term marijuana use causes a generalized loss in drive. This lack of drive is a slow-down in the limbic system—the system that includes, among other things, the hippocampus and amygdala. Theoretically, impaired function here would affect the ability to take in and retrieve information.

Booster: *Ondansetron*

Ondansetron (Zofran) is prescribed to decrease nausea. A side effect of this drug is an increase in memory power. This effect probably happens because ondansetron is a short-acting drug that blocks serotonin receptors in the brain. It's my belief that this action affects the level of cortisol (a known memory booster) in the brain.

Zapper: *Sedatives*

Sedatives are often prescribed to reduce anxiety, calm frazzled nerves, promote sleep, and ease the burden of chronic stress. In this high-pressured, fast-paced world, benzodiazepine drugs, such as Valium, Xanax, and Ativan, have become household names. They are embraced by many as miracle drugs that allow them to live normal lives and avoid debilitating tension. Unfortunately, they may also be responsible for lives filled with little memory of days past and little emotional flair. Many who have taken such sedatives for an extended period of time and then stopped taking them report that they have little recollection of what happened in their lives during that period of sedative use. Some benzodiazepines, such as Versed, exert such an intense amnestic effect that after intravenous injection, patients will have a full and apparently fluid conversation with another person and yet have no recollection of any of it the next day. It's probably not that they can't remember, but rather that the memories were never well-recorded.

One effect of the benzodiazepine class of sedatives is to diminish activity in the hippocampus and amygdala. This is probably one way they appear to reduce stress. One possible mechanism involves the LTP neurons that remain turned on after certain stimulating or intense events. If benzodiazepines allow fewer LTP neurons to get turned on, the perceived feeling of stress and anxiety may be less severe. Furthermore, users may not remember the stress as intensely because it won't trigger long-term memory incorporation as strongly. Unfortunately, not many other events will be remembered either.

Beyond anxiety and stress, sedatives reduce the intensity of all emotions. When a person is feeling mellow, the amygdala isn't triggered to respond to the many emotions that burn in strong and vivid memories. Again, the user is left in this neutral state, unable to remember the details of daily life. These effects on memory are expected only during the time a person is taking the sedative. Once he or she is off the drug, memory function should return to normal capability.

Zapper: *Stimulants (amphetamines, caffeine, and nicotine)*

Amphetamines (sometimes called "uppers") that include drugs such as Ritalin and others prescribed for attention deficit disorder, along with caffeine and nicotine, are short-term memory boosters but long-term zappers. The exact mechanism by which they can heighten awareness initially and destroy brain function eventually was explained in detail in Chapter 2. On the subject of memory, it's noteworthy to point out that the rush of alertness gained from these drugs, in the long term, may take its toll on the brain and then on memory.

Amphetamines, nicotine, and caffeine create harmful free radicals, disrupt sleep, and in the long run or with high use, dim memory and mimic the effects of stress. Because of the chronic stress-like effect stimulants have on the brain, it is shown that, like stress, over time they cause a decrease in brain mass. This alone decreases the brain's ability to hold onto memories.

A prominent anesthesiologist was giving talks on an important subject across several European cities. To help himself fall asleep in strange hotels and unfamiliar surroundings, he brought with him a certain benzodiazepine sedative (that has since been taken off the market). He used it for this trip because of its short action: You fall asleep and the effects of the drug are completely gone when you awaken.

This doctor was scheduled to speak in Paris on the last day of his speaking tour. On the train to Paris, he took one of these pills, intending to take a short nap. His recollection after taking the pill was waking up on the airplane heading back home. He was panic-stricken. It was two days later and he did not know if he had given his talk in Paris.

Upon arriving home, he checked his suitcase and found gifts from Paris for friends and relatives that he had no memory of buying. He telephoned a colleague who had also attended the conference in Paris and found that he had given a "fine talk that was well-received." As the facts unfolded, he found that after taking the sedative, he got off the train, found his hotel, went to dinner with several colleagues, gave his talk the next morning, and went gift shopping that afternoon. He still has absolutely no memory of those two days.

Boosters and Zappers in Foods

The most direct and easily available way to positively affect memory power is through diet. The same foods that clog arteries and cause disease when eaten in excess also affect memory. You can boost your ability to remember by reducing fats and protein, maintaining a moderate intake of sugars and carbohydrates, increasing vitamin B12, and loading up on antioxidant fruits and vegetables.

Booster: *Antioxidants*

Under ideal conditions, free radicals are kept in check by antioxidants released by cells of the immune system or by natural antioxidant substances found in the bloodstream. But when conditions are not so ideal (such as when you eat fats and proteins or are exposed to continuous emotional or environmental stress), you can help your body fight off memory-robbing free radicals by increasing your intake of certain fruits, vegetables, and supplements.

Vitamin C (ascorbic acid) is so vital to brain function that its levels are almost 15 times higher in the brain than in other areas of the body. Not only is it a well-known and powerful antioxidant, there is evidence that it can reduce the risk of plaque formation in the arteries (arteriosclerosis) and block the effects of free radicals that can reduce blood flow to the brain and impair memory. This vitamin is also necessary for the manufacture of neurotransmitters (the substances by which all nerve cells communicate with each other), especially acetylcholine, the most important neurotransmitter for memory processing.

Vitamin C is found in parsley, sprouts, citrus fruits, strawberries, broccoli, potatoes, kiwi, red peppers, cabbage, and leafy greens. Many experts recommend megadoses of vitamin C at 1,000 to 5,000mg per day. But be careful. Such high doses, if not accompanied by adequate water intake, may acidify the urine and enhance the formation of kidney stones.

Vitamin E is another commonly known antioxidant. In partnership with the mineral selenium, it neutralizes free radicals that accelerate brain aging. Vitamin E can also preserve memory, possibly by restoring damaged neurotransmitter receptor sites on neurons. Vitamin E not only prevents deterioration of the brain, but it may also help restore brain function.

Vitamin E is found in nuts and seeds, nut oils, peanut butter, wheat germ, whole wheat, and other grain sprouts. For antioxidant benefits, many experts recommend doses of as much as 800 to 1,600IU of vitamin E per day.

Selenium is an elemental metal that has antioxidant properties. In studies it has been shown to act synergistically with vitamin E as an antioxidant.

The Care and Feeding of Your Brain

Magnesium is a powerful free-radical scavenger that helps increase the antioxidative power of vitamin E. At the recommended daily allowance level, it is an indispensable brain-boosting nutrient.

You'll find magnesium in apples, blackberries, blueberries, celery, cherries, figs, grapes, oranges, lemons, limes, papaya, peas, plums, potatoes, squash, and walnuts.

Although magnesium is a notable memory-booster, I can't recommend taking high doses of magnesium in supplement form to increase memory power. The tests that support magnesium supplementation are shock or stroke models in animal studies that don't apply to daily use in humans. In a typical experiment, the animal is made to suffer a stroke and then a percent of brain function is preserved by pumping the "patient" with magnesium megadoses. I am not convinced that this translates into a recommendation for daily supplementation.

I believe, in fact, that magnesium supplements can be dangerous. The negative effects of excessive supplementation are easy to see in pregnant women with toxemia who are given megadoses of intravenous magnesium to prevent seizures. Along with the side effects of lowered blood pressure, relaxed muscles, cardiovascular and respiratory depression, the women get very tired and lethargic. There is no brain boosting going on here. Magnesium acts as an anesthetic. If taken in oral form, it also acts as a laxative and will cause diarrhea.

Look for magnesium in the foods you eat and avoid supplements.

Carotenoids are the most celebrated of the antioxidants. There are approximately 40 of these substances, which are most potent in scavenging loose free radicals. They consist of long carbon chains that bind particularly well to these renegade molecules. Carotenoids are found in carrots, sprouts, apricots, sweet potatoes, spinach, celery, squash, red peppers, tomatoes, oranges, and kale. There is a negative effect of carotenoid supplements that you should be aware of: A recent study of beta carotene supplements showed that it increased lung cancer rates in smokers. Because of this one study, it has been dropped off many of the lists of recommended antioxidants.

Flavenoids comprise another class of large, high-energy carbon structures that are powerful antioxidants. These can be found in onions, broccoli, cabbage, turnips, cauliflower, cantaloupe (and other orange-colored fruits), peppers, bean sprouts, and select herbs such as peppermint, spearmint, winter mint, and basil. (As a bonus: Broccoli, cabbage, turnips, and cauliflower are potent anticancer agents.)

Herbal remedies. Good herbal antioxidant-containing tonics to sip or sniff include green tea, black tea, alfalfa, rosehips, peppermint, nettles, hawthorn, goldenseal, fenugreek, cumin (in curry), capsicum (hot pepper), cinnamon, and basil. Of all of these, green tea has been the most closely studied for its antioxidant properties and has been found to be a potent free-radical scavenger.

Zapper: *Fats and proteins*

Excessive intake of fats and protein can cause the production of free radicals. Free radicals, remember, are waste products released when the body burns its fuel (food) for energy or when the body breaks down certain toxic substances (such as a burned steak). Because long-term exposure to free radicals affects memory functions, you can boost memory power by reducing your intake of fats (found in butter, oils, nuts, and processed bakery goods) and protein (found in fish, red meat, milk, eggs, and cheese).

Excessive intake of fats and protein also affect memory through a second mechanism. They can have detrimental effects on blood vessels. They cause plaque deposits, "narrowing" of arteries, and arteriosclerosis. These conditions restrict the flow of oxygen-filled blood to the brain, which has a profound effect on memory function.

Booster & Zapper: *Sugar and carbohydrates*

The way the body burns sugar and carbohydrates is quite different from the way it burns memory-zapping protein and fats. The process of burning sugar and carbohydrates actually results in the production of fewer, if any, free radicals. This difference gives sugars and carbohydrates the upper hand as memory boosters.

It is also interesting to note that sugar and carbohydrates can improve memory simply because they make you feel good. We know that memories are most vivid when they come into the brain accompanied by strong emotions (this combo triggers the amygdala to jump into action along with the hippocampus). Not too surprisingly then, anything that can create pleasurable feelings in the brain will poke the amygdala into creating memories. This happens naturally when the brain produces an ample amount of serotonin—the "feeling good" brain chemical. Memories are more easily made when serotonin levels are high. You can artificially create a positive emotional state by taking in high-caloried carbohydrates and sugar, which raise the brain serotonin levels. Feeling good will trigger the amygdala and the hippocampus to store memory.

Because of this relationship among serotonin levels, feeling good, and memory, you might think that it would have been easier to remember the things you studied in school if you had munched on chocolate cupcakes while you were studying. It's true—if you were to eat a high-sugar or high-carbohydrate snack while you were studying, the body's release of serotonin would have activated the pleasure center of the amygdala and burned that information into a retrievable memory.

Timing is everything, however, when you want to use sugar or carbohydrates to enhance memory. The initial rush will cause alert and clear thinking, but when the candy bar or cracker is gone, insulin will cause the blood sugar to drop off, leaving the brain less efficient and less able to focus. Or if you take in too much sugar or too many carbohydrates, the increased levels of serotonin will make you sleepy, lethargic, and less able to recall details. Studying with a candy bar the night before will give your brain time to grasp the facts and then work off the sugar drop before you take the test the next day. You could also study while eating a candy bar immediately before the test (and maybe even sneak one in during the test) so you could recall the information before you experience the fuzzy thinking caused by a drop in sugar or a rise in serotonin.

Booster: *Vitamin B12*

Vitamin B12 is "brain food." A shortage of vitamin B12 causes a domino effect that, bit by bit, breaks down brain function. In fact, a deficiency of vitamin B12 can lead to irreversible memory loss.

In plentiful supply, B12 is involved in the synthesis of methionine. This amino acid is involved in protein synthesis, which produces the protective sheath that surrounds neurons and enables them to record and retrieve memory. Without B12, none of this can happen.

A shortage of B12 is not common in most American diets. But for the elderly and for vegetarians, it is a reason for concern. Michael Freedman, Director of Geriatrics at New York University Medical

Center, believes that anywhere from 7 to 15 percent of older people suffer from B12 deficiency. This probably occurs because the acid content of the stomach decreases with age, so we have more difficulty absorbing B12. Vegetarians (vegan vegetarians in particular) have a problem maintaining B12 levels because plants can't make or store B12. These two groups of people have a particular need to take B12 supplements to maintain full memory function. (The new B12 supplements bypass the digestive tract because they are placed under the tongue for direct absorption into the bloodstream.)

Boosters and Zappers in Supplements

Supplements that claim to boost mental alertness and memory power are often referred to as smart drugs. It is estimated that more than 100,000 Americans take smart drugs by prescription, over-the-counter, or by mail order from overseas markets. The most popular supplements that may affect memory include acetyl-L-carnitine, DHEA, dilantin, DMAE, ginkgo biloba, ginseng, lecithin, piracetam, and phosphatidylserine (PS).

Booster: *Acetyl-L-carnitine*

Acetyl-L-carnitine (ALC) is an ingredient often listed in over-the-counter memory boosters. It is found naturally in the brain where it improves energy metabolism and reduces intracellular generation of the free radicals that are caused by oxidation of fatty acids. Human studies have suggested that acetyl-L-carnitine supplements may improve memory in healthy people. It also may offer promise in the treatment of Alzheimer's disease.

Questionable: *DHEA*

Naturally occurring DHEA (dehydroepiandrosterone), a steroid hormone raw material, is absolutely necessary for brain function. Although found throughout the body, its levels are five times higher in the brain than in any other tissues. As we age, however, the level of DHEA declines. By the time you are 70, you will probably have only about 10 percent of the amount you had in your 20s. Studies have shown that people with Alzheimer's have as much as 48 percent less DHEA than those without the disease.

Unfortunately, the naturally occurring presence of DHEA in the brain has led to the assumption that by artificially increasing the levels of DHEA, we can increase mental functioning. I don't think this is necessarily true. All we've shown scientifically is that correlation is not necessarily causation. Consider this analogy:

> Cows make cow manure. This is a fact (like the fact that the brain makes DHEA). If half the herd dies of mad cow disease, there will be less cow manure in the field. This is another fact (like the additional fact that there is less DHEA as the brain ages). But you can't bring the dead cows back by putting extra cow manure on the field—just as you can't bring back brain power by putting more DHEA into the brain environment.

Don't waste your money on this "smart drug." It is still in the early stages of animal testing, and the results say little about its ability to help you find your keys. It may even lead to testicular cancer and cause women to grow facial hair. If you see DHEA in a memory tonic, don't count on positive results.

Questionable: *Dilantin*

Dilantin, also known as phenytoin, is a miracle drug according to many believers who promote it with religious fervor. I, however, am not one of them. Dilantin is an approved seizure medication that should not be taken regularly because it has many side effects, including long-term problems with cognitive function, that are not mentioned in the trade books on smart drugs. There are enough good smart drugs on the market that you can stay away from this one and not miss anything.

Booster: *DMAE*

DMAE (dimethylamine ethanol) is another smart drug that is involved in the production of acetylcholine, the neurotransmitter necessary for memory. Studies have suggested that DMAE directly increases the power of short-term memory, which is very dependent on an adequate and constant supply of acetylcholine. DMAE is available outside the United States in supplement form and is also found naturally in anchovies and sardines (explaining why these fish have been called "brain food").

Booster: *Ginkgo biloba*

Ginkgo biloba is an herbal supplement extracted from the leaves of the ginkgo tree. Impressive studies have shown that this natural herb improves alertness and memory. This is the result of many mechanisms:

1. Ginkgo is a free-radical scavenger with antioxidant properties. This keeps the cells of the brain in top working order.

2. Ginkgo biloba is a vasodilator, meaning it opens the pathways in the vascular system to improve circulation, allowing blood to flow freely through the body. This increased blood flow enhances brain function by sweeping out free radicals as it flows through, and by bringing in more oxygen and nutrients. In short, ginkgo biloba allows the circulatory system to efficiently bring in the good stuff and take out the bad.

3. Ginkgo biloba inhibits platelet binding. When platelets in the blood bind together, they can cause it to clot and close up small blood vessels. When the blood can't flow freely to the brain in a person with arteriosclerosis, the brain can often suffer a relentless series of mini-strokes (completely unknown to the person) that over time severely affect brain function. This is known as multi-infarct dementia.

4. Long-term use of ginkgo increases the number of acetylcholine receptors in the brain. This means that when acetylcholine is released in the brain, it becomes more active because there are more molecules that receive it and affect its action. (Remember, acetylcholine is vital to memory function.)

Unlike many other compounds claiming to improve memory, ginkgo biloba clearly has been shown to have an affect. In 39 out of 40 trials, ginkgo has been proven to slow or improve symptoms of dementia of the Alzheimer's type. In fact, the FDA is allowing some companies to state on the label that ginkgo biloba does help memory. You'll also find a mention of ginkgo in the notable text, *Physicians' Desk Reference* (PDR).

Booster: *Ginseng*

Ginseng has been used medicinally for thousands of years in Asia. In America, it was Daniel Boone's primary crop in the 1700s. Today it is extremely popular for its supposed ability to "balance" brain function. Ginseng does this possibly by modulating chemical activities, such as the release of cortisol. Some cortisol is needed to help you deal with stress, but too much can damage brain cells. Ginseng may also regulate serotonin release. Some serotonin is good for keeping your mood up; too much will cause fatigue and lethargy. Working in this way with many systems of the body, ginseng supposedly enables the brain to maintain an ideal, stable state of arousal.

Booster: *Lecithin*

Lecithin consists mainly of the raw material phosphatidylcholine, which is a building block of acetylcholine (the neurotransmitter necessary for memory). It is also needed for repair and maintenance of the structure and insulation of neurons. Obviously, it's an important smart drug. Lecithin works best to prevent memory failure, but some studies have shown that it has promise as an agent of repair, as well.

Lecithin is nontoxic and has no known side effects. Its brain boosting ingredient, phosphatidylcholine, can also be found in the supplements choline bitartrate and choline chloride.

Caution

Acetylcholine is the primary neurotransmitter of memory. These receptors must be functioning in the hippocampus in order to have explicit memory. Anything that stimulates acetylcholine will improve memory; anything that inhibits acetylcholine will disrupt memory. That's why all substances that promote the production of acetylcholine are effective smart drugs. However, anything that increases acetylcholine in the brain over time, also increases the tendency toward depression. This may be because acetylcholine stimulates production of brain cortisol, which in excess promotes depression. Anyone with bipolar disorder or other depressive illnesses should be very careful when using supplements that boost acetylcholine, such as lecithin, piracetam, DMEA, and phosphatidylserine.

Booster: *Phosphatidylserine (PS)*

Phosphatidylserine (PS) is a substance that occurs naturally in the membranes of all nerve cells. It keeps fatty substances soluble and keeps cell membranes fluid. It also seems to assist glucose metabolism and increase neurotransmitter receptor sites. These are all very important chemical activities in the processing of memory. Two very frequently cited studies attesting to the remarkable effects of PS on memory include a 1991 study at Stanford and Vanderbilt Universities and a 1990 study at the University of Milan in Italy. Both found impressive results when PS was given to individuals with normal or impaired memory loss.

However, these and many other studies used PS that had been extracted from cows' brains. In the wake of mad cow disease scientists are now working exclusively with PS made from soybeans. There is no proof, however, that soybean PS is equivalent to cow PS. As of this date, the only study to use soy PS in humans was inconclusive.

In short, phosphatidylserine supplements may help us remember more, but the only type currently on the market hasn't been adequately tested.

Booster: *Piracetam*

Piracetam is another smart drug that affects memory. In clinical studies with Alzheimer's patients, with elderly people without mental dysfunction, and with healthy college students, piracetam proved effective in improving memory.

Piracetam boosts the activity of the neurons in the brain so they function more efficiently and use up less energy. This is a general memory booster. Most specifically, piracetam increases the effectiveness of the neurons that manufacture acetylcholine. It also appears to increase glucose metabolism. (Remember, glucose is the fuel of the brain.) It is also suspected that piracetam may enhance the brain's ability to use oxygen, as well as serotonin and dopamine, all well-known memory boosters.

Whatever the exact mechanism, it has proven effective in literally hundreds of studies. Although it is not presently available for sale in the United States, many advocates buy piracetam through mail-order companies from overseas or Mexico.

Piracetam is a safe drug, but it sometimes mimics the effects of stimulants, causing agitation and/or insomnia. It can also increase the effects of amphetamines and psychotropics, so talk to your doctor before combining these medications.

Boosters and Zappers in Your Lifestyle

Your daily schedule and a few of your daily habits can give you some insight into how well you can expect your memory to work. In particular, you should pay attention to the effects of exercise, sleep, relaxation, caffeine, nicotine, and alcohol.

Zapper: *Alcohol*

If you've ever drunk yourself under the table and woke up the next morning with no recollection of anything that happened the night before, you know first-hand that alcohol has a profound effect on memory. This extreme circumstance gives a clear-cut picture of what happens when the brain is exposed to any amount of alcohol.

The way alcohol affects long-term memory is varied and still under study. It is known for certain, however, that because metabolizing alcohol produces an excessive amount of free radicals, long-term use of it at high levels definitely impairs memory.

In the short-term, alcohol works very similarly to sedatives to inhibit the retention of memories. Alcohol and sedatives seem to affect the function of the same hippocampal receptors that affect neurons used to burn in retrievable memories.

Alcohol further affects memory by causing specific nutritional deficiencies. Some alcoholics have very poor diets that negatively affect not only memory but also general health. But that's not the result of alcohol directly. Alcohol itself directly causes a nutritional deficiency in even casual drinkers because it impairs the processing of some vitamins, particularly B1 (thiamin). The natural store of thiamin can be used up during the process of breaking down alcohol. This thiamin deficiency has a direct and profound effect on memory processing. As the store of thiamin is depleted, you are typically confused and disoriented. Thiamin deficiency of alcoholism damages a structure called the thalamus that is connected to the hippocampus and is also subtly involved in memory processing. Treatment with thiamin supplementation can alleviate confusion, but by this time, damage is likely to have occurred, resulting in permanent memory loss.

If you have a drink or two each day, you can give your memory a helping hand by taking a multiple vitamin that includes 50 to 100mg of thiamin.

> *I have a vivid memory of a rock concert I attended years ago. Sitting up close In the third row, I remember being awed by the guitar player—he was out-of-his-mind, fall-down drunk. He was physically escorted on and off the stage, yet he played flawlessly. His motor memory, burned deeply in the cerebellum (and not processed through the hippocampus), was functioning seemingly on its own. But I knew that the sensory events of the evening that were being processed through the hippocampus would be lost forever. This guitarist would have no memory of the details of that night: He wouldn't remember how he got on stage, what songs he played, or how the audience reacted. This was just fascinating to me.*

Zapper: *Coffee and cigarettes*

If you smoke cigarettes and drink coffee, you are setting yourself up for long-term memory loss. As explained under "Boosters and Zappers in Drugs," caffeine and nicotine are short-term boosters and long-term zappers. (See pages 59 to 60.)

In addition to the stress effect (and thus memory loss) caused by the long-term use of caffeine and nicotine, nicotine hits the brain with a double whammy. It is well-known that smoking affects the health of blood vessels. Over time, smoking will cause or enhance arteriosclerosis (the deterioration of blood vessels) and this will keep the brain from receiving a healthy blood supply. Not only does this lead to an increased risk of stroke, but it will also slowly, in step-by-step fashion, affect the brain's ability to think and remember.

Booster: *Exercise*

As we all know, exercise offers many health-promoting benefits. Let's add one more to the list: It can improve memory in several ways:

- Exercise changes the body's reaction to stress. This change lowers the levels of brain and body cortisol. Cortisol is a known memory zapper and its chronic presence at high levels is known to have a long-term effect on brain deterioration. Using exercise to keep cortisol levels down is an excellent way to protect memory function.

- Exercise balances the rest/sleep cycles necessary for healthy mental functioning.

- Exercise (especially aerobic exercise) improves the flow of blood to the brain. It also prevents arteriosclerosis—the deterioration of blood vessels that over time reduces the supply of blood and oxygen that feed the brain. The healthy flow of blood through vessels is vital to memory function.

- Exercise raises natural serotonin levels, reducing the likelihood of memory-zapping depression.

- Exercise moderates insulin release, preventing memory-zapping hypoglycemia when sweets are ingested.

Booster: *Relaxation*

Research in humans has demonstrated that high anxiety can temporarily erase or muddle recollection. Prolonged exposure to the hormones released during stress cause cells in the hippocampus to atrophy and even die (explained on pages 73 to 74). Because stress has such a strong negative effect on memory, learning to relax is one of the first steps taught in memory classes at the Aging Clinical Research Center at Stanford University School of Medicine, California.

If your memory is starting to slip, do yourself a favor and learn how to deal with daily stress and learn how to relax.

(For stress, see the relaxation exercises discussed in Chapter 6.)

Zapper: *Sleep deprivation*

Lack of sleep definitely affects the brain's ability to hold onto information. In fact, sleep deprivation causes the same long-term effects on memory as stimulants. This effect is probably caused by the depletion of the reserves of brain acetylcholine, norepinephrin, and serotonin, and by the effect of stress (cortisol release) on the hippocampus.

Without adequate rest, the body's natural balance of the these brain chemicals is disturbed, thus making it difficult to remember.

Sleep deprivation also affects the brain's ability to turn short-term memories into long-term memories. Although exactly how this process occurs is not fully understood, it is generally agreed that it happens during sleep, perhaps during REM (rapid-eye-movement) sleep when the eyes move rapidly under closed lids. Without deep, prolonged sleep, this process cannot occur fully and properly.

Zapper: *Stress*

We have been hearing for years how stress ages the body. We've been encouraged to learn how to relax, how to breathe deeply, how to shut down the stress response. Now you have another reason to learn how to deal with the tensions of everyday life. Stress is a primary memory zapper, especially when it's chronic.

When the body feels stress, certain neurons in the hippocampus actually release a steroid hormone called hydrocortisone, which restores balance by turning off the stress response. Repeated stress turns this system on so intensely that it cannot shut off easily (possibly because LTP neurons have some role here—see page 50 for details). Chronic brain exposure to hydrocortisone causes the common symptoms of stress overload, which include anxiety, irritability, inability to relax, and difficulty sleeping. In his book *Brain Longevity*, Dr. Dharma Singh Khalsa outlines the three ways hydrocortisone (or cortisol) damages the brain:

- ◆ It interferes with the supply of glucose, the fuel that powers the brain. When this happens, new memories are hard to lay down and existing memories are hard to retrieve.
- ◆ It causes an excessive influx of calcium into brain cells. Over a long period, this calcium creates free-radical molecules that cause dysfunction and eventually kill brain cells. In the long term, calcium build-up can produce neuronal cell loss and neuronal cell damage. When the brains of Alzheimer's patients are examined at autopsy, there is virtually always evidence of a great deal of calcium buildup in brain cells. This cell death is particularly notable in the hippocampus, and so memory is particularly damaged.

♦ It interferes with the function of neurotransmitters, making it difficult for different areas of the brain to communicate and put together or store a complete memory.

Because hydrocortisone is so damaging to brain cells over time, it explains why people who take hydrocortisone for chronic conditions, such as arthritis, asthma, and psoriasis, slowly lose mental power for clear, sharp thinking.

Stress also reduces the level of DHEA found in brain cells. DHEA is found in high concentrations in the brain, and as a precursor or building block of cortisol, is necessary to maintain proper neurological function. DHEA is so sensitive to body tension that clinicians often monitor DHEA levels to track the effects of long-term stress. What they find is that when the level of DHEA is low, the levels of cortisol are high (probably because DHEA is getting used up to make cortisol). Given these mechanisms, we can see that stress is toxic to your brain cells, and memory in particular.

Stress is not only experienced in tense situations; it can be manufactured in the body by things you eat. Stimulants, such as caffeine and nicotine, and free-radical-producing products, such as fatty processed cakes loaded with preservatives, put a tremendous amount of stress on the body that can trigger the stress response. Too much coffee and cake will give you the exact same symptoms as the chronic stress previously mentioned—anxiety, irritability, inability to relax, and difficulty sleeping—indicating that they too may cause the cortisol release system to go awry.

The destruction of brain cells from stress doesn't happen suddenly or dramatically. It happens gradually, over time—and it can be stopped. If you're worried about memory loss, take a big step toward keeping the cells of the hippocampus healthy by learning how to deal with stress and by adjusting your diet to ease up on the stress-producing caffeine and processed foods. (See also Chapter 6.)

Chapter 4

Sex: What's Fueling or Draining Your Sex Drive?

Forget what you've heard about rabbits. In all the animal kingdom, it is humans who are the most sex-obsessed. It's true! Humans are the only species to make sex a major recreational occupation. Unlike other animals that have sex only when the female is in estrus (when she is ovulating), male and female humans feel sexual desire and practice sexual activity even during nonestrus periods. The reason for this difference lies less in personal preference and more in a biological, survival-of-the-species explanation.

It is believed that our "sex obsession" has to do with the fact that the time to human maturity and the time required for supervision of the young is generally lengthy compared to other animals. (Cats, for instance, reach maturity in six weeks.) As a result, over years of evolution it has become advantageous for a human male and female to be together for years and to form a family unit to provide stability for the developing young. It is thought that because we are obsessed by sex, even during the nonestrus portion of the cycle, the bond between the male and female is enhanced.

The Holistic Brain

Finding a mate and reproducing are complex human behaviors that involve many different brain functions. This makes it difficult to isolate aspects of sexual behavior and arousal to singular brain functions. So keep in mind throughout this chapter that we will be talking about trends and trying to isolate subsystems as well as possible, but with the understanding that each works in concert with the other.

The Brain and Sex

The fact is, we exist biologically solely to reproduce. The drive for survival of the species is so strong that every part of the brain, from the neurons responsible for vision, sight, smell, touch, and hearing to those involved in memory, attention, emotion, and so on is in some way involved in sexual drive and behavior. In this section, we'll look at the three aspects of brain function that are most directly responsible for sexual activity: 1) the hypothalamus and its link to the sex hormones; 2) the neurotransmitters and their ability to keep us focused on the act; and 3) the two parts of the autonomic nervous system.

It is these three aspects of brain function that are most often affected by the foods, drugs, and lifestyle choices we make.

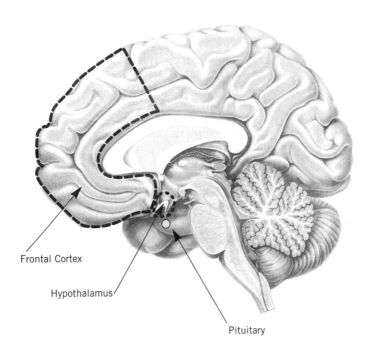

Frontal Cortex

Hypothalamus

Pituitary

FIGURE 4A

Sex Hormones

The hypothalamus is a nucleus near the lower portion of the brain above the brainstem. (See Figure 4A.) It is the hypothalamus that is believed to be the core of the mind-body connection because of the way it takes neural input from different parts of the brain and uses it to regulate many bodily functions. In the case of sexual activity, the hypothalamus receives input from the pituitary gland that regulates the release of the sex hormones known as the *luteinizing hormone* (LH) and the *follicle stimulating hormone* (FSH).

From the pituitary, LH and FSH pass through the bloodstream to reach the primary sex organs of the female (the ovaries) and the male (the testes). These sex organs then release the secondary sex hormones—predominant in males is *testosterone* and in females, *estrogen* and *progesterone*. (Because there is crossover in the synthesis of testosterone, estrogen, and progesterone, there are small amounts of each hormone in both males and females.)

In the male, the pituitary releases LH and FSH continuously, causing the testes to constantly produce sperm and release testosterone.

In the female, LH and FSH are released cyclically to control the ovarian release of estrogen and progesterone through the menstrual cycle.

> *A vagina and clitoris will develop in all mammals along with a cervix and uterus, unless exposed to testosterone in utero. Only when testosterone is introduced will the testes and penis develop. This explains the danger of certain external compounds that can imitate testosterone. Elements found in the environment as pollutants, such as the pesticide DDT, as well as barbiturates taken early in pregnancy, may introduce testosterone-mimicking substances to the fetus. This may cause differences in the development of the brain that affect sexual characteristics and behaviors. In laboratory animals, these testosterone-like pollutants cause masculinization of females and abnormal sexual development.*

Two other hormones released from the pituitary gland are also important in the sexual response: prolactin and oxytocin.

Prolactin, linked to the dopamine system, is clearly involved in the sex drive. Too much prolactin decreases libido and sexual response, and in pregnant women it is involved in initiation of lactation.

Oxytocin is released in females by the pituitary gland during orgasm and during nipple stimulation; it directly causes pleasurable contraction of the uterus when the nipples are stimulated during lactation and sex. Some studies show that it has a potential "aphrodisiac" effect on female sexual interest and arousal. Other studies, however, have shown that oxytocin is present in both male and females during orgasm, causing a reduction in sexual drive, perhaps accounting for the drop in desire for a quick repeat performance.

Nitric Oxide

Nitric oxide is a chemical released by cells lining blood vessels throughout the body that causes vasodilation. It is important to normal sexual function because it controls blood flow responses in both the brain and the sex organs. For instance, nitric oxide causes vasodilation (increased blood flow) in areas of the hypothalamus that trigger the pituitary to release the various sex hormones previously discussed. Further, it opens the blood vessels that cause penile erection and clitoral excitement. The effects of the drug Viagra involve the release of nitric oxide in the penis (see pages 85 to 86).

Sexy Neurotransmitters

The location of the neurotransmitters norepinephrine, serotonin, dopamine, and histamine receptors supports their involvement in sexual activity. In Chapter 2 we discussed how these neurotransmitters are active in keeping the brain focused and attentive by allowing for specific cortex regions to turn on while others shut off on demand. We discussed how PET scans reveal increased blood flow to the frontal region during moments of great concentration and awareness. Not coincidentally, PET scanning during sexual orgasm shows that this same area of the brain "lights up"—particularly the right side, which is most directly active when one is focusing on a specific task. This involvement of the attention-grabbing neurotransmitters in the sex process explains why the path to orgasm can be sabotaged by mental distraction.

Balancing the Autonomic Nervous System

Another factor involved in sexual function and dysfunction is the autonomic nervous system that controls involuntary functions throughout the body. This involves two distinct systems:

1. The sympathetic nervous system (the fight-or-flight system) is regulated by certain nerve tracts that start in the brainstem and go down the spinal cord. Along the spinal cord at each level there is a small collection of nerve cells (called ganglion) that stimulates various organs and blood vessels in the region by releasing norepinephrine and epinephrine. A specific set of fibers also goes to the adrenal gland on top of each kidney and triggers the release of epinephrine into the bloodstream. The sympathetic system speeds up the heart and increases the rate of breathing, the state of readiness, and the blood flow to the muscles.

2. The parasympathetic nervous system is involved in the relaxation response that balances the sympathetic system. The parasympathetic system causes the heart to slow down and lowers the respiratory rate. It also stimulates restorative functions of the body, such as salivation, swallowing, digestion, eliminating, and urination.

Normal sexual response depends on a delicate balance between these two systems. In males, during an erection a certain amount of relaxation of the veins in the penis allows it to engorge with blood and swell in size (thanks to the parasympathetic system). At the same time, there needs to be just the right amount of constriction of these veins at the outflow to trap that blood in the penis and cause erection. Ejaculating mainly involves sympathetic nerves, but this also requires a careful balance. In females, similarly balanced responses increase blood flow and swelling during arousal and mediate the vaginal muscle and uterine contractions of orgasm.

Homosexuality and the Brain

There is no doubt that a multitude of environmental and psychosocial factors may have a profound influence on sexual preference. But scientific studies have also suggested multiple physical differences in the brains of male and female homosexuals compared to heterosexuals. The evidence is complex, but in an effort to report it simply we can note that studies on homosexual men have found that:

- An area of the hypothalamus called the suprachiasmatic nucleus (SCN) is much larger and contains twice as many cells in male homosexuals as the SCN in the brain of a heterosexual person.
- The interstitial nuclei of the anterior hypothalamus are more than twice as large in heterosexual men as in homosexual men.
- The anterior commissure (a nerve tract connecting frontal halves of the cortex) is larger in homosexual men than in heterosexual men or women.

Sexual Disorders

There are no clear or simple answers to explain why some people engage in what might be called sexually deviant behaviors. Everything from foot fetishes to exhibitionism, from pedophilia to rape involves a complex host of psychological as well as physiological processes, all mediated through the brain.

There is some evidence that lesions on the brain's frontal lobe result in inappropriate sexual behavior, hypersexual behavior, transvestitism, and transsexual behavior. We also know that testosterone levels directly affect sexual desire in males. When testosterone is normal, there is a normal sexual drive; when it's low, there is a reduced sexual drive. And when the levels of testosterone are abnormally high, deviant sexual behavior often results. High levels of testosterone result in a relentless sex drive that often includes obsessional preoccupations and bizarre and complex sexual fantasies.

When this male hypersexuality interferes with normal living, it can be successfully treated with progesterone. Pedophiles, exhibitionists, and other patients with sexual disorders are often given the oral contraceptive Provera or the long-acting progesterone injection Depo-Provera to reduce the libido.

Sex Boosters and Zappers

There are many factors and substances that influence sexual drive and performance. Some of these are sex zappers that cause sexual dysfunction. In males, sexual dysfunction is characterized by the inability to have an erection, delay of orgasm, inability to ejaculate, or reduced or absent sex drive. In females, sexual dysfunction is characterized by reduced or absent sex drive, delay or inability to achieve orgasm, and pain with intercourse from insufficient lubrication that normally occurs with arousal.

Other substances are sex boosters—long known as aphrodisiacs. The history and lore of substances claiming to heighten sexual response and performance is long and fascinating, but most are hardly scientific. There is a belief among people in isolated areas of Mexico, for example, that pork tainted with parasites boosts sexual powers. (Don't try this at home!) But there are others that may actually work.

Boosters and Zappers in Your Own Body

It is difficult to neatly divide the natural substances in the body into sex zappers and boosters because many do both—depending on the amount and the timing. Balance is the key.

Booster & Zapper: *Hormones*

Prolactin is released by the pituitary gland in both males and females. In males, this hormone decreases sexual drive and erectile function; in females, it decreases the orgasmic response. Raised prolactin levels (and thus sexual dysfunction) are commonly found in patients with pituitary tumors, but moderate elevations of prolactin levels caused by no apparent disorder frequently occur as well.

The sex-boosting neurotransmitter dopamine can block the release of prolactin and improve libido and potency. We know this because the drug bromocriptine, which enhances the dopamine effect by acting like dopamine, improves sexual function in patients who have either too little dopamine (such as from Parkinson's) or too much prolactin (from pituitary tumors or kidney failure) in their system.

Testosterone is the number-one sex hormone in males. You may have heard people joke that a highly sexed man has an overload of testosterone. Well, it may be true! There is an interesting relationship between testosterone, dopamine, and prolactin. It seems that testosterone enhances the dopamine response so that people with high testosterone levels have high dopamine levels, which keep the prolactin in check and increase sexual drive and function. On the other hand, low testosterone levels result in low dopamine levels. Without enough dopamine to keep prolactin in check, prolactin levels increase, causing decreased sexual drive and function.

Estrogen and progesterone are the major hormones active in females. Responsible for monthly cyclical changes, the sudden drop of both before menstruation causes brain-based behavioral effects ranging from irritability to sex drive loss or enhancement. Menopausal loss in estrogen can have effects ranging from loss in vaginal lubrication and sex drive to deepening of the voice and hair loss (not exactly psychological aphrodisiacs). (See Chapter 9 for more details.)

Booster & Zapper: *Neurotransmitters*

Dopamine is the "sexiest" of all neurotransmitters because it seems to be the one most directly involved in sexual response, drive, and performance. It is the most likely natural brain substance involved in what we call "horniness." Dopamine neurons go to the hypothalamus, which controls the secretion of the pituitary sex hormones.

Patients with Parkinson's disease suffer cell loss in a major dopamine nucleus and therefore have decreased levels of brain dopamine. Studies of young patients with Parkinson's disease (ages 36 to 56) report diminished sexual drive and more difficulties with male erection and ejaculation and female orgasm.

Serotonin is also involved in the sex response. A normal and healthy supply of this neurotransmitter is necessary for normal orgasmic response. However, at high or low levels, serotonin is a sex zapper. This is seen in people who are given antidepressants that raise brain serotonin, such as Paxil and Prozac. Many experience orgasmic delay or absence. On the other hand, drugs that decrease levels of serotonin can cause inhibited sex drive and impotence.

Norepinephrine in the brain is involved in the state of alertness required for sexual function. In the body, it is the main chemical mediator of the sympathetic nervous system, which is involved in both the orgasmic response in males and females and the delicate balance required for male erection. But as with serotonin, too high or too low levels of norepinephrine are sex zappers. If you're a male and your norepinephrine is too high (perhaps because you're under too much stress), you won't be able to get an erection. If you're taking drugs that block the norepinephrine response in the body (such as beta blockers or antihypertensives), you can develop problems with impotence. If you're a female, this may affect arousal levels and ability to reach orgasm.

Histamine is involved in the attention centers active for normal sexual function. Certain antihistamines can actually prevent the orgasmic failure that occurs when serotonin is raised with drugs such as Prozac and Paxil. If someone is taking one of these selective serotonin re-uptake inhibitors (SSRIs) and is unable to have an orgasm, the antihistamine cyproheptadine (Periactin) often restores the balance needed for sexual function. (There is no evidence that taking antihistamines will help people to have orgasms—it is more likely to make them fall asleep.)

Booster: *Pheromones*

Pheromones are substances (steroid in nature) found on the skin that trigger a sexual response in the opposite sex. They are also responsible for synchronization of the cycles of women living in the same house or dormitory. The olfactory system senses the presence of pheromones (although they probably do not produce an actual scent) and sends a message to the frontal lobe, where so many other sex-related drives and behaviors originate. Pheromones are essentially an airborne aphrodisiac!

Recently, perfumes containing pheromones have been manufactured and advertised as aphrodisiacs. Don't waste your money. No specific human substance has yet been identified and produced synthetically.

Boosters and Zappers in Drugs

An increase or decrease in sexual drive and function is a common side effect of many popular drugs—over-the-counter, prescription, and illegal/recreational drugs. Virtually all aspects of the human sexual response can be affected by these drugs. Many affect both desire (libido) and performance (impotency, as defined by lack of erection and ejaculation). In fact, an important first step in the treatment of sexual dysfunction of any kind is to identify the drug/medication use of the patient. A few commonly used drugs that affect sexual drive and performance are discussed in this section. But they are not the only ones. Be sure to check with your physician or pharmacist about the effects on sexual performance of any drug you are taking.

Booster & Zapper: *Antidepressants*

A popular class of prescription drugs used to treat depression is the selective serotonin re-uptake inhibitors (SSRIs). These drugs, which include Prozac, Paxil, Zoloft, and Wellbutrin, increase brain serotonin. Orgasmic difficulties are prominent with these medications, although problems with libido, ejaculation, and erectile function are also common. In a cruel twist, these drugs can even sometimes increase libido, cranking up the sex drive, while zapping the ability to sexually perform.

Antidotes to the negative effect of SSRIs on sexual function can be found in several other prescription drugs. Periactin (an antihistamine), yohimbine (used to treat impotence), and amantadine (an antiviral and anti-Parkinsonian drug) have all been found to be safe and relatively effective in reversing SSRI-induced sexual dysfunction.

Another class of antidepressants that affect sexual function are the monoamine oxidase inhibitors. These cause problems similar to the SSRI drugs.

Zapper: *Antihypertensives*

Certain antihypertensive drugs can cause sexual dysfunction in both males and females. Impotence, decreased libido, impaired ejaculation, and gynecomastia (breast bud development in males) are all potential side effects depending on the agent prescribed. These include:

1. Drugs that work on the central nervous system. These drugs can cause a decrease in the outflow of norepinephrine projections from the brain down the spinal cord and have a negative effect on sexual function. This includes the antihypertensives Aldomet and Clonidine (also used to treat the massive norepinephrine outflow in narcotic addiction withdrawal).

2. Beta blockers. These drugs lower blood pressure by blocking the effect of norepinephrine and the epinephrine at receptors called beta receptors, but they can also cause impotence and decrease in sexual drive. These beta blockers include Inderal, Corgard, Tenormin, and Lopressor.

3. Diuretics. These drugs (often called "fluid pills") are used to lower blood pressure and are known to cause impotence in some people. Included are Lasix and hydrochlorthiazide.

Some other antihypertensives have little or no adverse effect on sexual function. These are the ACE inhibitors such as Captopril, Vasotec, and Lisinopril. The calcium channel blockers also have little adverse effect. The popular ones include Norvasc, Procardia, and Calan. Many people who need medication for high blood pressure request these drugs to avoid the negative side effects on sexual function.

Questionable: *Antiseizure drugs*

Antiseizure, also called anti-epileptic, drugs (such as Dilantin) are suspected of causing decreased libido in both sexes and impotence in males. It is unclear, however, which is the cause and which is the result. Seizure disorders usually occur in patients who have had some form of organic brain damage. This makes it difficult to tell for certain whether the sexual dysfunction experienced by these patients is caused by the drugs that treat the seizures or by the brain damage itself. It would be unethical to take these patients off their medication and to let them have their seizures to find out if their sexual drive improves. So for the present, the relationship between sexual function and antiseizure medication is speculative.

Booster: *Aphrodisiacs and performance enhancers*

The drugs most commonly prescribed to treat sexual dysfunction include Viagra, yohimbine, Papavarine, and prostaglandins.

Viagra (sildenafil citrate) clearly has amazing effects on improving potency in males. This miracle drug acts "simply" by dilating blood vessels in the penis. This allows increased blood flow into the penis and promotes erection. Viagra is also now being considered to aid female sex dysfunction by improving blood flow to the clitoris.

Physicians caution patients to consider the side effects of Viagra before jumping on the bandwagon. Viagra has been fatal to patients who are also on cardiac nitrates. These are vasodilating drugs that open up the blood vessels to the heart. The combination of the vasodilation caused by the two drugs causes a significant effect on blood pressure that can cause heart attack and death.

Yohimbine increases the outflow of norepinephrine from the brain and causes both increase in libido and improvement in sexual function. This has been well-established through clinical studies and it has long been appreciated as an aphrodisiac for both males and females. This derivative from the bark of the yohimbine tree has been used to treat both erectile dysfunction in males and orgasmic difficulties in patients who have a problem achieving orgasm because they are taking antidepressants that affect serotonin.

Although yohimbine is a proven aphrodisiac, don't run out to the supermarket to pick up the over-the-counter version and expect exciting results. Studies have found that the yohimbine in these products is actually a mixture of various botanicals or bark extracts that contain little or no yohimbine plant material. The purified preparation of yohimbine requires a prescription. (Be aware that it may worsen hypertension because it increases the flow of norepinephrine.)

Papavarine is a direct vasodilator injected into the caverns of the penis to open blood vessels and cause erection. The problem with Papavarine is the side effect of priapism—failure to lose an erection. This is not the dream state you might imagine. A prolonged erection causes extreme pain and will eventually cause cell and nerve damage to the penis.

Prostaglandins (Alprostadil) come in suppository form for males. This small pill is placed in the penile urethra. The specific prostaglandin in this pill causes vasodilation and hence erection.

Questionable: *Deprenyl and bromocriptine*

Deprenyl (Eldepril) and bromocriptine (Pavlodel) are most commonly prescribed to treat Parkinson's disease. Deprenyl raises brain dopamine levels and bromocriptine acts like dopamine. Therefore, theoretically, these drugs can increase sexual desire and improve sexual performance and erectile dysfunction. Studies have supported this belief, but evidence supporting this effect in subjects without Parkinson's is limited.

Zapper: *Illegal/recreational drugs*

Drug abuse of any kind almost always leads to a decline in sex drive and sexual potency. The following are a sampling of popular drugs and their negative effects on sexual drive and performance.

Amyl nitrite ("rush poppers") is a drug that, when used to treat cardiac problems by dilating blood vessels, causes a sense of "rush" to the brain. This drug is frequently abused. When it is inhaled from a vial, it rapidly enters the bloodstream, where it suddenly opens brain blood vessels and can increase feelings of sexual arousal. It is believed to be an aphrodisiac intensifying sexual desire, erections, and the rush during orgasm. Researchers have found that this drug is commonly used within the homosexual community.

Unfortunately, amyl nitrite can cause fatal overdoses. It lowers blood pressure to dangerous levels and can cause toxic substances to accumulate in the bloodstream.

Cocaine and crack cause marked elevation in brain dopamine. This, along with stimulation of the glutamine neurons in the brain, which increase feelings of excitement and self-worth, make these drugs seem to be powerful aphrodisiacs. However, long-term studies show a very long list of sexual problems in chronic users.

Amphetamines are also stimulants that cause an initial rise in neurotransmitters and an increase in sexual response. However, over time they decrease libido and sexual function.

Opiates (heroin and morphine) raise brain dopamine and directly stimulate their own receptors. Addicts rapidly lose interest in sex, preferring the high from the drug. Drugs that treat withdrawal cause impotence and impaired sex drive, as well.

Fenfluramine is a diet stimulant that shows the same pattern of initial boost, long-term zap found in other illegal/recreational drugs. I do not recommend taking any over-the-counter diet pills. Most are mild and ineffective stimulants. Prescription diet pills containing fenfluramine can cause severe cardiac problems.

Ecstasy is a so-called "designer drug" (clinically known as methylenedioxymethamphetamine or MDMA) that is commonly used as an aphrodisiac. Although it does enhance sexual drive and function, it is also a known nerve toxin and significantly degenerates the serotonin neurons so necessary for sexual and mental health. This is a dangerous trade-off: a few moments of increased sexual pleasure for the risk of permanent brain damage, anxiety disorders, memory problems, and chronic depression (caused by the destruction of the serotonin neurons). This is a dangerous drug that is not for recreational use.

Ecstasy has also been implicated in Parkinson-like disorders because of a side product of faulty synthesis of this drug. One of the side effects of improperly manufactured MDMA is immediate and permanent Parkinson's disease. There are many young people around today suffering this terrible condition because they were looking for a few moments of heightened sexual pleasure.

Marijuana may or may not affect sexuality; the results of research studies are mixed and often contradictory. In my opinion, the effect of marijuana on sex is a matter of personal belief. Some say this drug relaxes them so they are better able to perform sexually. Others feel they become too relaxed to become sexually aroused. As a physician, I cannot recommend the use of any illegal drug. There are no clear effects in either direction, short-term or long-term.

Booster & Zapper: *Nicotine and alcohol*

Initially, nicotine can be a sex booster, but in the end, nicotine is a definite zapper. In beginning smokers, it causes the release of dopamine, which improves sex drive and performance. In chronic smokers, the increased dopamine level becomes the norm and has no further influence on sexual function. Once addicted, missing a cigarette or two will cause a drop in dopamine, followed by loss of sexual drive and performance. Those who quit may experience these problems until the body readjusts.

Nicotine reduces oxygen in the blood and, over time, impairs blood flow to the brain and sex organs. Both can cause erectile impotence. In addition, the chronic lung disease associated with long-term smoking impairs sexual desire and function in males and females. Besides providing oxygen to the body, the lung is involved in the subtle hormonal secretion and breakdown necessary for healthy sexual drive. Also, people with chronic lung disease have high levels of CO_2, which causes chronic release and depletion of norepinephrine and epinephrine. This alone can impair sexual function.

Alcohol is both a sex booster and a zapper. There is an initial burst of dopamine that excites and stimulates sexual drive, but then suddenly the effects on the GABA receptors take over and there is an overall drop in everything, including sexual ability. It also upsets the balance between the sympathetic and the parasympathetic systems, causing impotency.

With long-term chronic use, alcohol has damaging effects on sexual drive and functioning in both men and women. Abnormalities in the metabolism of sex hormones are frequently observed in chronic alcoholics. Also, in males, because of certain metabolic changes that occur in the liver, estrogen levels increase and sexual interest and ability decrease.

Questionable: *Oral contraceptives*

Oral contraceptives introduce sex hormones (estrogen and progesterone) into the system. Study results are mixed and inconclusive. In some patients, oral contraceptives increase sexual drive and function; in others, they have no effect; and in still others, they decrease sexual behavior. Part of the difficulty in obtaining consistent results can be blamed on the many psychological effects of oral contraceptives. If a woman claims that oral contraceptives increase her sex drive, perhaps it is because it has removed the fear of pregnancy, or maybe it's because she's no longer encumbered with a diaphragm, creams, or her partner's condom. Maybe unencumbered sex increases her partner's drive, thus increasing her own sexual satisfaction. All these factors muddle scientific results. The bottom line: It is unknown if oral contraceptives affect sexual drive or function.

Zapper: *Sedatives*

Sedatives such as lithium and the benzodiazepines (Valium, Xanax, Ativan) impair libido and in males can cause impotence. A recent study found that when used alone, lithium caused sexual dysfunction in about 35 percent of patients being treated for bipolar disorder. When combined with benzodiazepines, the number of affected patients increased to 49 percent.

Zapper: *Tranquilizers*

The major tranquilizers (also called antipsychotics) such as Thorazine, Haldol, Prolixin, Mellaril, and others have an affect on sexual function because they decrease dopamine levels in the brain. They cause erectile problems in males and orgasmic dysfunction and decreased libido in both males and females. These drugs are prescribed to treat schizophrenia and severe manic depressive illness.

Boosters and Zappers in Foods

Just as certain drugs influence the way the brain reacts to sexual stimulation, so too can certain foods.

Myth: *Green M&Ms*

The FDA requires that safety studies, performed on rats, be conducted on all food dyes. In the early 1980s, there was some evidence released claiming that the green food dye used in M&Ms enhanced sexual drive and function. Since then, numerous studies (that involved pumping huge amounts of green food coloring into rats) have been conducted to support those findings—with little success. There does not seem to be any actual connection between little green candies and sexual performance.

Booster & Zapper: *Guarana, kola nut, and betel nut*

Tannin-rich beverages made from guarana, the kola nut, and the betel nut (from African, Asian, and Latin American countries) are believed to have aphrodisiac properties. These enjoy much popularity in their native countries and are now finding their way to North American shops and grocery stores. They are used in herbal tonics, compounds, teas, supplements, and ice-tea mixes.

These beverages are stimulants and have the same effect on sexual drive and performance as any stimulant: short-term boost, long-term zap.

Booster: *Herbs*

In ancient Chinese medicine, it is said that sexual dysfunction related to *chi* (energy, "vital sense") is generally helped by taking herbs that stimulate circulation and warm the body. Typically, such herbs include peppers, anise, and thyme. (Cayenne pepper is even sold as a supplement.)

The claim that garlic has the power to boost sex drive and performance probably has some merit. Garlic contains antioxidant properties that are known to increase blood flow. Anything that enhances blood flow (promoting the swelling of the penis and clitoris) may improve both male and female sexual function.

Although there are no scientific studies to support it, an online site called "Did You Know?" tells us a bit of interesting history about some herbal aphrodisiacs:

Cinnamon: We are told cinnamon was the attar used by the Queen of Sheba to captivate King Solomon.

Cloves: Because of the shape, cloves are considered an aphrodisiac for males, especially in Asia. Indonesian parents plant a clove tree when they bear a son, so both will prosper as they grow up together.

Ginger: A cousin of the gladiola, the ginger's pure white blossoms are thought to be a love potion, because a woman wearing the aromatic bloom is so alluring. Egyptian traders originally brought it to Rome as an aphrodisiac.

Almonds: Samson courted Delilah with fragrant almond branches. Ancient Persians perfumed almonds in jars with flower petals before using them in desserts.

Basil: Hindu males say it is an aphrodisiac because it resembles the female organ.

Mint: In mythology, the dainty nymph Mente was turned into greenery by her envious rival, Persephone, wife of Pluto. Pluto found Mente irresistible, particularly her aroma. Hence, mint was thought to be an aphrodisiac.

Zapper: *Hot dogs, cold cuts, and smoked products*

Hot dogs, cold cuts, smoked products, and most other packaged meats contain preservatives called nitrates (such as sodium nitrate or sodium nitrite). The link between these nitrates and cancer made big headlines a few years ago, but few know that the infamous "saltpeter" (known as a killer of sexual performance) is simply another name for sodium nitrate.

The zapping power of nitrates has to do with an interaction that occurs between nitrates and the natural vasodilator nitric oxide. Nitrated foods impair the effectiveness of nitric oxide, which is vital to normal sexual function. As Viagra prompts nitric oxide to open blood vessels and allow penile erection (as well as swelling in the female clitoris), nitrates block this effect.

Be careful as you down those hot dogs at your next barbecue—it doesn't take much of these preservatives to have a negative effect. Because nitrates are present in large amounts and are water soluble, they get into the blood stream very easily.

Booster: *Libido*

The commercial product Libido (also called Libid, Libbido, Erosom, and Ardorare), which is based on components derived from fertilized, partly incubated chickens' eggs, has been successfully used to treat diminished sexual desire in men. Studies have shown significant effects on the frequency of sexual intercourse, on increased self-esteem, on the level of happiness, and on stamina.

Booster: *Licorice*

There is some evidence that the extract from licorice has natural estrogen properties and may enhance the sexual activity in women after menopause. This property of licorice is a potent estrogen simulator and acts on estrogen receptors in a way similar to that of natural estrogen. However, postmenopausal women should be careful before they raid the candy store. The negative side effects of estrogen are also present in licorice extract: Breast and reproductive cancers have been attributed to an excess supply of this hormone.

Zapper: *MSG*

The food additive monosodium glutamate (MSG) has been found to have a toxic effect on the neurons in the area of the hypothalamus responsible for sexual drive and behavior. This is not going to be good for healthy sexual function.

If you are pregnant or are looking forward to a night of love-making after a romantic dinner, it would be wise to stay away from foods known to contain MSG. Chinese food has long been noted for containing this food additive, but many Chinese food restaurants now offer "MSG-free" dishes if you specifically ask. In other dishes, MSG is commonly called "natural flavors" and found in most commercial salad dressings, soup bases, and meat stocks, as well as dairy products, sauces, seasoning mixtures, frozen foods, teas, and many convenience foods.

Myth: *Oysters*

Oysters have long been thought to be natural aphrodisiacs. This rumor started because their shape resembles the structure and symmetry of the sexual organs. The same has been said about phallic-shaped vegetables, such as asparagus, cucumbers, and leeks. But, unfortunately, none of these have ever been shown to have any real effect on sexual pleasure.

You might not want to tell your partner this, however, because the psychological placebo effect can be quite powerful. Scientific studies have shown that when given a substance that is said to be an aphrodisiac (even though it is not) the majority of people will report an increase in sexual appetite and performance. So tell your mate that anything (from oysters to cucumbers to green M&Ms) is an aphrodisiac and you have better than a 60-percent chance of improving his or her sexual performance.

Boosters and Zappers in Supplements

Check the back of almost any consumer magazine and you'll find many ads offering supplements that claim to boost sex drive and performance. Beware! Most are bogus and some are far from harmless. The following will give you a look at a few "sex supplements" that are safe and can boost sexual performance and others that have dangerous side effects.

Booster: *Ginseng*

Ginseng is well-known for its ability to combat fatigue and physical stress. (Currently, sales of ginseng in the United States amount to more than $300 million annually.) Now comes the news that ginseng also shows promise as an aphrodisiac. There are a number of studies that tell us how ginseng may not only stabilize the effects of stress on the neurotransmitter systems of the brain (which keep the sexual response system healthy), but it also enhances nitric oxide synthesis, which contributes to ginseng-associated vasodilation, increasing blood flow in the penis (enhancing erectile function) and in the clitoris (enhancing sensitivity and likelihood of orgasm).

There are many different kinds and forms of ginseng. The content of each supplement differs, depending on the method of extraction, subsequent treatment, or even the season of its collection. Therefore, supplements from authentic ginseng root labeled as "standardized" are recommended.

Warning: *"Rock" or "love stone"*

A supplement called "rock" or "love stone," derived from toad venom or secretions, is commonly used as an aphrodisiac. Unfortunately, it contains bufadienolides, which are naturally occurring cardioactive steroids (similar to those in Spanish fly) that mimic the action of the cardiac drug digoxin. Used for recreational purposes, this drug can cause fatal cardiac dysrhythmias. This drug is not worth the risk: The New York City Poison Control Center reports that between 1993 and 1995, they were informed about the onset of illness in five previously healthy men after they ingested "rock." Four of these men died. The odds are not good.

Questionable: *Saw palmetto*

An herbal supplement extracted from the berry of the saw palmetto plant has been used to improve sexual performance. Although it has been shown to be an effective natural treatment for older men suffering enlarged prostate gland (which interferes with urination), it has not been established that this herb increases sexual drive or potency.

Warning: *Spanish fly*

Spanish fly, also called cantharidin, has been used for millennia as a sexual stimulant. This is a very dangerous product. Whether it really is an aphrodisiac is not worth mentioning, considering that it is purified from dead beetles and routinely causes death from cardiac complications. If it is not fatal, Spanish fly has other awful side effects: mouth burning, pain with eating, nausea, vomiting of blood, mucus erosion and hemorrhage of the upper gastrointestinal (GI) tract, vaginal and/or rectal bleeding, and kidney failure. This is not a romantic way to go.

Booster: *Vitamin C*

Several studies have shown that besides being an antioxidant (which improves blood flow and so naturally enhances healthy sexual functioning), vitamin C affects sexual function. It may work in the brain to slow the release of prolactin from the pituitary when dopamine is released. (Remember, prolactin is believed to inhibit the male sex drive and inhibit male sexual performance.)

Booster: *Vitamin E*

Vitamin E interacts with selenium to become a powerful antioxidant, cleaning up the blood vessels and allowing healthy blood flow to feed the sex organs. Together they have also been shown to improve sperm quality (an interesting point for those having fertility problems). In addition, vitamin E prevents the breakdown of nitric oxide, which in the hypothalamus and pituitary causes lower prolactin levels and may improve penile and clitoral vasodilation.

Boosters and Zappers in Lifestyle

It's not only the things we eat and drink that affect sex drive and performance. Things such as age, stress, boredom, and exercise all affect what happens under the covers.

Zapper: *Age*

Problems with sexual drive, arousal, and function often increase with age. A study at the Mayo Clinic of men between the ages of 40 and 79 compiled the results of a self-rated questionnaire on sexual concerns, performance, satisfaction, drive, and erectile dysfunction. In all five of these categories, the prevalence of problems and dysfunction increased with age. A comparison of men aged 70 to 79 years with men aged 40 to 49 years in this study suggested that older men were more worried about sexual function (46.6 percent vs. 24.9 percent), had worsened performance compared with the year before (30.1 percent vs. 10.4 percent), expressed extreme dissatisfaction with sexual performance (10.7 percent vs. 1.7 percent), had absent sexual drive (25.9 percent vs. 0.6 percent), and reported complete erectile dysfunction when sexually stimulated (27.4 percent vs. 0.3 percent). Studies in women have found similar dissatisfaction with sexual drive, arousal, and performance.

The reasons for this decline in sexual drive and performance are many, complex, and interrelated:

1. Dopamine levels and dopamine receptor-producing neurons decrease with age. This may be one of the major reasons for decreased sexual drive and performance as one ages (see page 82 for more details on dopamine).

2. Changes in the autonomic nervous system (as explained on page 79) can cause problems with penile erection in males.

3. Hormonal changes in postmenopausal women cause vaginal dryness and painful intercourse.

4. The side effects of medications frequently given to older people for cardiac problems, hypertension, and depression often cause sexual problems.

5. In monogamous couples, relationship complacency or the lack of novelty can decrease desire.

Not all elderly people experience a decline in sexual interest and function. But for those who do, the reasons are often a combination of physical and psychological factors.

Booster & Zapper: *Exercise*

A moderate amount of exercise is excellent for maintaining healthy sex drive and function. ("Moderate" generally meaning 20 minutes of aerobic activity three times a week.) This decreases stress and increases the body's and mind's resilience to the negative effects of stress. It also improves blood flow throughout the body, preventing arteriosclerosis (which interferes with adequate blood supply to the brain and sexual organs).

An interesting study at the University of California measured the effects of nine months of aerobic exercise on heart disease risk factors and sexuality. The results found the expected reduction in cardiac risk factors, but the effects on sexuality were surprisingly notable. An analysis of the subjects' diary entries revealed significantly greater sexuality enhancements in the exercise group (frequency of various intimate activities, reliability of adequate functioning during sex, percentage of satisfying orgasms, and so on). This research supports what many people already know—exercise doesn't make you tired; it gives you energy to do lots of other pleasurable things.

However, excessive exercise (such as when 30-year-old athletes run 30 to 50 miles a week) clearly has both short- and long-term negative effects on sexuality. It causes a decrease in the production of sex hormones by mimicking the effects of stress on the body, particularly as one gets older. (See "Stress" on page 98.)

Booster & Zapper: *Novelty and boredom*

Boredom zaps the libido. New and different things improve it. When a new substance, idea, sight, sound, or scent is introduced to the brain, levels of the neurotransmitter dopamine (essential to sexual drive) rise. Because of this relationship between novelty and dopamine, novelty definitely has an effect on sexual desire, excitement, and performance.

Almost any new stimulus has a direct aphrodisiac effect. There is evidence that women with new partners (even in adulterous relationships) tend to have a significantly greater number of orgasms. There is evidence that watching the same sexually explicit film over and over causes viewers to experience decreasing levels of arousal, but when these viewers then watch a new film with new actors performing identical sexual acts, the arousal level increases again.

This fact may be the enemy of monogamy for those who lack imagination. Having sexual relations in the same setting, same positions, same time, and so on, zaps the fun out of sex. (In fact, some suggest it may not be age that reduces sex drive, but rather boredom!) Complacency and inertia are the enemies of good sex. (That's why habitually watching late-night TV is a sex zapper.) To reignite the spark of excitement and novelty in a relationship, I recommend the book by Charles and Caroline Muir, *Tantra: The Art of Conscious Loving*

(Mercury House, Inc., 1990), which combines the traditional Eastern meditative approach with sex, adding something new and exciting to the way sex is performed. Also try *Getting the Love You Want* by Harville Hendrix (HarperPerennial Library, 1992).

Booster & Zapper: *Stress and meditation*

You cannot underestimate the negative effect of stress on sex. Everything from drive, to performance, to orgasm is affected by stress—especially chronic stress. A chronic stress state affects the outflow of the hypothalamus in the brain, which controls the pituitary and thus causes a decrease in the release of all sex hormones. The negative effects of chronic stress on sexual hormones are most dramatically seen in females who suffer a disruption in the normal menstrual cycle, resulting in longer cycles or amenorrhea (elimination of menstruation). This hormonal disruption in pregnant women under extreme stress may even cause miscarriage. The negative effects on sexual drive and performance may not be as noticeable in males, but they are definitely present in both sexes.

Any situation that relieves stress will improve sexual function. That's one reason the candle-light dinner, soft music, and tender words are all powerful aphrodisiacs and shouldn't be underestimated. They are nonaddictive, have no side effects, and serve as a calm interlude after a stressful day, allowing the body to relax and focus better on sexual desire.

Meditation is thought to increase the mind/body resistance to stress and, therefore, is a natural way of encouraging healthy blood flow to the brain and the sex organs and maintaining necessary levels of sex hormones.

An interesting study on the effects of meditation on sexual performance involved two married males who reported the complete absence of ejaculation during sexual intercourse. Intervention consisted of meditative relaxation exercises, together with supportive (brief) psychotherapy for the husband and wife in both cases. Normal ejaculatory competence was reported by both subjects following 10 to 12 months of intervention. This was maintained at follow-up 14 to 16 months later.

The calming effect of meditation is a terrific antidote to the sex-zapping effects of stress.

Chapter 5

Sleep: Tracking the Source of Sound and Troubled Sleep

There is no rest for the ever-vigilant brain. Through the use of the electroencephalogram (EEG) and positron emission tomography (PET) we have learned that even during sleep the brain is very active in coordinating the processes that rejuvenate the body.

Brain Changes Involved in Sleep

Although there is still much to be learned about brain function during sleep, we do know that there are five major areas of the brain involved in sleep.

1. The amine and cholinergic brain centers. The amine system includes projections from the brainstem to the cortex that supply the brain with the neurotransmitters serotonin and norepinephrine. Both drop drastically during the deepest sleep stage called REM and rise during waking.

The cholinergic system involved in sleep is a collection of brainstem neurons. As acetylcholine levels fall, drowsiness occurs. This system becomes highly active during REM sleep.

2. The hypothalamus. The hypothalamus regulates body temperature. Body temperature falls as you get sleepy and rises as you awake. This may be involved in triggering changes in the amine and cholinergic systems.

3. The thalamus. The thalamus (located centrally between the brainstem, cortex, and limbic system) receives many of the messages from the body and directs them to different parts of the brain.

Because it does this with a rhythmic firing of neurons, it works in concert with the hypothalamus to time and control the ultradian rhythms of the body that occur throughout each day in 90-minute cycles. Every 90 minutes, your body temperature, levels of alertness, and other brain functions vary in a consistent, repeated pattern. This rhythmic cycle coordinates the sleep cycles as well.

4. The pineal gland. The pineal gland releases the hormone melatonin, which promotes sleep in a cyclical pattern and in response to dimming light at the end of the day.

5. The pituitary gland. As the body prepares for sleep, the pituitary gland (controlled by the hypothalamus) releases less adrenocorticotropin (ACTH). ACTH is a hormone that causes the adrenal glands to release cortisol, so there is less of this stress substance to stimulate the body and brain.

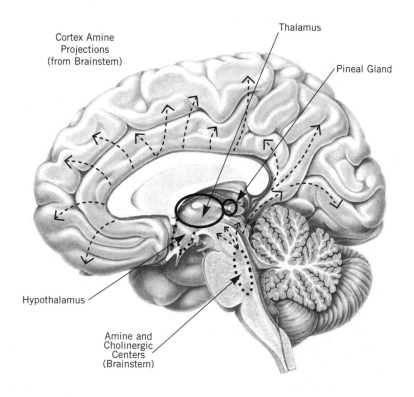

FIGURE 5A

Why Sleep?

Sleep is not a choice. The body demands it whether we like the idea or not. If we don't get enough sleep, we soon feel negative mental and physical effects. The National Sleep Foundation tells us that those who persistently don't get enough sleep report the following:

♦ Impaired ability to concentrate during the day.

♦ Memory problems.

♦ Difficulty coping with minor irritations.

Sleep deprivation robs the brain of the time it needs to do some "housecleaning." Part of this involves re-uptake (taking back) of serotonin and norepinephrine from junctions between brain cells to prepare the brain for waking. When you are sleep-deprived, you get a stress-like depletion of these substances that are so important for wakefulness, alertness, and good mood.

During sleep, the hippocampus also processes memory traces from the day. (See Chapter 3.)

Sleep Stages

Because of the body's circadian and ultradian rhythms, sleep has regular 90-minute cycles. Each cycle contains four stages of non-REM (or NREM) sleep and one REM period. (The acronym REM stands for "rapid eye movement.") Passing through these stages is like descending a staircase, with each stage of sleep becoming deeper than the previous.

Stage one is a transitional period between wakefulness and sleep, lasting only about three to five minutes. Massive coordinated nerve firing occurs so that rapid random nerve signals change to slower alpha waves. Alpha waves also occur in deep relaxation and meditation states. Soon they are replaced by even slower, more regular theta waves. Meanwhile, body temperature drops and voluntary muscles relax. Parts of the brain are still awake, so information from the environment still gets processed. Hence, you are easily awakened.

Stage two progresses into a deeper sleep. More time is spent here than in any other stage—about 30 to 40 minutes of the 90-minute cycle, or about 50 percent of the total sleep time.

In *stages three and four,* brain wave activity slows even further to produce large, wide delta waves. Stages three and four sleep are often referred to as "deep delta sleep," which amounts to only 20 to 25 percent of the total sleep time. Children, however, spend about twice as much time in these stages. (Growth hormone is released here, making these stages very important for children.) Time spent in stage four sleep decreases with age, sometimes disappearing completely in the elderly.

In these deep NREM stages, heart rate and breathing become very regular. Meanwhile, sensitivity to light and sound is almost gone, making it difficult to awaken.

Delta sleep helps restore and revitalize the body via increased protein production and tissue repair. Deprivation of deep delta sleep results in a feeling of uneasiness the following day. Delta sleep occurs during the first three hours of the night and disappears from the later sleep cycles.

After completing stage four of the cycle, the sleeper ascends through stages three and two. Rather than going back to stage one and waking, he or she enters the night's first REM sleep stage.

During REM sleep, event-based dreams of situations occur. The eyes move back and forth quickly beneath closed lids. (It is still unclear whether the rapid eye movements are a result of the eyes following the action taking place in dreams.) In early cycles, REM lasts about two to 10 minutes. As the night progresses, REM periods increase in duration.

Brain activity during REM sleep is very different from both the awake state and the NREM sleep state. Although brain wave activity resembles the rapid, random voltage of an awake state, brain function is very different. First, all voluntary muscles (except the diaphragm and eye muscles) are completely paralyzed. In fact, if you are awakened during REM sleep, you may have a few moments of terror as a specialized area of the brainstem blocks messages to your voluntary muscles, making it impossible for you to move.

REM sleep is believed to play an important role in maintaining the balance of brain neurotransmitters and in the long-term storage and consolidation of learning and memory. In addition, during REM, serotonin and norepinephrine release is almost completely stopped.

These functions are probably essential for the more complex brains of higher animals. It has been found that the higher up the evolutionary chain, the more time is spent in REM sleep. For example, reptiles and birds (who both have minimal cortex volume) sleep with barely any detectable REM sleep at all.

About one-quarter of the night is spent in REM sleep with most occurring in the latter half. With each 90-minute cycle, REM becomes increasingly longer until it lasts for almost an hour prior to waking.

Sleep Disorders

When the brain systems involved in sleep don't work in a balanced coordinated manner, sleep disorders develop.

Insomnia

Insomnia, (defined as trouble falling asleep or staying asleep) is a problem that plagues 70 million Americans of both sexes and of all age, race, and socioeconomic groups. The reasons for insomnia are many and often perplexing. The most common causes are:

- Physical problems (such as chronic pain or respiratory problems).
- Emotional disturbances (such as stress or depression).
- The side effects of medications or foods (such as pain relievers or coffee and colas).
- Lifestyle habits (such as smoking, drinking, or too little or too much exercise).
- Daily schedules that upset the natural circadian rhythms (often caused by shift work and jet lag).

Many of these things cause insomnia because they trigger changes in the way the brain balances the amines, acetylcholine, body temperature, hormone release, and circadian rhythms. Proper care and feeding of the brain is often the best remedy for insomnia.

Chronic Fatigue Syndrome

Researchers in England have found that most patients with chronic fatigue syndrome (CFS) have sleep disorders that are likely to contribute to daytime fatigue. It was reported that compared to those who do not suffer this syndrome, chronic fatigue patients spend more time in bed, sleep less efficiently, and spend more time awake after initially going to sleep. Sleep disorders may be important in understanding this syndrome.

Although CFS has been thought to be related to viral infections, there is scanty scientific evidence to support this. Patients with CFS often have either a history of prior psychiatric illness or a personality-type that makes them more vulnerable to stress. Nevertheless, there are clear differences between sleep patterns in these patients and in those who suffer the fatigue from chronic depression. This suggests some physiological cause.

Sleep Apnea

Sleep apnea occurs as the body becomes paralyzed during REM sleep. Here, the mouth, palate, and throat all relax and in some people cause an obstruction to airflow. As a result, these people wake up to catch their breath, causing an interruption in REM sleep. Diminished REM sleep causes daytime fatigue and many of the stress symptoms of sleep deprivation.

Why can't we remember all our dreams? The dreams you remember most vividly are those that occur during REM sleep just before waking. The drastic REM changes in neurotransmitters prevent adequate short-term storage of dream events. When we wake up and think about a dream we just had, it then gets incorporated into memory. Also, during REM, dreams occur in real time and the replay in the hippocampus of the memory traces from the day occurs in real time and is thought to aid memory. But in the non-REM stages of sleep, there is a replay of events and general feelings at high speeds, about 10 times faster than real time. Maybe our sense of awareness and focus is unable to catch these traces that run by so quickly, hence the dreams of NREM sleep are described more as feeling states and not events.

Sleep Boosters and Zappers

So many things we eat, drink, and do have a direct (and often profound) effect on the ability to sleep soundly and awake refreshed.

Boosters and Zappers in Your Own Body

There are natural chemicals released by the body that influence sleep and wakefulness. These include amines (serotonin and norepinephrine), acetylcholine, adrenaline, melatonin, and ACTH.

Zapper: *Adrenaline*

The body pumps up its production of adrenaline when it needs to reinforce the stress response. When you are feeling great excitement, fear, or anger, you can feel the rush of adrenaline coursing through your system. This defense mechanism is an enemy of sleep. It excites and awakens all the body processes that should be shutting down for sleep. It raises blood pressure, respiration rate, and body temperature; it also increases the production of acetylcholine. Long term, this stress response, if repeated often enough, can deplete brain serotonin and norepinephrine, causing the early morning awakening seen in depression. That's why your mother was right when she warned you not to get "wound up" before bedtime.

Booster & Zapper: *Amines and acetylcholine*

Healthy wakefulness requires a good balance between the aminergic (amines) and cholinergic (acetylcholine) systems. In simple terms: Changing levels of brain amines (mainly serotonin and norepinephrine) causes sleepiness, while high brain levels of acetylcholine cause stimulation and wakefulness. As you fall asleep, the amine levels rise and the acetylcholine levels fall. During REM sleep the process reverses itself. The amines drop and the acetylcholine levels rise. Upon waking, both amines and acetylcholine rise. Any disruption of this delicate balance will cause sleep problems.

Zapper: *Depression*

Insomnia is a very common feature of depression. It is believed that about 90 percent of patients who are depressed have insomnia (often experiencing middle-of-the-night and early-morning awakenings).

Only about 10 percent have hypersomnia, meaning they sleep long or more than usual.

Depression is associated with depletion of the brain amines serotonin and norepinephrine, both essential in the control of normal sleep patterns.

Booster: *Melatonin*

Melatonin is a hormone that sets the body's clock to the cycles of night and day. When the sun goes down, the eyes cue the pineal gland to start releasing melatonin. In response, body temperature falls, metabolism slows, and we prepare to drop off. As the morning light appears, the gland reduces its output, allowing the body to gradually come back to life. If melatonin is not produced in an adequate or timely way, sleep problems will develop. When this happens, a synthetic form of melatonin can be bought over-the-counter to help regulate the sleep cycles. (See "Supplements" for more information.)

Boosters and Zappers in Sleeping Pills

Sleeping pill is a very broad term used to refer to any chemical agent that produces drowsiness. Although each agent may differ in the way it influences sleep, each works by depressing the central nervous system in some manner.

Sleeping pills may help you sleep through the night, but you should be aware that there is a clear-cut difference between drug-induced- and nondrug-sleep. It has been found that sedative sleeping pill medications (barbiturates, benzodiazepines, and other older hypnotics such as chloral hydrate) distort the normal sleep patterns by altering the time spent in the various sleep stages. Sleep medications often reduce sleep stages three and four (deep sleep), as well as REM sleep, all causing daytime tiredness. They also increase the time spent in shallow sleep stages (stages one and two), causing more periods of wakefulness during the night. This too causes daytime fatigue.

Such sleeping pills are useful in treating mild and transitory cases of insomnia, as might occur after a stressful event or a trip to another time zone. Long-term treatment with sedative sleeping pills alone almost never works. Close medical supervision and adoption of lifestyle and behavioral changes, including treatment of underlying medical or psychological causes, is necessary.

Booster & Zapper: *Over-the-counter medications*

Popular over-the-counter (OTC) sleeping pills include Sominex, Nytol, and Compoze. Their sleep agent is an antihistamine, commonly used to treat congestion. It is a mistake to think, however, that because these sleeping pills can be purchased without a prescription, they are harmless. Antihistamines block histamine, an amine involved in the awake state, working in concert with other amines such as serotonin and norepinephrine. Their affect on alertness and wakefulness can be profound.

OTC sleeping pills are effective for the short-term treatment of some types of insomnia. They work quickly but only for a short period, so they will help you fall asleep, but will not help stop frequent nighttime awakenings. They also often cause morning grogginess.

Booster & Zapper: *Prescription medications*

Prescription sleeping pills are effective treatment for occasional short-term insomnia. However, they are only effective for a few days. Individuals who try to use these pills for long periods of time may become dependent. These side effects include:

- ◆ *Tolerance.* The brain rapidly adapts to the GABA receptor stimulation that occurs after taking these sedatives. Within three to 14 days, the brain adjusts by lowering GABA release (a sedative neurotransmitter) and sleeping problems return. The natural inclination at this point is to increase the dosage, which will further stimulate GABA receptors until GABA levels fall even further (causing more tolerance). Eventually, GABA levels are so low that the pill is no longer effective.

- ◆ *Rebound.* Rebound insomnia occurs when pills are discontinued and the symptoms of insomnia become much worse than before the medication. Although rebound is temporary until GABA levels return to normal (anytime from several days to several weeks), it tends to reinforce insomniacs' belief that they cannot sleep without medication. This pushes them to return to medication and sets the stage for dependency.

♦ *Dependence.* Very gradually, people who take sleeping pills find that they need the pill to maintain a sense of physical and psychological ease. Even though the medication may have lost its beneficial effects (because of tolerance), they believe they cannot stop taking the pill. At this point, a longer-acting change in the number of brain GABA receptors probably occurs.

♦ *Withdrawal.* When sleeping pills are discontinued after long-term treatment, many people suffer withdrawal symptoms. These include general malaise, vision problems, and increases in anxiety and insomnia. Some people experience depression. In extreme cases, discontinuation can produce seizures.

Sedatives and antidepressants are commonly prescribed to treat sleep problems. *Sedative* is a term commonly used to include two kinds of drugs: barbiturates and benzodiazepines. They each act through enhancement of the GABA receptor and are only effective for transient or short-term insomnia, for which prescriptions should, if possible, be limited to a few days, occasional or intermittent use, with courses not exceeding two weeks.

1. *Barbiturates.* Once the first line of treatment for insomnia, barbiturates have now been almost completely abandoned for this use. They have a higher level of toxicity than other available hypnotics, they are more likely to interact negatively with other medications. They also pose a greater risk for developing tolerance and dependence. An overdose of barbiturates can severely depress the central nervous system and lead to death.

2. *Benzodiazepines.* The benzodiazepines (Valium, Xanax, Klonipin, Ativan, and Dalmane) cause fatigue and sleepiness. Their effect, like other sedatives, is to initially help one fall asleep by enhancing the GABA inhibitory receptors in the brain. However, tolerance quickly develops, along with a rebound of insomnia when discontinued.

Prescription antidepressants with sedative effects are usually recommended when insomnia is associated with a depressive or anxiety disorder. Those used for this purpose include doxepin (Adapin,

Sinequan), trazodone (Desyrel), amitriptyline (Elavil), and nortryptaline (Panelor). Many physicians prescribe antidepressants rather than benzodiazepines for treating insomnia even in nondepressed patients, because the potential for abuse or physical dependency is significantly lower. These can be taken long term with minimal tolerance, and withdrawal is less severe.

Although most antidepressants have inherent direct sedative properties, their lasting effectiveness in treating insomnia comes from their treatment of sleep disorders related to underlying anxiety and depression.

Boosters and Zappers in Drugs

Disruption in sleep is a common side effect of many drugs: over-the-counter, prescription, and illegal drugs, and caffeine, nicotine, and alcohol. Some cause insomnia; others cause drowsiness.

Booster & Zapper: *Alcohol*

Initially, alcohol has a sedative effect that leads to rapid sleep. But using alcohol as a sedative is a mistake. Alcohol-induced sleep is followed by arousal, sleep fragmentation, and a prominent decrease in REM, removing much of the restorative value of sleep.

The initial sleep-boosting effect of alcohol is also ineffective because it is only temporary. You will need to continuously increase the amount of alcohol needed to bring on sleep. If you eventually decide to stop using alcohol as a sedative, you may experience a rebound effect (similar to that of sedative sleeping pills), making it even harder to fall asleep.

Chronic alcoholics tend to experience little or no REM and are plagued by frequent awakenings. The result is daytime drowsiness. Even after quitting drinking, sleep problems may not end immediately. With alcohol withdrawal, sleep problems actually worsen, but they improve in the long run (sometimes in months or years).

Zapper: *Caffeine*

Caffeine is a known enemy of sleep. Through the process of vasoconstriction and vasodilation (discussed in Chapter 2), caffeine causes brain cell activation in areas that are being used and decreases blood flow to areas where it isn't needed. This heightens the sense of awareness and alertness.

This solution to daytime tiredness, however, can make it difficult to sleep at night. Thus, caffeine can fuel a chronic cycle of sleepless nights and tired days.

Two to three cups of coffee within five hours of bedtime will disrupt almost anyone's sleep (even if he or she is not aware of it). Drinking more than six cups a day may lead to chronic insomnia. As we age, sensitivity to caffeine increases.

Zapper: *Illegal/recreational drugs*

Most psychoactive drugs interfere with sleep. This especially applies to illegal drugs, which are almost never taken in moderation.

Marijuana. Marijuana exhibits both depressant and stimulant characteristics and so has unpredictable effects on sleep. Some are excited; others are sedated. In either case, it is known that Delta-9 tetrahydrocannabinol (THC), the psychoactive compound found in marijuana, alters brain neurotransmitters involved in sleep and produces changes in brain-wave patterns. It has been documented that individuals using marijuana spend less time in REM sleep, but spend more time in stage four sleep. Less REM time eliminates much of the restorative effect of sleep and its ability to enhance memory.

Stimulants. Amphetamine (speed) and its relatives (crack and cocaine) are powerful stimulants that intensify the brain chemicals involved in wakefulness, thus reducing the time spent in deep sleep and REM sleep. They also delay sleep onset, increase the chances of waking after sleep onset occurs, and decrease total sleep time. Withdrawal from stimulants can lead to REM rebound (an increase in REM sleep), which is sometimes accompanied by nightmares.

Cocaine and crack are more potent, addictive stimulants that produce an intense sense of euphoria, only to be followed by severe depression. The euphoria probably comes from elevation in brain dopamine (remember, this is a neurotransmitter that plays a role in sleep and wakefulness). As dopamine levels rise, brain melatonin falls.

Discontinuing the use of these stimulants produces very sleepy, fatigued feelings as the body adjusts to functioning without artificial stimulation.

Heroin. Heroin is a highly addictive, narcotic depressant that inhibits intellectual and motor functioning. It also raises brain dopamine and causes a decrease in both deep sleep and REM sleep with frequent awakenings. Discontinuing the use of heroin causes a massive release of adrenaline, preventing sleep altogether, and when sleep does occur, REM rebound can cause nightmares.

Zapper: *Nicotine*

At low blood concentrations, nicotine can cause mild sedation and relaxation (explaining why some people grab a cigarette when they need to calm down). But at higher concentrations, nicotine is a stimulant that arouses and excites the nervous system. It's no wonder that insomnia ranks high among the complaints voiced by smokers.

Nicotine can affect sleep in two ways:

First, because nicotine is a central nervous system stimulant that affects the processes of vasoconstriction and vasodilation, it produces almost the same effects on the body as caffeine (explained on pages 109 to 110). The result is general arousal, including increases in blood pressure, heart rate, and brain-wave activity—all of which can negatively affect sleep.

Secondly, nicotine craving interrupts sleep patterns. As an addictive drug, nicotine is craved by the smoker's body even during sleeping hours. This may cause smokers to awaken in the middle of the night craving a smoke. If they have a cigarette, the nicotine will arouse the central nervous system, further aggravating the insomnia.

Keep in mind that cigarettes are not the only source of nicotine that will affect a sound sleep. People who smoke cigars or pipes, or who chew tobacco or snuff, or those who inhale snuff through their nostrils, are also at risk.

Booster & Zapper: *Over-the-counter medications*

There are many medications that are available without a prescription that disrupt normal sleep. The warning labels on all over-the-counter medications contain information on this possible side effect. Following are descriptions of some of them.

Cold and allergy preparations. Many medications that relieve congestion, runny nose, sneezing, watery itchy eyes, and coughing cause drowsiness because they contain antihistamines (NyQuil and Benadryl, for example). Antihistamines block histamine in the brain, one of the amines required for the alert state.

On the flip side, allergy and cold preparations that contain pseudoephedrine (such as Sudafed), a norepinephrine releaser, can cause insomnia if taken close to bedtime.

Diet pills. Diet pills frequently cause insomnia if they contain amphetamines or other stimulant substances. (See "Stimulants" on page 110.)

Pain relievers. Pain relievers, such as Dristan, Excedrin, and Anacin, cause insomnia because they contain caffeine. (See the sleep-zapping effects of caffeine on pages 109 to 110.) Always check the label if you plan to take a pain reliever before bedtime.

Booster & Zapper: *Prescription medications*

There are a number of medications prescribed by physicians for various ailments that can disrupt normal sleep. A few examples are listed here, but if you're having any sleep problems and are taking medication of any kind, be sure to ask your doctor or pharmacist about this relationship.

Antidepressants. Many popular antidepressants enhance the release of brain serotonin or norepinephrine. This can cause drowsiness, sometimes even a state of hypersomnolence (excessive sleepiness). Tricyclic antidepressants such as Elavil (amytriptaline) and Panelor (nortriptaline) most often have this effect.

The newer antidepressants called selective serotonin re-uptake inhibitors (SSRIs) prevent the process of clearing the brain of serotonin, leaving it around to have a calming effect. They include Prozac, Wellbutrin, Zoloft, and Paxil.

SSRIs make most people sleepy, but make some people more awake. Additionally, some people have more pleasant dreams, while others have nightmares. Very often, changing from one SSRI to another will change the side effects experienced.

Asthma medications. Many of the asthma inhalers (such as Ventolin and Proventil) act like epinephrine on the lung. OTC medications such as Primatene Mist are actually epinephrine solutions. Because they stimulate beta receptors (one of several sites of epinephrine action) and some get into the bloodstream, they can cause many of the symptoms of stress (such as shaking, rapid pulse, anxiety, and increased alertness). Taking these medications at bedtime can have the same effect as stress or physical activity.

Steroid preparations are also given for asthma (such as Asthmacort) with a similar effect on sleep. The steroid gets into the bloodstream and brain and produces a stress-like activation. This steroid effect is delayed and may occur hours after taking the medication.

Hypertensive medications. Some medications prescribed to treat high blood pressure and heart attacks affect sleep. The worst offenders are the beta blockers (Inderal, Corgard, Atenolol, Metoprolol). They block the beta receptors normally activated by norepinephrine. This can cause drowsiness and even nightmares.

Another antihypertensive drug affecting sleep is clonidine, which decreases central nervous system norepinephrine release and causes general sleepiness.

L dopa. Drugs used to treat Parkinson's disease, such as L-dopa, raise brain dopamine levels and have a negative effect on sleep. Besides directly stimulating alertness, as dopamine goes up, pituitary release of prolactin falls and may cause a decrease in brain melatonin (needed for sleep).

Lithium. This drug is often given to schizophrenic patients and those suffering manic-depressive illness. It interrupts REM sleep and causes intense fatigue.

Oral contraceptives. Because oral contraceptives simulate pregnancy in the body, they can directly cause sleepiness. Progesterone, the main ingredient, has been shown to enhance anesthetics, as well.

Steroids. Steroid medications (such as Prednisone and Asthmacort) prescribed to treat inflammation, asthma, and other conditions first cause insomnia because they have stimulant properties. Later, after chronic use, these drugs can cause depression, resulting in early-morning awakening.

Boosters and Zappers in Foods

Some of the foods we eat can have a profound effect on the quality of our sleep. The answer to sleep problems is often found right in the food pantry.

Booster: *Carbohydrates*

Carbohydrates help you get a good night's sleep for three reasons: 1) They directly raise brain serotonin levels; 2) they cause a release of insulin, which lowers glucose and enhances the tendency of the brain to want to fall asleep; and 3) insulin released in response to carbohydrate intake has been shown to raise blood tryptophan—the amino acid converted to serotonin in the brain.

If you're having sleep troubles, you might try eating a complex-carbohydrate snack (such as crackers, cereal, bread, or pasta) before bed. Starchy carbohydrates have a better effect on sound sleep than sugary carbohydrates. You should also avoid fat; it can slow the digestion and release of these carbohydrates.

Zapper: *Chocolate and cola*

It is well-known that having a cup of coffee before bedtime will zap sleep, but don't forget the other common foods that contain caffeine. Having a chocolate bar or a can of cola before bed will fill your system with enough of this stimulant to keep you awake for hours. Chocolate contains xanthines—substances similar to caffeine. All colas contain caffeine and should be avoided before sleep, but diet soda may actually be worse for two reasons: 1) The sugar that would otherwise exert its sedating influence as a carbohydrate is absent; and 2) there is mounting evidence that NutraSweet (commonly used to sweeten many diet drinks) may be a direct stimulant to the brain.

Zapper: *NutraSweet*

The artificial sweetener NutraSweet (aspartame) is a stimulant that lowers brain serotonin and should be avoided before sleep and by all insomniacs. Also, long-term use may cause PMS, hunger, and even depression. It has also been reported to cause headaches—another factor in problem sleep.

Myth: *Protein*

Protein-laden foods contain certain amino acids that have inherent stimulant properties. All meats can keep you awake because of their high protein content.

It is a myth that meats (such as turkey) high in tryptophan make you sleepy. Although they do contain this sedative-like property, the amino acids in protein foods have the stronger effect of wakefulness.

Myth: *Warm milk*

Sorry, but scientifically, your mother was wrong. Milk is high in protein, which makes it harder to fall asleep. However, the power of suggestion may override this fact. If you associate warm milk with home and warmth, and sound, secure sleep, the expectation of a good night's sleep following a glass of warm milk can make it happen.

Boosters in Herbs and Supplements

Some herbs and supplements have a tranquilizing effect that will help you achieve sound sleep. A few of the herbs commonly used to encourage sleep are listed here.

Booster: *B vitamins*

There are at least three B vitamins important in the sleep process. An adequate daily supply of these vitamins will encourage peaceful sleep; a shortage can zap the sleep process. Because B vitamins have mild and temporary stimulant properties for some people, avoid taking them before bedtime.

Vitamin B3 (niacin) is sometimes used to relieve insomnia caused by mild depression. It has been found that niacin prolongs REM sleep and decreases the time spent awake by insomniacs.

Vitamin B6 (pyridoxine) acts as a natural sedative on the nerves and is instrumental in maintaining the proper level of magnesium in the blood. When B6 is deficient, the amino acid tryptophan is not used properly by the body, preventing adequate serotonin synthesis.

B12 is another B vitamin that has been used to treat insomnia. Researchers from the National Institute of Mental Health recently reported in the journal *Sleep* that they were able to maintain normal sleep-wake cycles in a patient who had been an insomniac for 10 years simply by administering B12 supplements.

Most multivitamins supply adequate daily amounts of these B vitamins. B12, however, may not be adequately absorbed in elderly patients and may not be adequately available in some vegetarian diets. In these cases, a B12 supplement is advised. Newer sublingual preparations that get absorbed under the tongue are available and recommended.

Booster: *Chamomile*

Chamomile (also spelled camomile) is the most frequently used of the sleep-inducing herbs. Both chamomile tea and chamomile preparations are used for the depressive effect they have on the central nervous system. Because chamomile has been reported to expel gas from the stomach and bowels, it may also be effective for those who lose sleep because of indigestion or gas pains.

Booster: *DHEA*

DHEA may be found to be a wonderful supplement to promote sound sleep as more research is done. It seems that it may enhance REM sleep. Those who take DHEA report increased and more vivid dreaming (a sign of more intense REM sleep). Some "experts" have urged caution with this supplement because of a theoretical link with testicular cancer. However, no evidence has been found to support this cautionary warning at this time.

Booster: *Hops*

Hops is a type of grain that, when ground into a liquid and fermented, is one of the components of beer. Hops itself, before fermentation, contains substances that promote sleep. It is usually combined with other herbs (such as valerian root and passion flower) to calm nerves. Loose hops have also been stuffed into pillows, taking the place of down, to help induce sleep (although no scientific studies substantiate this effect).

Booster: *Kava kava*

Kava kava contains substances called kavapyrones that may reduce anxiety and promote sleep. They seem to act by raising both serotonin and norepinephrine, but they should never be taken by anyone already on antidepressants or anti-anxiety medications. It has even been reported that a person taking kava kava and the sedative

Xanax together lapsed into a coma. Because of this kind of potency and interaction, kava kava should be taken only under the supervision of a physician. Kava kava is available over-the-counter and bears warning labels about interactions with antidepressants and anxiolytics (sedatives).

Booster: *Lavender*

A study published in the British medical journal *Lancet* recently reported that the sweet smell of lavender oil helped four elderly insomniacs fall asleep more quickly and sleep longer. Three of them stopped taking sedatives completely. This is an intriguing study that probably has something to do with the fact that the olfactory bulb (the nose's nerve center) connects directly to the limbic system, which mediates drive and arousal states. The reticular activating system sends projections of serotonin- and norepinephrine-producing neurons to the limbic system, as well as to the cortex. (Avoid burning lavender-scented candles at night. Besides being a fire hazard, the extra light impairs sleep!)

Booster: *Melatonin*

As the sun sets, the brain is triggered to release the natural substance, melatonin, involved in helping the body fall asleep. Melatonin affects the daily cyclical rhythms and seems to promote the fall in body temperature that occurs as the body prepares for sleep. Its action is mainly on the hypothalamus.

Melatonin is now available as a supplement and offers hope as a nonaddictive sleeping pill that does not interfere with the production or release of serotonin, norepinephrine, or dopamine.

Many studies have been conducted to test the effectiveness of melatonin on sleep and the results are very encouraging. Study participants who take melatonin before bedtime often fall asleep more quickly sleep soundly through the night, and sleep longer in the morning. The studies conducted thus far find melatonin to be safe for short-term use.

A most effective dosage is 1 to 3 milligrams taken at bedtime. Don't overdo it, because too much melatonin can make you feel groggy in the morning.

Booster: *Passion flower*

Passion flower is used around the world as a mild sedative that reduces nervous tension and anxiety. Passion flower may also be effective in combating muscle cramps that disrupt and limit sleep.

Booster: *Skullcap*

Skullcap is a supplement preparation made from *scutellaria baicalensis*, which may dampen the stress response and promote sleep in insomniacs. It also has variable effects on the bone marrow and should be avoided by people with blood disorders or anemia and by those undergoing cancer chemotherapy.

Booster: *Tryptophan*

Tryptophan is a naturally occurring amino acid. Inside the body, tryptophan is carried to the brain where it is converted into the neurotransmitter serotonin (which induces sleep). Synthetic tryptophan was pulled from the market in 1990 after a contaminated form of the product, made in Japan, was associated with a rare blood disease. Later, the supplement was replaced by a version called 5-hydroxy-L-tryptophan which sold over the counter and was promoted as a remedy for depression and insomnia. Now, low levels of a similar contaminant have been found in this product also. Tryptophan is an important sleep inducer that may be back on the shelves soon if the manufacturing process is improved enough to isolate safe preparations.

Booster: *Valerian root*

Valerian root has been used for centuries as a mild sedative. Before barbiturates were invented in the early 1900s, valerian root was the most widely used sedative. In World War I it was used by troops on the front lines to prevent shell shock, and in World War II it was used by civilians experiencing stress and anxiety from air raids. Valerian root is most often used to treat sleep disorders that stem from anxiety and nervousness.

Its history supports its effectiveness. Many OTC "natural" sleep remedies contain valerian root.

Boosters and Zappers in Lifestyle

There are many daily habits and practices that either boost or zap restorative sleep.

Booster & Zapper: *Exercise*

If you are not sleeping well at night and are tired during the day, the last thing you'll feel like doing is getting up to exercise. But that's exactly what you should do to get a better night's sleep and feel energized during the day.

There are numerous reasons exercise promotes sound sleep:

1. Exercise is known to raise baseline serotonin levels in the brain. (This alone will improve sleep patterns.)
2. Those who exercise regularly seem to be more resilient to the exhausting effects of stress on the brain.
3. Vigorous exercise increases the core body temperature by about two degrees Fahrenheit. Exercise performed in the late afternoon or the early evening will force the body temperature to dip much lower during sleep—a strong sleep booster.

On the other hand, ill-timed exercising can make it difficult to fall asleep. Exercise promotes the release of adrenaline and lactic acid; both are stimulants that prevent sleep. If performed too close to bedtime, exercise will cue the brain to switch to an awake and excited mode, chasing sleep away.

Zapper: *Jet lag*

If you travel from one time zone to another, you will feel your biological clock in action. With jet lag, your internal clock is out of sync with the new environment.

You can't prevent jet lag, but you can minimize the effects by following this advice from the National Sleep Foundation:

- Ease yourself into the new time zone for a few days before you depart.
- Rest as much as possible in transit.
- Plan an easy schedule for your first day or two after arrival.

Booster & Zapper: *Power naps*

Normal ultradian body rhythms cause changes in body temperature every 90 minutes. This fluctuation is most pronounced in the afternoon between 2 and 4 p.m.—that's when most people feel a surge of fatigue. In some cases, the best way to fight this feeling of tiredness is to give in to it—take a nap. Power naps can reduce the effects of chronic stress that interfere with nighttime slumber. They seem to allow the body to forget some stress patterns that build up during the day. A quick nap can improve alertness, sharpen memory, and generally reduce the symptoms of fatigue.

Short naps of 15 or 20 minutes are very effective, but the ideal is 90 minutes, allowing you to go through a full sleep cycle with a REM episode.

On the other hand, naps too close to bedtime can zap your chances of getting of good night's sleep. Also, naps that last longer than 90 minutes can confuse the wake/sleep cycle that controls tiredness and wakefulness.

Booster: *Relaxation exercises*

Anything that reduces stress usually improves sleep. Be sure to read about the stress-zapping power of abdominal breathing, progressive muscle relaxation, meditation, and spiritual prayer in Chapter 6.

Booster: *Sex*

Sex has several benefits with regard to sleep. Most people report a significant decrease in stress and anxiety, particularly after orgasm. (This is probably the only exercise that you should do before bedtime.) In addition, physical contact itself reduces stress hormone levels in the bloodstream.

Zapper: *Shift work*

Shift workers cannot work in concert with their own body rhythms. They need to sleep when their clocks are set for wakefulness, so they tend to sleep badly and not enough. If you occasionally work the night shift, it's better to work the shift for several weeks before changing to another. This gives the body time to adjust to the new pattern—at least for a while. Changing shifts every few days creates a chronic stress syndrome that further interferes with sound sleep.

Booster & Zapper: *Sleep schedule*

The ultradian rhythms coordinate the rise and fall of body temperature, hormones, and neurotransmitters. The timing of these patterns is consistent every day, but a daily schedule that is inconsistent works against this internal clock that is so crucial in regulating sleep and wakefulness. If you want to fall asleep easily and wake refreshed, it is best to go to sleep and wake the same time every day, or nearly as possible—no late-night outings, no sleeping in on weekends. These disruptions in the pattern upset the body rhythms and cause sleep problems.

Zapper: *Stress*

Stress is thought to be one of the major causes of insomnia. It is not just the worrisome thoughts that keep you awake. Two brain physiological reactions zap normal sleep cycles:

1. Chronic stress depletes brain amine supplies (serotonin and norepinephrine) necessary for normal sleep cycles.

2. Stress also stimulates the adrenals to release the stress hormones epinephrine and cortisol. Both feed the stress response and cause general psychological arousal. Further, long-term repeated elevation in brain coritsol levels over time can even cause brain cell death.

Excessive sleep deprivation can actually cause these stress symptoms. Extreme sleep deprivation can even result in paranoia, memory loss, and confusion. The stress effects of sleep deprivation can generate a cycle of poor sleep and daytime fatigue.

The information in Chapter 6 on "relaxation" will help you create a lifestyle that controls stress.

Zapper: *Television*

Watching evening and especially late-night television is a triple whammy to sound sleep. Here are some reasons:

1. It causes you to regularly engage in sedentary lifestyle, causing weight gain and avoiding the stress-busting effects of exercise.
2. The artificial stimulation of witnessing violence and even the novelty of a sitcom can cause general arousal and excitement.
3. Falling asleep with the TV on (really a light on that makes noise) interferes with natural melatonin production and causes more waking during lighter stages of sleep.

Booster & Zapper: *Weight maintenance*

Sleep needs are directly proportional to body weight in adults. As your weight decreases, your need for sleep decreases. Therefore, if you are overweight, you may find that you need more sleep than you have the time to take. This can leave you feeling fatigued during the day. Losing weight will reduce your need for sleep and will thus boost your daytime energy. However, be aware that sudden, extreme weight loss will simulate stress and impair sleep.

Chapter 6

Stress, Fear, Anxiety: Causing and Calming the Jitters

Feeling stressed? Afraid to ask for a raise? Anxious about your finances? The mind/body response to these kinds of situations can be traced to the survival instincts of our animal ancestors. If an animal can fight to protect its offspring, flee predators too dangerous to fight, or recognize a potential threat rapidly enough to walk in a different direction, he or she will live to reproduce more offspring—the goal of any living organism. This "fight-or-flight" response to stress, fear, and anxiety is an impulse still present and necessary in all of us and involves a complex interaction between the entire brain and the body.

Sometimes this response is immediate and profound—we feel our heart race, our breath quicken and our palms sweat. Other times, the response to low-level, daily frustrations and fears is virtually unnoticeable on a conscious level. In either case, the brain is hard at work receiving sensory signals, sending alarm messages throughout the body, raising neurotransmitter levels, producing stress hormones, and pushing the production of natural stimulants. All of these actions occur in concert with every situation, action, drug, food, supplement, and lifestyle choice that promotes stress.

The Anatomical Structure of Fear and Anxiety

In the brain, the main players mediating the stress response are the following:

♦ The limbic system, particularly the amygdala and hippocampus.

♦ The cerebellum.
♦ The cortex.
♦ The thalamus.

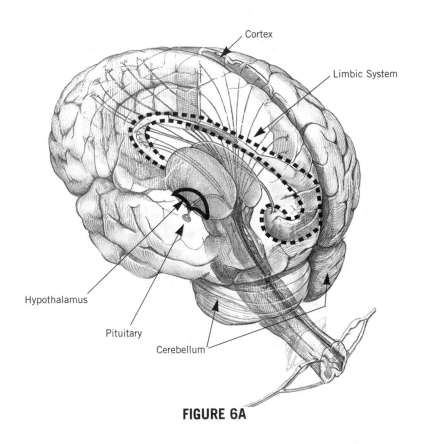

Cortex

Limbic System

Hypothalamus

Pituitary

Cerebellum

FIGURE 6A

The amygdala is thought to be the center of the conscious stress response. It is an almond-shaped nucleus of the limbic system sitting at the front tip of each hippocampus, leading into the frontotemporal cortex. (See Figure 6A.) This small nucleus takes in thought information from the cortex, feeling and drive states from the hippocampus, and sensory input from the thalamus. It then sends signals back to the hippocampus, mediating arousal and drive; to the reticular activating system in the brainstem to release serotonin, dopamine, and norepinephrine; up to the cortex and hippocampus, calling these areas to attention; and to the hypothalamus, which acts as a mediator between brain and body. All this action happens the moment your mind perceives a stressful situation.

In addition, the cerebellum plays an important role in the stress response. This clamshell-shaped brain region behind the brainstem has traditionally been thought to be the center of balance and coordination of the brain. Newer evidence now points to its role in taking complex environmental cues and processing them rapidly and sending alarms to the cortex about danger. Very recent research suggests that this may mediate rapid reactions such as the avoidance of a car jumping lanes on the highway or the "bad" feeling one gets from the unscrupulous, used-car salesman. Both may involve complex but rapid processing that is inaccessible to the conscious mind.

These signals to the cortex and amygdala and other structures from the cerebellum may involve "alarm" type signals. Like a house alarm that goes off when a window is broken, a simple "worry" signal may be sent before these dangerous stimuli are processed and identified in the cortex. Hence, this may explain such phenomena as rapid fearful facial reactions quickly covered in a poker game, and panic attacks and phobias that defy thought (for example, "there are no monsters in the basement"). It seems in such circumstances that the fear and anxiety, the rapid heart rate and shallow breathing, the dry mouth and sweating, all get out of control before we consciously comprehend the situation.

Conducting this complex stress response is the cortex, which processes thoughts about outside events in response to various sensory inputs, mainly from the eyes and ears. (Smell and taste are not used in humans to the degree they are used by other mammals. For example, the wolf that smells blood a half-mile away or that can detect an invader by the smell of dried urine on frozen ground.)

The now-abandoned technique of psychosurgery called "frontal lobotomy" gives us a unique look at the relationship between the function of the cortex and the stress response. This procedure involved cutting many connections between the frontal cortex and amygdala. The result was a docile, unstimulated person incapable of worry and anxiety, but also incapable of being stimulated into any activity much beyond eating and sleeping.

Extremely happy and exciting events can have similar effects on the body as stressors. A commonly used example of positive stress is the feeling of "falling in love." Compare the rapid pulse, heavy breathing, "butterflies" of the stomach, sweaty palms, dry mouth, and wide pupils that occur when the lover encounters the beloved, with the bodily reaction that occurs in a victim who encounters the violent criminal on a dark street. The comparison is shockingly similar.

There are many clear examples of the negative consequences of stress during happy times that are almost stereotypes: the "pillar of society" who dies in bed with the young sexy bombshell; the "lucky" fellow who dies from a heart attack at a surprise birthday party or after winning the sweepstakes. Even the major acne outbreak before the big date is a stress signal.

Stress, Fear, and Anxiety Boosters and Zappers

Stress has an exceptionally strong influence on both mental and physical health. The things that boost stress and harm the brain impair healthy functioning of almost all body systems if overutilized. The things that eliminate stress and boost the brain by promoting the relaxation response usually enhance the health of these same systems if regularly called into action. Knowing the facts about stress can have a profound effect on your overall well-being.

Remember that the long-term effects of stress on the body include:

- High blood pressure.
- Irritable bowel.
- Stomach ulcers. (Although recent evidence points to the presence of particular bacterial organisms in ulcers such as *C. pylori*, chronic stress produces an immune depression that may allow this to grow, particularly when combined with a diversion of nourishing and oxygenating blood flow away from the gastrointestinal tract.)
- Coronary artery disease.

◆ Cancer. (There is growing evidence in both animal studies and human population studies to suggest that stressful periods and even depression lower resistance to tumor growth.)

◆ Infections (via immune depression).

◆ Unmasking of dormant immune disorders (such as lupus, rheumatoid arthritis, multiple sclerosis).

◆ Impaired memory. (See Chapter 3.)

◆ Impaired sexual function. (See Chapter 4.)

◆ Insomnia. (See Chapter 5.)

◆ Depression and burnout. (See Chapter 8.)

This long, yet incomplete list gives you an idea of the possible consequences of neglecting the role that stress is playing in your life.

Boosters and Zappers in Your Own Body

When the brain perceives stress it sends out alarms and signals that produce the physical stress response and at the same time gear up the body to fight back.

Booster & Zapper: *Amine neurotransmitters*

The stress response causes release of the amine "attention and focus" neurotransmitters, particularly serotonin and norepinephrine, to call the mind to attention so it can deal with the stressful threat and decide to flee, fight, or problem-solve. Initially, this increased attention and alertness helps the body battle stress, fear, and anxiety. But chronic stress-induced release of serotonin and norepinephrine amines causes an eventual depletion of these brain chemicals. A reduced amines supply leaves the brain unable to call itself to attention and manage the stressful situation. Instead of solving the problem, the stress worsens.

When this happens, the proverbial "all hell breaks loose." Bills pile up, angry clients keep calling, an ignored spouse begins to ignore you, creditors knock on your door, your spouse files for divorce, the school principal calls about your child's behavior, and you arrive at work on Monday morning to find a memo that says the boss wants to see you. And you say, "So what's new?" This newly developed apathy only prolongs stress, opens the body to physical disorders, depression, and immune dysfunction. Your lower-back pain progresses to full-blown disability and that chronic cough develops into a florid bronchitis. You start entertaining thoughts of suicide or you retreat to mind-numbing drug addiction or alcohol.

This exaggeration demonstrates how important a healthy and balanced supply of amines are in helping a person adapt to the complex stresses of human society.

Booster & Zapper: *The autonomic nervous system*

The involuntary or autonomic nervous system (beginning at the brainstem and sending projections to most major organs) is busily at work responding to stressful stimuli. The responses mediated through this system are the ones most recognizable by all of us when facing stress. It has two "yin and yang"-like halves. The sympathetic and the parasympathetic systems.

Traditionally, the sympathetic portion of the autonomic nervous system of the body mediates the fight-or-flight symptoms. It sends norepinephrine neurons out from nuclei along the spine that influence all major organs and cause the release of adrenaline (epinephrine) from the adrenal glands. Adrenaline causes rapid heart rate, dry mouth, increased blood pressure, dilated pupils, sweating, redirection of blood flow to the muscles and away from the digestive tract and skin (causing the pale look of terror), and muscle tremor.

The parasympathetic portion of the autonomic system is responsible for the restorative functions of the so-called "relaxation response." These functions are believed to be suppressed during stress. This slows the heart rate, allows normal digestion, causes relaxation of sphincter valves allowing urination and defecation, stimulates salivation, and allows for normal sexual function.

Booster & Zapper: *Beta endorphin*

Stress also causes the pituitary to release beta endorphin, a very potent analgesic (pain-fighter), similar in action to the opioids morphine and heroin. Opioids act on specific neuron receptors in areas of the brain and spinal cord that zap the effects of stress and mediate pain. (See Chapter 7.) This release of beta endorphin may help an injured animal fight or run to safety by preventing the pain from overcoming it. This ability to block pain is thought to be related to "runner's high" that occurs when a certain threshold of exhaustion is passed during long runs.

This suppression of pain is accompanied by an immune suppression mediated by adrenal gland release of cortisol. Although this combo prevents swelling and additional pain at injured sites, if left on, it allows for more damage. Also while the immune system is down, infections can creep in and tumors can develop.

Booster & Zapper: *Cortisol*

In the stress response, a complex process that begins in the hypothalamus causes the release of the stress hormone cortisol into the bloodstream. Cortisol can cause a simple stressful situation to have negative consequences on the body lasting from several hours to weeks and months if the stress is repeated and chronic (such as an annoying house mate, or a painful lower back) or if the stress is severe enough (such as witnessing a violent crime or the death of a loved one).

Initially, cortisol release during stress has several good purposes. It suppresses the immune system, which, if you are in a fight or running from a predator, keeps a small injury from swelling up, preventing you from fighting back or getting away. Cortisol also causes the level of blood sugar to rise, making it more available for use in the brain and muscles for energy and quick action. Cortisol reaches the brain and, acutely, acts as a stimulant, heightening your sense of awareness.

In the long term, however, the release of cortisol in severe or chronic stress will take an undesirable toll on the brain and the body. In animals, the long-term exposure to stress beyond the animal's control, or in a repeated fashion, results in a depression-like syndrome called "learned helplessness," where the animal loses drive, interacts less with other animals, becomes slower in movement, and eventually even dies. In the brains of such animals, release of cortisol becomes continuous. Neurons that release cortisol in the hippocampus remain activated for extended periods, causing burnout or depression. (See Chapter 8 for more information on learned helplessness.)

It is primarily cortisol that mediates the many negative effects of stress, such as immunosuppression (related to the development of infections, autoimmune disorders, and cancer), mental depression, and arteriosclerosis leading to heart disease.

Booster & Zapper: *DHEA*

Stress reduces the level of DHEA found in brain cells. DHEA is found in high concentrations in the brain, and as a precursor or building block of cortisol, is necessary to maintain proper neurological function. DHEA is so sensitive to body tension that clinicians often monitor DHEA levels to track the effects of long-term stress. What they find is that when the levels of DHEA are low, the levels of cortisol are high (probably because DHEA is getting used up to make cortisol.) There is some evidence that DHEA therapy may help in reducing the effects of stress in mood. (See Chapter 8.)

During my fourth year in medical school, I had the good fortune of being asked to speak at the National Institutes of Health on some research I had done on stress physiology. Unfortunately, I developed a fever and sore throat 24 hours before my presentation. But I was not going to let that stop me and so I drove to Bethesda, Maryland, the next day.

Before I was called to the podium, my heart raced and palms sweated in anticipation of presenting data on stress to an audience that included at least two of the world's leading experts. My raw sore throat was aggravated by the dry mouth of stress. Even worse, my body ached and I felt dizzy.

I was introduced, stood up, and faced the predator-audience, ready to "stay and fight" but wanting to "flee" home to bed. Suddenly everything changed. I remember realizing that my sore throat had miraculously disappeared (although my voice was still a bit scratchy). I no longer felt achy and dizzy. The talk proceeded without a hitch.

After fielding questions from the audience, I sat down, and as if signaled by the applause, the raw sore throat, aching muscles, and dizziness returned with a vengeance! I struggled through my drive home, stopping twice along the way, and then slept for the next 12 hours. Clearly the fight-or-flight response of giving my presentation called forth enough cortisol and beta endorphin to suppress the pain of my virally inflamed throat and muscles. As soon as the stress was over, so was the temporary pain relief and sense of well-being, and I actually felt much worse than before.

Boosters and Zappers in Drugs

We can explore the individual mechanisms and pathways of various drugs on the brain's stress response to gain a general impression of how each affects levels of stress, fear, and anxiety. Stimulating one set of nerve cells or relaxing another has some effect on the entire system.

Booster & Zapper: *Alcohol*

Alcohol has effects on the brain similar to the sedative prescription drugs, the benzodiazepines. That's why so many people "drink to relax." In fact, there have been studies that promote the health benefits of moderate alcohol intake, which I define as a maximum of one to two drinks of wine or beer. (Hard liquor is potent, and in the case of martinis, for instance, one drink has the equivalent alcohol content of about four beers.) The positive benefits of moderate use may partially relate to reduced effects of stress on the body.

Your decision to indulge, however, must carefully weigh the following considerations:

1. Alcohol always presents an addictive potential with severe withdrawal symptoms.
2. Impaired motor performance can and does cause automobile death and injury.
3. The control of the stress-blocking effect is quite unpredictable.
4. There is a stimulating effect at low doses.
5. If anxiety is part of a depression, alcohol may actually worsen the symptoms.
6. If taken before bedtime, REM sleep is diminished along with much of the restorative value of the sleep.
7. Alcohol can cause heart rhythm problems, particularly in patients who already have heart disease.
8. Alcohol may also have negative long-term health effects besides alcoholic liver disease, including cancer, brain cell loss, and diabetes.

9. If taken in first trimester pregnancy, alcohol can cause a number of fetal facial and brain anomalies.
10. Although alcohol can dull the sharp edges of stress, its other effects on the body make it a poor choice as a stress zapper.

Booster & Zapper: *Amphetamines and other stimulants*

Amphetamines and other stimulants initially enhance feelings of euphoria by stimulating the glutamate receptors. But overstimulation of glutamate receptors seems to be harmful to brain cells—a state called excitotoxicity. When activated, glutamate receptors cause calcium ions to enter nerve cells, increasing their excitability. Eventually, this process may result in cell death. A chronically overexcited brain (as with chronic use of stimulants, such as amphetamines and cocaine) literally becomes worn out through gradual cell death.

Chronic use of stimulants in an uncontrolled fashion also depletes amine neurotransmitters. This depletion can cause depression and even psychotic symptoms such as paranoia and delusions. (Amphetamines such as Ritalin are carefully controlled in the treatment of attention deficit disorder.)

Zapper: *Antidepressants*

The antidepressants, which will be discussed in more detail in the chapter on depression (Chapter 8), are extremely effective in removing anxiety and agitation when it is a part of a major depression episode. Antidepressant medications counter the stress response by raising levels of serotonin (these include Prozac, Pexil, Wellbutrin, and Zoloft) and/or norepinephrine (including Panelor, Elavil, Tofanil, Phenelzine, Parnale, Nardil), and probably even dopamine. There is some evidence that they may also be effective at treating chronic anxiety states and the anxiety associated with obsessive-compulsive disorders and phobias.

Zapper: *Beta blockers*

Beta blockers, used to treat high blood pressure, exert strong effects on the body's autonomic fight-or-flight sympathetic response to stress and anxiety. Beta blockers are named for their action of blocking the stimulating effects of epinephrine and norepinephrine on beta-adrenergic receptors in organs, including the heart, the muscles, the adrenal glands, the sweat glands, and the salivary glands.

These drugs are very effective at blunting the voice tremor, dry mouth, rapid pulse, sweaty palms, and general anxiety state associated with performance before a group. Many professionals I have spoken with use beta blockers such as Inderal, Tenormin, or Lopressor regularly to get rid of these stage fright symptoms. These drugs slow down the heart and significantly lower its workload and oxygen demand, protecting it from the potential damaging effects of stress-induced tachycardia (rapid heart rate.)

The major downside of beta blockers is their danger for asthma sufferers. They can provoke untreatable bronchospasm.

Zapper: *Buspar*

Buspar (buspirone), another anti-anxiety drug, is in a class by itself. Unlike sedatives, it has no effect on GABA receptors in the brain, and unlike beta blockers, it does not affect the beta-adrenergic receptors in the sympathetic nervous system of the body. It seems to act on serotonin receptors and possibly dopamine receptors, as well. Buspar is particularly good at treating the anxiety associated with depression. Its anti-anxiety effect is not as strong as the benzodiazepines, however, so it is recommended only for low-level anxiety symptoms.

Booster: *Caffeine*

Caffeine acts by generally stimulating brain neurons—this is not good for stress and anxiety. Caffeine raises a compound inside cells called cyclic AMP, which has an effect similar to norepinephrine. Norepinephrine calls the mind to attention, which initially helps the body battle stress, fear, and anxiety. But chronic release causes an eventual depletion of this brain chemical, leaving the brain defenseless against stress.

Zapper: *Clonidine*

Clonidine is an antihypertensive drug that blocks the outflow of autonomic sympathetic signals from the brain to the body, preventing the fight-or-flight response altogether. Like beta blockers, clonidine has the added benefit of eliminating the stress response. Clonidine is prescribed with caution because although it causes general relaxation, it may also cause excess sleepiness and may prevent necessary blood vessel constriction required to prevent fainting when you stand up.

Zapper: *Illegal drugs*

Opioids such as heroin bind to opiate receptors in the brain to produce a profound sense of well-being and relaxation. However, these drugs are so highly addictive that a single "trip" can make a person a lifetime addict, disrupting all aspects of behavior and daily functioning.

Marijuana is known to produce a state of "mellow" relaxation and even indifference to outside potential stressors. There are specific THC (tetrahydrocannabanol) receptors in the brain that closely parallel the regions where GABA neurons (activated by the benzodiazepine sedatives) occur—the cerebellum, the hippocampus, and the cortex. Little else is known about exactly how these receptors fight off the stress response.

As a physician, I cannot recommend the use of this illegal drug to combat the stress response. I find it particularly worrisome that the discontinuation of marijuana is followed by a withdrawal syndrome of increased anxiety, insomnia, motor restlessness, nausea, and muscle cramps. In addition, marijuana carries the added danger to health caused by possible contaminants and impurities found in the leaves. PCP (phencyclidine, or angel dust) for instance, a dangerous stimulant, has been reported to be a common contaminant. Smoking marijuana also causes the same harmful effects on the lungs as cigarette smoking.

Booster & Zapper: *Ketamine (Special K)*

Ketamine is an anesthetic drug that causes euphoria by causing dopamine release. But as a frequently abused drug often mixed with alcohol, ketamine increases the behavioral hazards of intoxication and directly stimulates the sympathetic nervous system by causing norepinephrine release in the body and brain and thus mimicking all the symptoms of stress activation. It also stimulates a subset of opiate receptors that cause profound brain dissociation in states such as amnesia and disorientation, placing the user in great danger. Because of this drug's popularity, I want to emphasize its very dangerous side and I strongly advise against its use.

Booster & Zapper: *Nicotine*

The initial morning cigarette is calming, but if the next smoke is delayed too long, withdrawal causes irritability, lowered performance levels in complex mental tasks, aggression, and increased appetite—all triggers for stress, fear, and anxiety.

Nicotine activates the brain by stimulating acetylcholine receptors present on neurons throughout the brain and in the autonomic nervous system. This general activation, through a different mechanism, has an end result similar to caffeine—it arouses the brain to attention, while decreasing blood flow so that blood is available only to active areas. This causes an alert, upbeat state. But this hyperstimulation may lead to excitotoxicity of brain cells, causing cell death. There is good evidence that long-term smoking mimics the stress response, lowers brain cell count in the cortex, and increases the risk of Alzheimer's disease. These facts, along with its addictive nature and association with cancer, lung disease, heart disease, and stroke make nicotine a poor choice as a source of relaxation.

Zapper: *Sedatives*

The most commonly used sedatives are benzodiazepines and barbiturates. Benzodiazepines are the prescription drugs most widely used to combat anxiety. These include Valium, Xanax, Ativan, Klonopin, Dalmane, Librium, and Versed. All are potent activators of the gamma-amino butyric acid (GABA) receptors on neurons (nerve cells).

GABA is an inhibitory neurotransmitter in the brain. This means that it dampens the responsiveness of any other neuron it touches. Benzodiazepines make receptors throughout the brain even more sensitive to GABA. Just as stimulants enhance the tendency of brain cells to act, GABA receptors decrease or inhibit brain cell action.

The GABA neurons that are involved in the stress response are found particularly in:

♦ The cerebellum. Activating GABA receptors in the cerebellum depresses the early-warning alert system that provokes the stress response.

♦ The thalamus, which sorts many of the sensory inputs and sends them to various points in the brain. When activated by benzodiazepines, the GABA receptors inhibit the nerve cells' ability to respond sharply or quickly to incoming signals of stress.

♦ The hippocampus and the entire cortex. These areas of the brain are flush with GABA-mediated circuits that act as a general buffer of nerve activity in thought, sensations, attention, and emotion.

Hence, a person taking benzodiazepines experiences a slowing of the reactivity of at least these four major components of the stress system in the brain. The result is that a person becomes less reactive to the environment and therefore calmer and more relaxed.

You might think that this dulling of the stress response might impair the performance of mental tasks. But if a person suffers from excess anxiety, the decreased reaction to stress actually improves mental performance. Still, these drugs must be used only under close medical supervision. Too much can cause impairment, amnesia, and confusion.

If you suffer from what appear to be panic attacks, anxiety attacks, phobias, serious social shyness, or generalized anxiety and worry, consult a psychiatrist about taking benzodiazepine drugs. They can be very helpful in treating stress, fear, and anxiety, if used properly. But be careful. If taken regularly for a period of several months, and then suddenly discontinued without gradual tapering, benzodiazepines can produce withdrawal symptoms. Besides rebound anxiety, this can result in seizures (massive uncontrolled firing of brain neurons) through a general loss of brain inhibition.

Barbiturates, which act on several neurotransmitter systems, are less specific in their action against stress. They produce a state that gradually approaches general anesthesia with global brain inactivation. Hence, they should not be used to treat anxiety problems.

Booster: *Steroids*

Steroids, such as Prednisone (used to treat severe inflammatory conditions such as asthma and rheumatoid arthritis), and even inhaled steroids like Asthmacort and Fluouent, all affect brain activity.

Short-term use of these drugs generally causes stimulation and can interrupt sleep and increase anxiety. When taken for several days, they can dampen nerve cell release of neurotransmitters, dull brain activation, and lead to depression.

Boosters and Zappers in Foods

Stress, fear, and anxiety are mildly sensitive to foods. Although you'll see here a collection of foods that are known to reduce stress, I believe that no foods are potent enough to be used specifically for this purpose. Food is best eaten in frequent small amounts throughout the day in response to stomach hunger and not in response to anxiety. Those who use food to battle stress often end up battling obesity.

Booster: *Artificial sweeteners*

The artificial sweetener NutraSweet (aspartame) is a stimulant that directly aggravates the stress response in the brain by causing general brain stimulation. Overuse and long-term use may cause depletion of amines such as serotonin, producing depression. To avoid these effects, avoid foods that contain this artificial sweetener, including diet colas, diet yogurts, and sugar-free gelatin products.

Booster & Zapper: *Carbohydrates*

Complex carbohydrates, such as the wheat in a bagel or cereal, moderate stress by elevating serotonin levels. Although the calming effect takes a while to achieve, complex carbohydrates ease stress better than simple carbohydrates (sugars in sweets) because they don't cause blood sugar levels to fluctuate so wildly (because of insulin imbalance) or cause the rebound effect of actually producing stress through lower sugar levels.

Booster & Zapper: *Free-radical-producing and -reducing foods*

Free-radical-producing products, such as fatty processed cakes loaded with preservatives, put additional stress on the body. Free radicals are highly reactive molecular fragments that bear an extra electron and bond with virtually any biological carbon-based substance they come into contact with. Free radicals bind to proteins, to membranes, to DNA, and to the proteins that help repair DNA, weakening the cells and impairing cell function. Damaged cells release stress-inducing substances such as cytokines, causing the hypothalamus of the brain to activate the stress process. That's why too many packaged cakes, or cookies, or white bread will give you the exact same symptoms as the chronic stress symptoms—anxiety, irritability, inability to relax, and difficulty in sleeping.

There are a variety of foods known to reduce the presence of free radicals in the body. Vegetables that contain bioflavenoids are especially helpful in this process. These include cabbage, broccoli, turnips, cauliflower, and beets. (Also see "Antioxidants" on pages 139 to 140.)

Zapper: *Fruit*

Fruits are the perfect food for reducing stress. They contain both complex carbohydrates such as pectin and sugar in the form of fructose. There is not enough simple sugar to rapidly raise blood sugar and insulin, and there is just enough complex sugar to prolong the positive effect of mediating higher blood sugar and serotonin release to the brain. This combination makes it wise to have some fruit, such as a peach, before you face predictable daily stresses, such as rush-hour traffic.

Booster: *Monosodium glutamate (MSG)*

Like NutraSweet, MSG acts as a stimulant and with overuse or long-term use may deplete supplies of serotonin, which can trigger depression. MSG is responsible for the famous "Chinese restaurant syndrome" of headache, dizziness, and poor concentration. It acts directly on the excitatory receptors throughout the cortex that respond to the neurotransmitter glutamate. Repeated overstimualtion with glutamate in animal models produces brain cell death called "excitotoxicity." MSG is found in many packaged foods, such as nacho chips and soup mixes, and is often disguised in the ingredients as "natural flavors."

Booster & Zapper: *Sweets*

Sweets are known to both raise and lower mood, depending on amount and duration. A little sugar has one response; a lot has quite another.

Sugar raises brain serotonin levels, which causes a more relaxed state. That's why people who are depressed and have a depletion of this neurotransmitter tend to crave sweets. In an emergency, for a momentary stress reducer, you might try a candy bar (one of my personal favorite strategies) to shake off the jitters.

However, sweets cannot be used as a long-term fix for stress because after a rapid rise that boosts feelings of well being, the pancreas makes lots of insulin, which rapidly lowers sugar levels. Mood generally follows this rapid drop as this sugar-lowering mechanism overshoots the mark.

Boosters and Zappers in Supplements

There are a number of readily available substances that can be taken to reduce the destructive effects of stress. (And watch out for the ones that cause it!)

Zapper: *Antioxidants*

"Antioxidant" is a term for substances that absorb or scavenge free radicals. Generally, they are found naturally in the bloodstream or are released by cells of the immune system when needed. But when emotional or environmental stress compromises the strength of the immune system, you can boost the supply of these stress-reducing substances through supplements (or in the foods that contain them, as mentioned earlier.)

There are many antioxidant preparations available, including the following:

Vitamin C (ascorbic acid) is so vital to brain function that its levels are almost 15 times higher in the brain than in other areas of the body. Not only is it a well-known and powerful antioxidant, there is evidence that it can reduce the risk of plaque formation in the arteries (arteriosclerosis) that can reduce blood flow to the brain. This vitamin is also necessary for the manufacture of neurotransmitters (the substances by which all nerve cells communicate with each other.) Many people recommend the antioxidant benefits of megadoses of vitamin C at 1,000 to 5,000mg per day. But be careful: Such high doses, if not accompanied by adequate water intake, may acidify the urine and enhance the formation of kidney stones.

Vitamin E is another commonly known vitamin-antioxidant. In partnership with the mineral selenium, it neutralizes free radicals that accelerate the stress process. For antioxidant benefits, many recommend doses of as much as 800 to 1,600IU of vitamin E per day.

Selenium is an elemental metal that has antioxidant properties because its outer electron shells will accommodate electrons common in the damaging of free radicals. In studies, it has been shown to act synergistically with vitamin E as an antioxidant.

Carotenoids are the most celebrated of the antioxidants. There are approximately 40 of these substances, which are most potent in scavenging loose free radicals. They consist of long carbon chains that neutralize and bind particularly well to these renegade molecules. There is a negative effect of carotenoid supplements you should be aware of, however, a recent study of beta-carotene supplements showed that it increased lung cancer rates in smokers. Because of this one study, it has been dropped off of many of the lists of recommended antioxidants. However, the theoretical value of these substances makes them still worth considering if you are not a smoker.

Bioflavenoids are another class of large, high-energy carbon structures that are powerful antioxidants. They are present in green tea, pine-needle derivative supplements, and in vegetables such as cabbage, broccoli, cauliflower, beets, and turnips. Also, they may be responsible for the heart-protective effects in red wine.

Herbal remedies. Good herbal antioxidant-containing tonics to sip or sniff include green tea, black tea, alfalfa, rosehips, peppermint, nettles, hawthorn, goldenseal, fenugreek, cumin (in curry), capsicum (hot pepper), cinnamon, and basil. Of all of these, green tea has been the most closely studied for its antioxidant properties and has been found to be a potent free-radical scavenger.

Booster: *Aphrodisiacs*

Many of the real and supposed aphrodisiac substances discussed in Chapter 4 also have stimulant properties that aggravate stress, fear, and anxiety. This includes yohimbine, which acts directly on the sympathetic nervous system, causing elevations in heart rate and blood pressure. Also watch out for guarana, which is a direct stimulant like caffeine.

Zapper: *Chamomile*

Chamomile is best known for its ability to promote sound sleep. Because of its effects inducing relaxation, it may reduce the effects of stress by relaxing the body after a stressful day, allowing for a more restorative sleep.

Zapper: *DHEA*

In the brain, DHEA is low during stress while cortisol is high. This leads some to believe that DHEA supplements can balance the scales and reduce the effects of stress on the body. Until more studies and scientific knowledge are gathered about this relationship, I do not recommend using DHEA to treat stress or anxiety.

Zapper: *Ginseng*

Ginseng modulates the release of the stress hormone, cortisol. (Some cortisol is needed to help you deal with stress, but too much can damage brain cells.) Ginseng also modulates levels of the stress and attention amine neurotransmitters in the brain such as serotonin and norepinephrine. This herb has been used for thousands of years in traditional Chinese medicine for calming stress, but keep in mind that it may require several weeks to months of therapy to have this effect. (Although there is a history of personal testimonials confirming the ability of this herb to calm stress, studies have been done only in animals, with no hard evidence yet in humans.)

Zapper: *Kava kava*

Kava kava contains substances (kavapyrones) that have been shown to reduce anxiety. They seem to act by raising serotonin and norepinephrine, but they should never be taken by anyone already on antidepressants or anti-anxiety medications. Because of possible severe interactions, kava kava should be taken only under the supervision of a physician. Kava kava is available OTC and bears warning labels about interactions with antidepressants and anxiolytics (sedatives.)

Zapper: *Valerian root*

Valerian root has been used for centuries as a mild sedative to treat anxiety and nervousness. You'll find a passage in the diary of

Anne Frank in which the young girl says, "I take valerian pills every day against worry and depression." The history of this supplement supports its effectiveness.

Boosters and Zappers in Lifestyle

Our days are filled with stress. Getting rid of the stress is not the answer to reducing the negative effects it has on our body. Learning how to deal with stress can prevent a full-blown stress response. A few lifestyle choices you can make to keep stress and anxiety in their place include moderate exercise, adequate sleep, distraction, relaxation exercises, and intimacy, along with avoidance of coffee, cigarettes, recreational drugs, and social isolation.

Zapper: *Acupuncture*

Because certain acupuncture points increase serotonin levels, the result is often a generalized decrease in the stress response. Most often this is a welcomed side effect of an acupuncture treatment for some other problem (such as backache or joint pain.) Recently, a patient told me that since starting acupuncture treatments with me for a chronic lower backache, she has gotten rid of the constipation that has plagued her for 20 years. This reduction of stress-related problems is typical of acupuncture patients.

Zapper: *Diversion*

Diversion is a very effective stress reducer. Once the stress response is activated, a conscious shift in mental thought can stop the snowballing process of negative effects. Diversion can be accomplished in many ways. A few are listed here.

Cognitive thought arguments (made popular by authors such as Aaron Beck, Albert Ellis, and Martin Seligman) stop short internal arguments. Let's say, for example, that you find a long line at the post office; we'll call that "A" for the activating event. Next comes "B" for the beliefs that follow: "The postal worker is wasting too much time. I'll be here forever." Then comes "C" for the consequences of the event: "I can't stand this. I'm going to lose my temper. I'm in such a hurry and now I'm going to be late." Cognitive thought arguments attack "B"—the assumptions of the belief system: "I can't control how much time the worker takes. Maybe he is working very hard; maybe he is having a bad day. I certainly will not be here forever. In fact, if I'm here more than 30 minutes I'll be surprised." This method can be very effective in preventing a full-blown stress attack.

Mindless household chores and any positive, helpful activity that gets one's mind away from personal problems can prove extremely effective in the stress response. Accepting busy work diverts you from the stressful thoughts while helping you adapt and take a "breather" from your problems.

Charitable activities are very capable forms of diversion. They promote social interaction while shifting attention away from one's own problems and bodily reactions.

Social interaction with upbeat people who share your interests and concerns is a fun way to head off stress. When you're feeling stressed, avoid sarcastic, dependent, or overly dominating or critical types. It's also not the time for a political or religious debate.

Take in a movie. Light dramas and love stories are good diversions that take your mind off the problems causing you stress and anxiety. (Stay away from violent, action and pornographic films—they up your stress response!) For the best diversion, try a comedy. Laughter is proven to change the physiology of stress in the mind and body.

Booster and Zapper: *Exercise*

Sometimes the best defense against stress, fear, and anxiety is a good physical workout. Exercise interrupts the stress response by raising baseline serotonin levels in the brain, giving the body a healthy store of ammunition to battle stress. Experts agree that those who exercise regularly seem to be more resilient to the exhausting effects of stress on the brain.

At the same time, too much exercise (such as running 40 to 50 miles a week) will give stress a helping hand. When you exercise excessively, muscle demand outstrips oxygen supply and metabolism changes. This so-called anaerobic muscle metabolism, in addition to producing lactic acid (a metabolic byproduct that stimulates the stress response and causes cramps), creates free radicals, cell damage, and further stress activation through release of cytokines from damaged cells. Also, the mere act of placing the body in overdrive maintains the stress response to supply blood flow to vital organs while muscles use up much of the body's fuel. I recommend aerobic exercise for 20 to 30 minutes at least three times a week for peak stress-reducing effect.

Zapper: *Relaxation exercises*

The best way to reduce stress, fear, and anxiety is to direct your body to call to action all the functions and processes that are directly opposed to stress and create a state of relaxation. Stress cannot get the upper hand when the body is relaxed.

Try some of the following exercises next time you're stressed:

♦ *Abdominal breathing.* Voluntary control of breathing has been used for centuries to reduce stress and anxiety. Get comfortable, close your eyes, relax, and take a deep breath from the bottom of your stomach. Breathe in as you silently count to five and repeat for at least five minutes. Let the air go easily to the count of five. Some practitioners recommend a relaxed smile when exhaling.

♦ *Progressive muscle relaxation.* Stress causes muscles to tense which also makes it difficult to relax. To counter muscle tension, practice this exercise: Find a comfortable place to lie down. Focus your attention on your right hand. Clench it into a fist, squeezing it as hard as you can for about five seconds. Open the fist and allow your muscles to relax. Repeat the exercise for the left hand, and the muscles in your arms, neck, shoulders, abdomen, buttocks, thighs, calves, and feet. Finally, squeeze and relax your facial muscles, including your eyes and forehead. Visualize the center of your mind about six inches above your head. By intentionally pairing tension with relaxation and visualization, you are conditioning your body to do the same naturally the next time your muscles tense.

Meditation is a great stress reducer in many ways:

♦ Meditation reduces levels of stress hormones, such as cortisol, which encourages the stress response.

♦ Meditation duplicates the cyclical brain pattern that occurs at the onset of sleep. In the last moments before sleep, brain activity reaches a slower, coordinated firing that produces alpha waves. These same waves are produced during the passive concentration of practiced meditation.

♦ Meditation helps to decrease the activity of the sympathetic nervous system while increasing parasympathetic nervous system activity (the release of acetylcholine to various organs). This so-called "relaxation response" reduces tension and anxiety, slows respiration and heart rate, and lowers blood pressure.

This relaxation exercise is a good introduction to any meditation exercise, including spiritual prayer. It is best to relax the mind after the body is adequately relaxed. Simply visualizing a placid scene while letting thoughts out of your mind can help. All good meditation requires practice and may be difficult the first few times.

Zapper: *Sex*

Regular sexual activity is thought to help promote relaxation and inhibit frustration. A stress-buffering effect on the brain caused by physical contact occurs. In addition, the release of pituitary prolactin after orgasm buffers the stress effect of dopamine released in sexual pleasure. Further, the prefrontal area of attention and focus also used for orgasm and pleasure in sex, by necessity, cannot be used simultaneously to arouse the brain to stress. It is a way of letting go or diverting stress-producing thought patterns.

The use of sex as a "drug" to treat anxiety, mask frustration, or block anger, however, is not recommended. This focus on orgasm as a tension reliever rather than as a source of mutual enjoyment and intimacy may potentially make the bedroom a place to express negative emotions such as anger. This gives short-term release at the cost of long-term frustration. Keep in mind that it is feelings of shared love and closeness itself that reduces stress hormone levels.

Booster & Zapper: *Sleep*

Many of the lifestyle choices that increase or reduce stress are the same ones that inhibit or promote sound sleep—stress being a stimulant that disrupts sleep. In fact, sleep deprivation can produce all the symptoms of mild to severe stress and intensify anxiety and irritability. Be sure to read about the stress-related effects of power naps and a routine sleep schedule in Chapter 5.

Booster & Zapper: *Social relationships*

Being with people or being alone can have an effect on how the mind and body respond to stress and anxiety. Social isolation can produce a stress-like state. We are social animals by nature and require a certain amount of positive interaction with other human beings. Animal studies have shown that physical contact somehow dampens the hormonal stress response of brain and body. Young experimental monkeys deprived of physical contact cannot socialize properly with normal monkeys, and they develop symptoms of chronic stress.

On the flip side, disharmonious or codependent relationships increase anxiety levels and can cause the symptoms of chronic stress so destructive to healthy living.

Chapter 7

Pain: Making It Stop

We all know what pain is—it's that body signal that makes us scream out loud, jump up and down, clench our teeth, grimace, and voice a few expletives. For something so commonly experienced, it's surprising how little the average person knows about what causes it, what stops it, and how the brain mediates it all.

This chapter will address the kind of pain that is a symptom of a diagnosed problem: headache, migraine, arthritis, lower-back pain, TMJ (temporomandibular joint syndrome), pain from recent surgery or trauma, cancer-related pain, and the like. In these instances, the gamut of therapies available to reduce pain is enormous; I will attempt to give a general overview of the possibilities.

Warning: This chapter is not meant to prescribe remedies for pain that is new, unfamiliar, persistent, or worsening. This kind of pain signals a developing, potentially serious problem that needs medical attention from a competent physician. From personal experience, I know that overlooking the necessity of a thorough medical evaluation for pain can be disastrous.

For example, relative of mine with bone pain sought advice from a practitioner who gave surface trigger point treatments (a method of injecting a local anesthetic or another compound to loosen the knots of a muscle spasm in chronic musculoskeletal pain). The pain did not get better. After several months, another practitioner recommended a bone scan that revealed metastatic lung cancer that had infiltrated her spine and shoulder. At that point, the cancer was beyond the hope of any conventional treatment. Only when you're sure what's causing the pain should you attempt to eliminate it.

The Quest for Pain Relief

I am a physician anesthesiologist, working day after day to relieve surgical pain. I am an important member of the surgical team. (You can be sure, surgery won't start before I get there.) In fact, before the advent of anesthesia, surgeons were primarily technicians whose level of skill was based on how fast they could perform their surgery, and thus shorten the time the patient spent in extreme pain.

This pain was tantamount to torture, so people chose a surgeon by how fast he could work. Then in the 1840s, at the Massachusetts General Hospital in Boston, a dentist named William T.G. Morton was experimenting with a substance called ether. He gave it to a young man who was having a tumor of one of his salivary glands removed. While inhaling the ether from a specially made sponge, the young man experienced no pain as his gland was removed. This procedure changed medicine forever. Many of the methods used today for treating pain have been developed by researchers like Morton in the field of surgical anesthesia.

Fortunately, you don't need the near-comatose state of general anesthesia to treat most painful afflictions. This chapter will cover methods of pain management that allow the brain to remain conscious and awake while experiencing pain relief or "analgesia."

The Brain and Pain

Pain is a warning signal produced by nerve endings under these circumstances:

+ Most soft tissue body structures such as skin, connective tissue below the skin, muscles, tendons, ligaments, visceral organs, joint capsules, and periosteum (the fibrous covering of bone), are flush with nerve endings called *nociceptors* or pain fibers that exist specifically for sensing damage even to single cells. They connect to the spinal cord, where they are turned on when a broken cell releases substances called *prostaglandins.*

+ Nerve endings sensitive to temperature register pain under extreme stimulation. Hold your hand in either boiling or freezing water and you'll feel these nerve endings in action.

♦ Nerve endings that sense a pulling or stretching in hollow organs such as the stomach, intestines, bladder, and in the coverings of the brain (the meninges), will signal pain. Extreme stretch in the involuntary muscle of these hollow organs can produce intolerable pain. Classic examples of this pain are felt when a stone is trapped in the kidney and ureters, when a gallstone clogs the gallbladder and bile tubes from the liver, when a newborn passes through the narrowest portion of the uterus and cervix in labor, and when a blood vessel bursts in the head, placing extreme pressure on the meninges surrounding the brain.

> It is an interesting fact that the brain itself has no pain fibers. Once a neurosurgeon penetrates the skull and the meninges, major brain surgery can be conducted on an awake patient with no pain!

The Reason for Pain

Why did we evolve to have such mechanisms of apparent torture? The answer to this question becomes obvious when we look at the consequences of a daily innocuous activity—such as walking—in a person without the capability of sensing discomfort.

Advanced syphilis (almost nonexistent nowadays) results in *tabes dorsalis*, a crippling degeneration of the knee joints caused by a loss of nerves in the spinal cord carrying sensory information to the brain during walking. In the same way, the rare condition *asymbolia*, where patients cannot experience pain, also results in similar joint changes. People who suffer from diabetic neuropathy of the legs can develop deep foot ulcers to the bone from similar wear and tear of walking without pain sensation caused by the breakdown of sensory nerve fibers. In each case, the lack of pain causes further injury.

Let's say a person steps wrong and gets a sore knee. Without the sensation of pain, he will continue to put pressure on this knee while walking, instead of favoring the leg and limping. These kinds of minor injuries occur regularly and we compensate for them, often on an unconscious level. Without the warning signal of pain, all our body parts used regularly would wear out like a pair of old sneakers.

Getting Pain to the Brain

Pain signals make their way to the brain through the spinal cord in one of two ways. The message travels through fast insulated "wires" (myelin-covered nerve fibers), causing pain sensations that are sharp, sudden, and whose location is very specific. These fast fibers also connect directly to motor nerves at the spinal cord level, causing you, for instance, to pull away your hand from a flame before your brain has even registered pain. This prevents you from getting seriously injured in the time it would take you to voluntarily decide to withdraw your hand.

The pain message can also travel through slower noninsulated thin "wires" that result in a delayed pain that is dull and nonspecific in location.

There is a modulating system in the spinal cord that regulates these impulses. If you remember our discussion on stress, the alarmed brain releases cortisol to dampen the stress response in the brain. Each level of the spinal cord functions like a miniature brain. (In fact, in lower animals, the brain is just a larger spinal cord segment.) Hence, at each level there is a built-in, inhibitory gate mechanism for dampening pain signals before they reach the brain. It is this gating mechanism that is responsible for much of the effectiveness of the pain therapies discussed in this chapter.

Pain signals that do make it past the dampening gates in the spinal cord reach various parts of the brain. Some pain fibers, particularly the slower, narrower, noninsulated fibers, send many connections to the brainstem. The brainstem areas stimulated by pain include the following: 1) the nuclei that send signals back down the spinal cord to control autonomic (involuntary) sympathetic fight-or-flight responses to pain such as release of adrenaline, fast pulse, sweating, and high blood pressure; 2) the brainstem nuclei that send parasympathetic stress signals back down the spinal cord and other nerves that cause pain-induced vomiting, fainting, and indigestion; 3) the brainstem reticular activating system that sends serotonin and norepinephrine projections to the cortex to increase alertness (try to fall asleep in extreme pain).

Other pain signals are routed directly to the brain. The sensory switching area called the thalamus sits just above the brainstem and below the cortex, sends signals to the cortex for specific localization of pain. The hypothalamus at the base of the brain also receives slow pain fibers, causing the pituitary to release the stress hormone ACTH into the bloodstream (stimulating cortisol release by the adrenal glands) and the natural painkiller beta endorphin.

Messages also reach the limbic system (hippocampus, amygdala, and other central brain structures mediating drive states, emotions, and memory) and result in the emotional response that is so important in helping a person formulate a response to pain.

Two extreme examples demonstrate the importance of this emotional "flavor" of the pain response: Patients who undergo frontal lobotomy, where limbic connections to the frontal cortex are severed (which is known to deaden emotional response), suffer little pain even in the face of extreme injury. There are also accounts of indescribable torture during the Spanish Inquisition of the Middle Ages, where victims with tremendous religious faith (and therefore a strong emotional and interpretational element attached to reception of pain) survived daily bodily mutilation and literally exhausted their torturers.

> *Long-term chronic pain has the same effect on the brain and body as severe stress: physical exhaustion, depression, insomnia, fatigue, and even more severe psychiatric symptoms.*

Pain Boosters and Zappers

Because pain interferes with the quality of life and daily functioning, it has sparked a multimillion dollar industry. Thousands and thousands of physicians, researchers, pharmaceutical companies, and individuals are searching to understand the cause and the cure for pain. There are a number of ways to boost and zap in your own body, in drugs, in adjunctive therapies, in foods, in herbs and supplements, and in lifestyle choices.

Boosters and Zappers in Your Own Body

When the brain receives a pain signal from the body, it immediately activates a number of systems that function to address this internal disturbance.

Zapper: *Cortisol*

Cortisol is released from the adrenals when stress or pain signals cause the hypothalamus to stimulate the pituitary to release the hormone ACTH into the bloodstream. Cortisol dampens the stress response in the brain and also dampens the inflammatory response of swelling, vasodilation, and prostaglandin release in areas of injury. (The decrease in "good" prostaglandin production by the stomach lining may be how too much stress or too much cortisol-like steroid medications, such as Prednisone, can cause ulcers).

Zapper: *Endorphins*

The endorphins are the most potent pain-relievers known to man. They are amino acid chains (peptides) produced in the brain, pituitary, and spinal cord. They stimulate specific molecules called opiate receptors on nerve cells that inhibit the pain response at the spinal cord level (the gating neurons, for instance) and in the brain. Endorphins also cause release of dopamine in the brain, which may mediate a pleasurable sensation and dull the response to pain. They also reach opiate receptors in the limbic system, where a dampening of the stress response occurs in addition to an emotional feeling of happiness and well-being.

The effects of these endorphins on opiate receptors may be the reason that during extreme stress or injury people describe feeling "numb all over." It may also explain the feeling of intense joy during near-death and high-stress experiences.

Specific endorphins include: 1) beta endorphin, which is released by the pituitary gland into the bloodstream during stress and pain, 2) dynorphin, which is released in various regions of the brain and spinal cord, and 3) enkephalins, which are one of several specific spinal cord neurotransmitters that help produce the gating response to dampen pain signals there. Narcotics such as morphine, Demerol, heroin, and methadone, act directly on these opiate receptors and produce similar effects.

Zapper: *Gamma-aminobutyric acid (GABA)*

GABA is a neurotransmitter that causes general inhibition or slowing of nerve activity in the brain and spinal cord. This includes a slowing of pain and stress signals. Located in the cortex, limbic system, and cerebellum, GABA neurons (although not direct pain relievers) affect the interpretation of pain because when the anxiety level about a painful event is decreased, the pain itself becomes more tolerable. Benzodiazepines such as Valium, Ativan, and Xanax act on these receptors.

In the spinal cord, GABA slows signals from nerves that control muscle tone and tension. Specific drugs that block spinal cord GABA receptors decrease painful muscle spasm associated with chronic back pain, spinal cord injury, and other neurologic disorders.

Booster: *Mediators of inflammation*

When tissues are damaged, many other substances besides the prostaglandins are released. Some of these attract immune system components such as the white blood cells that further release the mediators such as bradykinin and histamine. All of these are thought to increase the pain response. Clearly, when inflammation from injury is a cause of pain, drugs that block inflammation, such as the steroids, can decrease pain.

Zapper: *Progesterone*

Progesterone, the female sex hormone that surges in the mid- and late-menstrual cycle and remains high during pregnancy, has a direct anesthetic effect on nerves and the brain. As a result, pregnant women need about half the amount of pain relievers to produce the same analgesic effect as nonpregnant women. Even isolated nerves in the laboratory, when exposed to progesterone, are more susceptible to local anesthetics. This probably has some role in helping women deal with the painful stretch that occurs in the uterus, cervix, and pelvis during labor and delivery. (See Chapter 9 for more details.)

I am currently doing research to determine if awareness under anesthesia occurs more commonly in women during the early menstrual cycle, when progesterone levels are at their lowest and therefore not dampening pain response. The hypothesis is that with less progesterone, patients under anesthesia might experience more pain stimulation and be more likely to wake up.

Booster: *Prostaglandins*

Prostaglandins are the substances produced within cells and released during tissue damage or inflammation. They directly stimulate pain receptors in tissue. Pain relievers, such as aspirin, acetaminophen (Tylenol), and nonsteroidal drugs (Motrin and Advil), block their production.

Besides mediating pain, some prostaglandins have other functions, such as protecting the stomach lining from its own acid. This is why people who regularly take aspirin or nonsteroidals (which block prostaglandin production where needed) can develop stomach ulcers.

Zapper: *Serotonin and epinephrine*

In Chapter 2 we spoke of the importance of the two amine neurotransmitters, serotonin and norepinephrine, that are spread throughout the cortex by nerve projections from small nuclei in the brainstem and which help mediate arousal and attention. These nuclei also send projections down the spinal cord and help the gating mechanism dampen the effects of pain.

Adrenaline (epinephrine), when released during extreme stress, also reaches the spinal cord through the bloodstream and stimulates alpha-adrenergic receptors or spinal cord pain-gating neurons. The effect is increased analgesia (pain relief) during the stress response. (See Chapter 6 for details about the stress response.)

Booster: *Substance P*

Substance P is a neurotransmitter in the spinal cord and brain that transmits many of the pain signals from one neuron to the next. Newer classes of drugs that block substance P are currently under study but not yet available.

The legendary pioneer in the field of anesthesia research, Henry K. Beecher, studied wounded soldiers on the battlefields during World War II. These injured men required less pain relief from morphine, for example, than patients with similar injuries in a more protected hospital setting. Clearly the extreme stress of battle and acute injury activated some internal pain-relief system. These observations led to much of the work in the formulation of a theory of spinal cord gating systems, and the later discovery of endogenous opiates.

Boosters and Zappers in Drugs

The drug industry is bursting with pain-relief formulas. A few of the more commonly used ones are mentioned here, but be sure to talk to your physician to determine what is best for you. Never use someone else's pain medication for your own aches and pains.

Booster: *Alcohol*

Alcohol is known to cause or worsen headaches. This happens because the breakdown of aldehyde produces brain vasodilation, which causes a generalized opening of the blood vessels in the brain. This sudden rush of blood puts pressure on the meninges of the fibrous tissue surrounding the brain, causing pain.

Zapper: *Anticonvulsants*

Anticonvulsants (seizure medications) are effective at treating pain problems involving chronic activation of pain circuits that seem to be burned into a spinal cord "memory." These types of pain problems result from nerve injury from surgery or trauma, limb amputation (causing phantom limb pain—pain felt where the limb "used to be"), herpes zoster infection of the skin, chronic headache syndromes, and even some cases of long-standing chronic back pain.

These drugs are thought to interrupt this pain cycle that persists after the original injury or painful cause is removed. The anticonvulsants used for this purpose include Dilantin, Neurontin, and Tegretol. These drugs are often used as a last resort because they have many undesirable side effects.

Zapper: *Antidepressants*

Antidepressants have a significant role in the treatment of chronic pain problems. Far and above the fact that most patients with chronic pain suffer from depression and benefit from its treatment, the antidepressants boost the amount of natural neurotransmitter serotonin and norepinephrine available to block pain in the spine.

Normally these neurotransmitters are made in nerve projections that originate from the brainstem. These act on the gating pain-blocking neurons in the spine and the brainstem. The tricyclic antidepressants (Elavil, Pamelor, Desipramine), which tend to increase norepinephrine more than serotonin, seem to be more effective at treating chronic pain problems than the SSRI (selective serotonin re-uptake inhibitor) antidepressants, such as Prozac and Paxil.

Zapper: *Aspirin and acetaminophen*

Aspirin and acetaminophen (Tylenol) inhibit prostaglandin production so when cells are damaged or when inflammation occurs, less pain results. Aspirin is a more potent pain inhibitor than acetaminophen because it decreases the inflammatory response. Very often, these are both combined with narcotics, producing a very effective analgesic combination (for example, Percocet combines acetaminophen with oxycodone; Percodan combines aspirin with oxycodone).

Although very effective pain relievers, both drugs have negative side effects. Aspirin causes stomach ulcers because (unlike acetaminophen) it weakens the protective prostaglandin lining. Acetaminophen overdose can produce permanent liver damage and death.

A new type of aspirin called COX-2 Blocking Aspirin will be introduced to the market shortly. This drug blocks the enzyme that makes the prostaglandins that produce pain and inflammation (COX-2), but not the enzyme that makes the prostaglandins that protect the stomach (COX-1). That is the good news. Unfortunately, this new class of aspirin doesn't prevent arteriosclerosis like regular aspirin does.

Headaches, specifically migraines, are vascular in origin and involve the dilation of blood vessels in the brain, putting pressure on and stretching the meninges. Many analgesics are quite effective at treating headaches, but are often combined with more specific medications that control the blood vessel dilation. For instance, Imitrex (sumatriptan) is the first of a new class of drugs that acts like serotonin on brain blood vessels, causing vasoconstriction and decreasing this pressure on the meninges. The antihistamine Periactin may also have similar serotonin-like properties. Oxygen therapy is also effective, presumably through a similar effect.

Zapper: *Benzodiazepines*

Although the benzodiazepine anti-anxiety drugs (Valium, Ativan, Xanax) don't directly interrupt pain transmission, they do enhance the action of the GABA neurotransmitters (responsible for feelings of relaxation), thus decreasing anxiety. It is known that when you feel relaxed, you can tolerate pain better than when you are anxious.

Zapper: *Caffeine*

Caffeine causes vasoconstriction in the brain. This tightening of blood vessels is often an effective remedy for headache pain that is caused by the dilation of brain blood vessels, which puts pressure on and stretches the meninges. For this reason, caffeine (along with aspirin or acetaminophen and a barbiturate sedative) is a major ingredient in pain remedies such as Fiorinal and Fioricet. Caffeine is also used in over-the-counter pain remedies such as Excedrin and Anacin.

Booster: *Capsaicin*

Capsaicin, made from cayenne pepper, causes the sensation of pain. It is used to treat the pain of herpes lesions, possibly by overloading the tissue pain fibers and thereby inactivating them.

Zapper: *Local anesthetics*

Local anesthetics such as Novocaine and Lidocaine (used for dental injection, and spinal and epidural anesthesia) cause local numbness and pain relief by blocking nerve transmission wherever they are specifically injected or applied. Throat lozenges and numbing mouthwash (Chloraseptic, for example) contain a local anesthetic called *phenol* that has this same effect on nerve transmission.

Zapper: *Marijuana*

The active ingredient in marijuana, THC (tetrahydracannabanol), activates specific receptors in the brain. These receptors tend to occur in the same places that GABA receptors are found and may have a similar effect on pain interpretation as the benzodiazepines. As a physician, however, I cannot recommend the use of illegal drugs to decrease pain.

Zapper: *Muscle relaxants*

Muscle spasm is a component of many skeletal pain problems, such as disc herniation of the lower back. Spinal GABA activators that relax muscles, such as Flexeril, Baclofen, and Robaxin, act on

GABA receptors of the spine, decreasing the muscle spasm that worsens such skeletal pain problems.

Booster: *Naloxone*

Naloxone is used to treat narcotic overdoses. It blocks many of the opiate receptors and immediately reverses the pain relief offered by the narcotic. Naloxone even makes the pain relief from acupuncture less effective.

Zapper: *Narcotics*

Narcotics such as morphine, Demerol, heroin, and methadone, act directly on the opiate receptors in the spinal cord and brain that produce the gating mechanism to dampen pain signals. They also cause euphoria through dopamine release and produce a sense of well-being through receptors in the limbic system of the brain. Whether purified from the opium poppy (morphine and heroin) or synthesized in a laboratory (Demerol, methadone), the narcotics or opiates are by far the most potent pain-relieving drugs available.

When taken voluntarily without the presence of pain, narcotics are highly addictive. It is thought that when one self-administers these drugs for the recreational euphoric effect, a permanent change takes place in the brain, making the person an addict for life. Although there is no scientific proof for this, it is a fact that narcotic addictions are among the most difficult to treat and have a very high relapse rate.

Fortunately, narcotics rarely cause addiction when given for pain. In fact, in serious pain problems such as terminal cancer and sickle cell crisis, patients are more often undertreated than overdosed for fear of producing addiction. Common oral narcotic preparations administered to relieve pain include codeine, oxycodone, and MS Contin.

Zapper: *Nicotine*

Although it probably doesn't have direct analgesic properties, nicotine in cigarettes stimulates the sympathetic autonomic nervous system to release epinephrine and norepinephrine. It also stimulates the parasympathetic autonomic system to produce a sense of relaxation. Both these actions dampen the perception of pain.

However, nicotine is highly addictive and withdrawal can cause problems—from weight gain to anxiety to severe depression. Further, it causes cancer, heart disease, and lung disease, making nicotine a poor choice as a pain reliever.

Zapper: *Nonsteroidal anti-inflammatory drugs (NSAIDs)*

Nonsteroidal anti-inflammatory drugs (NSAIDs) are common pain relievers that include Motrin, Advil, Naprosyn, and Feldene. They are often used to treat arthritis and low-back pain. They all work by decreasing prostaglandin production, thereby decreasing both pain fiber stimulation in tissue injury and tissue inflammation.

Like aspirin, NSAIDs weaken the protective stomach lining and, further, they block prostaglandins needed to maintain bloodflow to the kidneys. In high doses or with chronic use, NSAIDs can result in kidney failure. This is important to remember because these are available over the counter and should be avoided by those with kidney disease.

Zapper: *Ultram*

Ultram is a weak opiate receptor activator (able to deaden pain) and it also increases both brain serotonin and norepinephrine, inhibiting the perception of pain in the brain and spinal cord. Ultram is used to treat chronic pain problems as long as patients are not taking antidepressants. The combination can produce seizures.

The placebo effect is "alive and well" in pain management. If a person believes he or she will get pain relief, the interpretation of the pain is different and the pain is less. This makes it hard to effectively evaluate new pain medications, and more importantly, to determine whether supplements and herbal remedies truly have some physiological effect. Here is one place that animal studies may have more value. The animals receiving a placebo, if not already trained, do not know what to expect.

Boosters and Zappers in Foods

Both the mechanism of pain (necessary to alert you to potentially serious problems) and the natural body systems that control pain rely on the healthy functioning of brain systems and spinal cord nerve endings. A balanced, varied, nutritious diet gives the body the nutrients, oxygen, and enzymes it needs to activate these systems with a high degree of efficiency. Although there is not enough scientific evidence to recommend any specific diet over another as "pain relieving," it would be wrong to assume that food plays a minimal role in pain production and management. Everything you eat feeds the brain systems that are integral to the way you perceive and tolerate pain.

Booster: *Capsaicin*

Capsaicin, the active ingredient in red pepper, is thought to act like substance P, a neurotransmitter in the spinal cord and brain that transmits many of the pain signals from one neuron to the next. Capsaicin causes a localized burning sensation.

Zapper: *Carbohydrates*

Carbohydrates (such as sugars in fruits and vegetables and starches in whole grains and pastas) may have a transient positive effect on pain tolerance by raising brain serotonin levels. An increase in serotonin elevates mood and may diminish some of the stress that aggravates pain.

Booster: *Food additives*

Food additives can cause or worsen headaches by causing brain vasodilation. These include monosodium glutamate (MSG), found as a "natural flavor" in many processed foods; nitrates, found in packaged meats such as hot dogs and cold cuts; and possibly aspartame, found in the artificial sweetener NutraSweet.

Booster: *Ketones*

Ketones are waste products of partially metabolized fat and are known to aggravate the pain response. They are produced by the body when fat is burned at an accelerated rate. To dieters, this may sound like a positive thing, but rapid weight loss through fasting is bad for the body in many respects and bad for one's ability to tolerate pain.

Boosters and Zappers in Herbs and Supplements

Since the beginning of recorded time, people have looked to natural substances to relieve pain. In this section, you will find a variety of herbs and natural supplements that are thought to reduce pain or the stress and anxiety associated with it.

Zapper: *Aloe vera*

Aloe vera contains the compound alocetin B, which, when applied topically to inflamed tissues, is believed to inhibit prostaglandin production. Prostaglandins, remember, are the substances that directly stimulate pain receptors in tissue and are the target of pain-killing aspirins.

Zapper: *Anxiety busters*

Stress, fear, and anxiety are known to support and aggravate pain. That's why the herbs and supplements that reduce anxiety are also often used to control pain. A few such herbs include:

- ◆ Kava kava, an extract of the plant *Piper methysticum*, contains lactone compounds that act similar to GABA in the central nervous system. Remember that GABA neurons, although not direct pain relievers, affect the interpretation of pain by lowering levels of anxiety. (Do not take kava kava if you are on antidepressants. See Chapter 8 for details.)
- ◆ Valerian root also causes relaxation and elevates mood. In this way, this herb may be useful in easing the perception of pain.
- ◆ Skullcap is thought to have similar anxiety busting properties as kava kava and valerian root, and thus has the same secondary effect on pain perception. In addition, skullcap may be particularly effective in treating migraines. The flavenoid compounds in this herbal preparation seem to have anti-inflammatory properties that can reduce the pressure on the meninges that are known to accompany migraine.

The Care and Feeding of Your Brain

Zapper: *Chamomile*

Chamomile, available as a supplement and an herbal tea, contains spiroether, thought to relax both voluntary muscle (causing general relaxation and less spasms) and involuntary muscle (helping in the spastic pain of gastrointestinal illness and menstrual cramping). In a German study, colicky babies given chamomile became significantly more relaxed and less distressed by pain.

Zapper: *Cloves*

Cloves contain a phenol-like substance called *eugenol*, that has local anesthetic properties. If chewed, they may ease the pain of a toothache.

Zapper: *Cod liver oil*

Cod liver oil, and other fish oils with omega-3 fatty acids, may slow prostaglandin production in tissues and act similar to aspirin and NSAIDs when taken orally.

Zapper: *Feverfew*

For chronic pain that stems from a condition involving inflammation, such as arthritis, migraine, or musculoskeletal pain, many people use the herb feverfew, which has anti-inflammatory properties.

Zapper: *Lavender oil*

Lavender oil, if applied on the temples, is thought to have a calming effect in headache sufferers from its scent.

Zapper: *St. John's wort*

St. John's wort has a growing reputation for treating depression (see Chapter 8 for more details). When taken as a supplement, this herb raises brain amine levels of serotonin and norepinephrine through its effect as a weak inhibitor of the enzyme (monoamine oxidase) that breaks them down. This action treats the depression of chronic pain and also has direct effects on pain transmission.

As an oil, St. John's wort may have local properties of decreasing inflammation when applied topically to inflamed tissues. Like aloe vera, it is believed to inhibit prostaglandin production, though scientific evidence for this claim is unavailable.

Zapper: *White willow bark*

White willow bark (*Salix alba*) is commonly used for any ailment or condition that is treated by conventional medicine with aspirin. The active ingredient of aspirin, salicylic, is derived from this source (although aspirin is now probably cheaper).

Zappers in Adjunctive Therapies

A discussion of pain cannot be complete without a look at adjunctive therapies that are commonly used to treat various kinds of pain. These therapies are all proven effective in certain circumstances and are often part of programs offered by renowned pain clinics throughout the world. Each one requires a trained (and sometimes licensed) practitioner for safe and effective application.

Zapper: *Acupuncture*

Acupuncture was first recognized in the United States on a large scale when a *New York Times* reporter accompanying Richard Nixon to China in 1972 underwent an emergency appendectomy, after which his postoperative pain was relieved by acupuncture treatment. This ancient healing art has been extremely well-studied and is generally accepted as the most effective alternative therapy for pain management.

The successful pain blocking probably involves a combination of several physiological mechanisms. The noxious effect of needle puncture on the skin causes release of endorphins into the bloodstream and serotonin into the brain. Further, the spinal-gating mechanisms are directly enhanced. But more mysterious effects may be at work, as well.

For instance, simply needling points at random has been proven not as effective, ruling out a placebo effect or the endorphin and serotonin effects alone. In fact, acupuncture points can effect parts of the body at a distance where there are no nerve connections or neural relationships between points. Whatever its exact mechanism, acupuncture is an effective tool in treating pain.

Zapper: *Chiropractic and massage therapies*

Chiropractic therapy is a program of healing based on the belief that displacements of the spine cause pressure on nerves, which create pain or symptoms in other parts of the body. Treatment often involves adjustments and manipulations to the spinal cord.

Massage is a very soothing way to relieve muscular pain. Massage works on the soft tissues, muscles, and ligaments of the body. It stimulates circulation, activates the function of the nervous system, and helps to lower blood pressure—all known pain relievers.

Chiropractic manipulations and massage can be used to prevent pain states. By relaxing tense muscle fibers, both techniques improve circulation, allowing blood to flow freely and toxins to be released and eliminated. Increased circulation also brings more oxygen and other nutrients throughout the body, promoting a stronger, healthier body system.

Zapper: *Distraction*

It seems that our mind can hold only one topic in consciousness at a time. You can choose consciously to attend to your pain by thinking about it, or you can choose consciously to think of something else. When you feel your pain taking up an undue degree of your mental attention, distract your mind away from the pain by going for a walk, talking to a friend, watching TV, or playing cards. Even listening to music has been shown to decrease the need for pain medication. Anything that requires your mental and physical attention can be used as a cognitive distraction strategy.

Comedies are the best films for distracting attention from pain. In addition to diverting, they cause laughter, proven to change the physiology of stress and relieve pain. Sustained laughter may very well stimulate the release of the body's natural painkillers, endorphins. It's also believed that the nervous system can hold only one kind of sensation at a time; it cannot simultaneously react to pleasure and tension.

Therefore, laughter can transmit a positive and joyful message that overrides those of anxiety, stress, depression, and pain. At the same time, laughter provides a source of distraction that keeps the body's focus away from pain, relaxes the muscles that aggravate pain, and offers temporary but welcome pain relief. So cultivate your sense of humor and laugh often!

> *In his book* Anatomy of an Illness as Perceived by the Patient, *Norman Cousins wrote, "Ten minutes of genuine belly laughter had an anesthetic effect that would give me at least two hours of pain-free sleep."*

Zapper: *Hypnosis*

Experts in the field believe hypnosis can be used as an effective adjunct to pain therapy and can lessen the total requirement of pain medication. Hypnosis is particularly effective in easing pain that is exacerbated by stress, tension, or anxiety, or is psychogenic in origin. Through hypnosis, deep states of relaxation can be attained. This allows tense muscles to relax and blood circulation to flow smoothly, thus easing the pain of tension-based problems.

Hypnosis should not be used alone as a treatment for chronic pain, but in combination with other modalities. If you do decide to use hypnosis as treatment for pain, be sure to find a legitimate hypnotherapist through the American Society of Clinical Hypnosis.

Zapper: *Psychotherapy*

There are many different kinds of psychological therapy that can help a person suffering chronic pain. The most commonly used is cognitive-behavioral therapy. This focuses on changing negative or non-coping thoughts and actions caused by persistent pain and repeated treatment failures. Cognitive-behavioral therapy tries to focus attention away from the pain so it doesn't dominate their lives.

When obsession with pain allows it to become the controlling life force, a sense of helplessness and hopelessness can result. Researchers have long noted the connection between these feelings and depression. A combination of cognitive and behavioral therapy can help.

Cognitive therapy for pain is based on the belief that people who think they can control their pain, who avoid thinking the worst about their condition, and who believe they are not severely disabled function better than those who do not. This therapy will help you recognize your own negative self-talk (such as, "This is awful; I can't stand this") and replace them with positive, realistic ones (such as, "I'm not going to let this pain ruin my day"). Your brain often responds to your thoughts when determining how to perceive pain.

> *The emotional context of pain is very important in how pain is perceived. For instance, the Lamaze method of childbirth specifically involves conditioning the mother to expect and work with pain rather than fear it. Similarly, children planning surgery who are given a tour of the surgical facility beforehand and are told what to expect are less apprehensive at the time of surgery and more comfortable in the recovery room. It is a hard scientific fact that those who feel they are in control of the situation and who know what's going on need less pain medication.*

Behavioral therapy will teach you that certain learned behaviors promote and aggravate pain. It is designed to break the unwholesome behavior patterns of chronic pain patients that have previously been rewarded: drug-taking, avoidance of activity, dependence on others, preoccupation with pain. Behavioral therapy encourages and rewards the very opposite of these behaviors: responsibility, independence, activity, and the desire to free oneself from pain and not be bound to it.

> *The way we perceive the amount of control we have over our pain can affect the amount of pain we feel. This has been shown in hospital patients who need medication for pain relief. Some patients are given a method of electronic morphine delivery after operations called PCA (patient controlled analgesia), in which they can press a button to deliver a dose of intravenous pain medication whenever they feel they need it. It has been found that these patients require medication less often and in smaller doses than those who are at the mercy of the doctors and nurses who decide when they need the next dose of pain medication.*

Zapper: *TENS (Transcutaneous Electrical Nerve Stimulation)*

The TENS unit is a battery-operated device that delivers a low-voltage electrical current through electrodes placed on the skin. The application of a weak alternating current to painful regions involves stimulation of the spinal gating mechanism and release of endorphins at low frequencies of current and brain serotonin pathway stimulation at higher frequencies.

Some of the conditions that have been successfully treated with TENS include musculoskeletal discomfort, dysmenorrhea, rheumatoid arthritis, phantom limb pain, musculoskeletal headache, and postoperative pain.

Boosters and Zappers in Lifestyle

No one is a helpless victim of pain. We all have the ability to do something about the way we perceive pain and directly affect the role pain plays in our lives. Physical exercise and relaxation therapies are two of the most commonly used lifestyle choices people make to take control of their pain.

Booster & Zapper: *Exercise*

People in pain generally are not the first ones to jump off the couch and say, "Let's go exercise!" Unfortunately, this fact worsens the pain condition because exercise can actually equip the body to better deal with the physical and emotional aspects of pain.

As soon as your physician gives you the okay to exercise (whether walking, cycling, swimming, playing tennis or golf, or whatever), get out there and move. You will immediately gain a number of benefits. Regular moderate exercise raises brain amine levels. By releasing substances that affect emotions, such as adrenaline, serotonin, and norepinephrine, you will boost your mood and relieve the pain-enhancing states of tension and depression.

Exercise produces better sleep—a real benefit to anyone who has difficulty sleeping because of a pain condition. Sound sleep also allows the body the restorative time it needs to repair and rejuvenate and battle the source and stress of pain.

Exercise is wonderful preventative medicine. When done properly, it prevents predisposition to painful arthritis, bone degeneration, and obesity (a stress on the skeletal system). More advanced methods of exercise involving controlled bodily stretch and movement (as experienced in yoga and tai chi) may be especially beneficial in this regard.

On the other side of the issue is the fact that excessive, unsupervised exercise can worsen pain conditions. "No pain, no gain" is simply not true. Remember, pain is a signal from our body that something is wrong. You should work through that pain and ignore it only under the direct supervision of a physician or physical therapist (and even then, speak up loud and clear if he or she pushes you beyond your tolerance level). Although some stiffness and muscle soreness is natural at first, you should not do any exercise that sharply aggravates an existing pain condition.

Zapper: *Relaxation Exercises*

Relaxation exercises can control the involuntary workings of the nervous system that are known to support and aggravate pain. These techniques can help you manage pain by influencing blood pressure, heart rate, respiration, and metabolism—all seemingly involuntary physiological functions that power the chronic pain cycle.

In addition to their effect on bodily functions, relaxation techniques can break the stress pain cycle. Reducing stress reduces pain in several ways. Self-regulated stress management improves your sense of control over your pain. Cognitive therapists assure us that the way we think about our pain affects the way we feel it. Relaxation techniques put you in charge; they give you an active role in managing your pain. This alone reduces the feelings of helplessness and hopelessness that support and maintain pain.

Relaxation exercises enhance sleep. Chronic pain robs us of sleep. Relaxation techniques calm the body, improve circulation, lower anxiety levels—all of which promotes peaceful rest. Relaxation reduces the sensation of pain by decreasing muscle tension. Studies have shown that stress-related muscle tension often is the greatest at the body's most vulnerable site—the source of chronic pain.

Relaxation therapy improves overall well-being. If a stress response is chronic, the constant presence of adrenaline pumping into your system begins to wear down the body's immunological system. You need a strong and healthy body to manage chronic pain. Relaxation techniques can help you achieve that physiological state. Look in

Chapter 6 for a detailed discussion of relaxation therapies, such as abdominal breathing, progressive muscle relaxation, meditation, and spiritual prayer.

Your emotions and your personal beliefs related to the pain can affect how you perceive it. A sense of purpose or the placement of the suffering in some logical context based on religious faith has been proven to increase resiliency and shorten recovery time in painful traumas, surgery, and other bodily stressors.

Chapter 8

Depression: The Extreme Side of Stress and Burnout

Has anyone ever told you that depression is "all in your head"? Well, it's true! Depression involves prominent physical changes in the brain. These changes make it clear that depression is no joke. It's not a plea for attention; it's not something you can just "shake off." It's a very real affliction. Unfortunately, many relatives and friends of a depressed person misinterpret the fact that depression is "all in your head."

They reason, "If only John would just go out and have some fun, he would forget about all this nonsense. Sometimes I think he actually wants to be miserable." "Why don't you just get out of bed and stop crying. Go enjoy your children, they need you! Stop it with this selfish behavior." Certainly, this is said with good intentions and may even be helpful advice for battling occasional bouts of the normal blues. But it makes a person suffering true depression, with all its accompanying guilt and conflict, feel even worse.

This is why we have to draw the line between sadness and depression. Much of the well-touted advice of pop psychologists and motivational self-help speakers and books, that says you can cure yourself by reciting some mantra or focusing on some diversion, usually won't work for a person with real depression (although I highly recommend such diversions for removing oneself from sad and stressful situations).

In depression, a storm in the brain has taken on a life of its own that is not easily calmed by will power. Yes, there are some people who find it easier in life to be miserable and seek the pity of others and some who enjoy the secondary gain of being able to use depression as an excuse to avoid responsibility. There are even others who out of superstition are actually afraid to admit they are happy. We have all met such people. The problem is that, very often, truly depressed people begin to believe they are one of these types. They buy into the labels of "faker" or "lazy" or "weak." Tragically, some feel deserving of no less than death by suicide.

Mental illness such as depression bears an unfair stigma despite all the mounting scientific evidence of its genetic and neurochemical nature. Depression is as much a real illness of the brain as is epilepsy or a tumor for roughly 20 percent of the adult population, and it carries a mortality rate between 10 and 20 percent by suicide if left untreated. In fact, in 1993, the American Psychiatric Association ran an ad campaign saying, "The way our society deals with mental illness is insane." It's time we understood clearly how drugs, foods, supplements, and lifestyle choices all can influence the way the brain influences mood.

Depression and the Brain

During repeated or severe stress, your brain sets off many alarms that call it and the rest of the body into action. The cerebellum helps recognize dangerous outside conditions. The amygdala coordinates much of the sensory information coming into the cortex and relays it to the rest of the limbic system, creating an emotional state of hypervigilance, fear, and anxiety.

The body becomes aroused through the hypothalamus at the base of the brain where stress hormones are released (by the pituitary just below it) and from where signals activate the autonomic nervous system of the body and the reticular activating system of the brainstem. This brainstem arousal system alerts the cortex and the limbic system into attention by way of the amine neurotransmitters. All these modes of stimulation gear up the brain and body for serious evasive or aggressive action. They dictate how we will deal with the physical changes that cause depression.

Depression Boosters and Zappers

Depression doesn't just appear one day and exist in a vacuum. It is greatly influenced by the daily workings of the brain, as well as by the drugs, foods, and supplements we put into our body. Later you will also see how depression can be influenced by lifestyle choices.

Boosters and Zappers in Your Own Body

Depression is not simply the result of feeling bad. It is the result of changes in brain function. You may be surprised to learn that these changes can be caused by various physical health conditions, including chronic pain, genetic disorders, the action of the immune system, stroke, and hypothyroidism. Depression is also caused by the changing levels of melatonin, neurotransmitters, sex hormones, and stress hormones.

Booster & Zapper: *Chronic pain*

All patients who suffer from chronic pain (as occurs from severe musculoskeletal back problems, neurologic pain syndromes, and so on) become depressed to some degree. (See Chapter 7 for details.) Although you might think that people in constant pain have a good reason to be depressed, the depression is most likely not something they could mentally fully control even if they tried. It is generally believed that the long-term, noxious stimulation to the brain and spinal cord caused by chronic pain sets up a long-term stress response known to physiologically cause depression. Further, the fact that the person in pain is helpless to alleviate the problem makes the whole situation worse (see "Learned Helplessness" on page 190).

Booster & Zapper: *Genetic disorders*

It is well-established that mood disorders run in families, and not just dysfunctional and codependent ones. Twins separated at birth and raised in very different family environments have similar rates of depression, manic depressive illness, and schizophrenia. Clearly, there are inherited tendencies that make certain individuals more susceptible to depression, especially when exposed to severe stress or a series of chronic stressors. This may be caused by an individual variation in one's ability to make more serotonin and norepinephrine when these neurotransmitters become depleted during stress.

Theoretically, if this were so, while one person might be able to resist stress by creating more amine neurotransmitters as needed, another person with a genetic predisposition towards depression may have less of an ability to produce the same amount of these brain chemicals at will. This explains why individual reactions to extreme chronic stress vary from one person to another—why one person reacts by becoming clinically depressed and another in the exact same circumstance is able to remain mentally healthy.

Booster: *Hypothyroidism*

There is a clear correlation between thyroid gland function and depression. In fact, because hypothyroidism is common as people grow old, testing for thyroid function is a requirement in the workup of the depressed elderly patient and should be part of the workup of any new adult-onset depression.

The thyroid gland is responsible for maintaining the normal metabolic rate of the body's cells. Because brain cells are the most metabolically active of all cells in the body (they use the most fuel, glucose, for their weight), they are sensitive to changes in thyroid hormone levels. Hypothyroidism causes general decrease in cortex activation, almost simulating the depletion of the amine neurotransmitters previously described.

Booster & Zapper: *The immune system*

Phillip Gold, M.D., of the National Institutes of Health describes the action of the immune system to stress hormones as similar to the brain's reaction. During acute stress, the immune system is activated and placed on alert. However, the shut-off mechanism, part of which involves the release of cortisol, eventually becomes ineffective so that like in the brain, the prolonged state of activation exhausts the immune system.

This imbalance makes the immune system less able to fight disease and at the same time releases all sorts of alarm substances that cause everything from muscle and joint aches to infections, and even cancer (a clear association between depressive episodes and cancer years later has been established).

One of the alarm systems that is another byproduct of this imbalance is the continued release of active immune substances called cytokines. Cytokines reach the brain and further depress the release of the neurotransmitters serotonin, norepinephrine, and dopamine (so necessary to balanced mood states). In fact, the effect of these immune cytokines on the brain may be an additional factor involved in the chronic fatigue of depression. Many studies have re-iterated the fact that autoimmune diseases such as multiple sclerosis, lupus, and rheumatoid arthritis, as well as certain cancers, can be linked to either specific stressful events or bouts of severe depression.

Booster & Zapper: *Melatonin*

The pineal gland (fed by inputs from the vision centers and from the hypothalamus) secretes melatonin when you fall asleep to help regulate the body's circadian day/night cycles. (See Chapter 5 for more details.) This process can get thrown off kilter during the winter months (especially in northern regions), when the amount of daylight decreases markedly. This change in melatonin levels seems to be at least partially involved in a very common form of depression called Seasonal Affective Disorder or "SAD."

SAD has all the features of depression we've described except two: Individuals with SAD tend to eat and sleep more, not less. Otherwise, SAD is just as severe a depressive disorder as any other type of depression.

Exposure to "full-spectrum lighting"—not just the white light released by fluorescent or normal incandescent light bulbs, but rather a special type of light that releases some of the higher near-ultraviolet ranges simulating sunlight—has been successfully used to treat this kind of depression. These full-spectrum lights are turned on early in the morning, simulating the time at which the sun would rise in the summer months. Presumably, this helps to shut off melatonin release and regulate its effects on the circadian rhythms of the hypothalamus.

Booster & Zapper: *Neurotransmitters*

Under stress, a few thousand nerve cells that begin at the brainstem fan out, sending projections that release the stimulating neurotransmitters norepinephrine and serotonin to trillions of connections between billions of nerve cells all over the cortex and limbic areas.

If the stress is extreme or chronic, eventually the system begins to wear down. The exact reason for this is uncertain: Either you just run out of the amines norepinephrine and serotonin to keep the system activated, or these neurotransmitters are so elevated for so long that the system can no longer respond normally to them. Or, it could be both.

Adding to the mix is the action of the enzyme monoamine oxidase that chews up the neurotransmitters serotonin, norepinephrine, and dopamine. Because serotonin and norepinephrine are involved in the brain's call to arousal during stress, the excess of monoamine oxidase found in depressed people explains why they don't feel alert and easily aroused. Because dopamine is involved in invoking the brain's attention during novel stimuli, its destruction by monoamine oxidase is probably responsible for the anhedonia (lack of enjoyment of usually stimulating activities) of depression and the motor retardation or slowness that depressed people feel.

The depletion of these neurotransmitters also causes the body to become physically exhausted. The disrupted amine levels make normal sleep cycles impossible, causing anxious early-morning awakenings or excessive sleep with daytime fatigue.

This relationship between depression and neurotransmitters is the reason antidepressants work: They raise the amount of these depleted amines by preventing their cleanup or their breakdown.

Booster & Zapper: *Sex hormones*

There clearly are brain changes that occur when levels of the female sex hormone progesterone fall. Progesterone is elevated in pregnancy, and during ovulation, and normally cycles up and down in fertile women with normal ovaries. After delivery of the child, it falls; before menses, it falls along with estrogen; and at menopause, both progesterone and estrogen cease their up and down cycles.

This may explain the phenomena of postpartum depression, mood disorders associated with premenstrual syndrome (PMS), menopause, and birth-control pills (which contain progesterone-like substances). Progesterone is a potent neuro-active hormone that even has anesthetic properties. Clearly, changes in this hormone's level of exposure to the brain will affect the mood state of the brain.

Much of the evidence supporting this case for hormone-related depression is controversial and still under investigation. (See Chapter 9 for more details.)

Booster & Zapper: *Stress hormones*

Normally, cortisol, a steroid hormone released in the brain and by the adrenals, is used as a negative feedback switch to shut off the stress response. But after many prolonged or frequent stress reactions, the cortisol loses its effect and the stress "switch" remains turned on. This explains reports by depressed patients who, despite seeming very quiet and slow on the outside, say they feel paralyzed by an intense inner storm of bad feelings such as fear, worry, anxiety, obsessive thoughts, guilt, and anger. They seem to be stuck in the internal fight-or-flight mode. As a result, they are less able to enjoy restorative and pleasurable activities, and they become depressed.

Booster: *Stroke*

People who suffer strokes often become depressed. Although you might think this is a natural reaction to having suffered permanent damage to an area of the brain, it is far too common a reaction to attribute the depression to simple sadness about one's plight.

One explanation for the depression focuses on a possible depletion of the amine neurotransmitters necessary for balanced mood states. Because a region of the brain is damaged, the amine projections that run through that region, as well as those that supply other regions but touch on or pass through the damaged area, may also be destroyed. This presumably results in an impaired amine neurotransmitter reserve and a predisposition towards depression.

Boosters and Zappers in Drugs

The brain functions that affect depression are very sensitive to many drugs. Those discussed here that can both boost and zap depression are alcohol and illegal/recreational drugs, caffeine, corticosteroids, diet pills, and nicotine. Those that can increase depression include antihypertensives and birth-control pills. Those that zap depression are monoamine oxidase inhibitors, tricyclic antidepressants, SSRI antidepressants, amphetamines, and sedatives.

Booster & Zapper: *Alcohol and illegal/recreational drugs*

Alcohol and many of the illegal/recreational drugs initially boost mood but then zap it. The most commonly used drugs that have this effect are cocaine (including crack cocaine), amphetamines, and narcotics (morphine, heroin, methadone).

The initial euphoria experienced after taking these drugs results from a sudden release of dopamine into the brain, particularly into the limbic system involved in mood control. This is also thought to be the major reason these substances are so addictive.

Long-term, repeated used of these drugs, however, has negative long-term effects. Besides their inherent toxicity and the dangers of overdose, these stimulants negatively affect mood in two ways. They mimic the stress response on the body and they interrupt the normal cycles between activity and rest. This produces added wear and tear on the brain and can even cause severe emotional consequences such as paranoia and delirium.

In their act of stimulating the brain to attention, they use up and eventually deplete the amines dopamine, norepinephrine, and serotonin necessary for a balanced mood state. All of these drugs produce a certain amount of tolerance, that is, the amount needed to stimulate the brain's dopamine "excitement" pathways becomes higher and higher eventually producing a physical dependence and a withdrawal syndrome if they are stopped.

Cocaine and amphetamine withdrawal results in intense fatigue. Alcohol withdrawal can produce seizures, hallucinations, and even death. Narcotic withdrawal produces autonomic overload with sweating, racing heart, severe anxiety, and loss of bowel control. Withdrawal from any of these drugs can result in depression.

A high proportion of chronic alcoholics suffer from frequent bouts of severe depression. The reason for this is clouded in a "chicken or the egg" circumstance. Is alcohol's effect on brain cells the cause of the depression? Or do people who have a tendency to be chronically depressed look to alcohol to help boost their moods? I suspect that there is an element of both.

Certainly a depressed person may feel a bit better when having a few drinks, but the long-term effects, tolerance, and outright brain cell toxicity and cell death that occur with chronic use of high amounts probably impairs the ability of the brain to replenish amines used in stress, thereby worsening depression.

Zapper: *Amphetamines*

Amphetamines (sometimes called "uppers" for their stimulating effects) were more widely used to treat depression before the advent of antidepressant medication. Although they don't alleviate the cause of the depression, and may actually worsen it in the long term, they do help motivate depressed patients who might otherwise remain bedridden, paralyzed by their internal stress and conflicts.

They are still used as an adjunct therapy in situations where the sedative side effects of antidepressants are troubling, yet where the medication is otherwise successfully treating the depression. Amphetamines should not be given along with the monoamine oxidase (MAO) inhibitors, because both are stimulants and, when used in combination, could raise blood pressure to dangerous levels.

Zapper: *Antidepressants*

There are three major classes of antidepressant medications used to treat depression. All work to raise brain levels of one or both of the amines norepinephrine and serotonin. Recent research points to the importance of dopamine levels, as well, in controlling depression; dopamine is also affected to some extent by these drugs. These classes are: 1) monoamine oxidase inhibitors; 2) tricyclic antidepressants; and 3) SSRIs (selective serotonin re-uptake inhibitors).

Monoamine oxidase inhibitors were the first antidepressants. They were discovered because certain anti-tuberculosis medications improved mood in patients. These drugs (including Parnate and Nardil) inactivate the brain enzyme monoamine oxidase that chews up the three amine neurotransmitters, dopamine, norepinephrine, and serotonin. As a result, a depleted state is avoided, or at least the cycle of depression is broken by raising the levels of these substances in the cortex and limbic structures.

These drugs can be quite dangerous. Although they are extremely effective at treating most variants of depression, when taken with certain foods that contain amine-like substances called tyramines (common in aged cheese, red wine, and cured meats), or with the narcotic Demerol or other stimulants, and even with certain brain-active supplements such as kava kava and St. John's wort, a dangerous elevation in blood pressure, and even seizures and death, can sometimes result.

These are all substances that raise brain amines, which rise to dangerous levels when added to MAO inhibitors. Newer MAO inhibitors, being tried experimentally, do not possess similar risks, allowing patients to lead more normal lives.

Tricyclic antidepressants are the long-standing foundation of the antidepressant therapy drugs. They are effective in most patients, especially those whose depression is very "textbook" in nature or whose depression stems from chronic pain states. These drugs include Pamelor, Elavil, and Tofranil. They all act to raise norepinephrine and, to a lesser degree, serotonin, and possibly even dopamine.

Normally, in the "cleanup process" of the brain and in an act of biological conservation and recycling, these amine neurotransmitters, when released among nerve cells in the cortex and limbic structures, are taken back up by the cell that released them. The process is referred to as re-uptake, and in addition to buffering the stimulant effect of the neurotransmitters released, the act of taking them up (re-uptake) makes them available for the next round of stimulation.

By inhibiting re-uptake mainly of norepinephrine, the tricyclic antidepressants allow the levels of this amine that sit freely around nerve cells to increase, enhancing an otherwise depleted state. It's like reusing waste water in desert habitats. Although this occurs immediately, it takes several weeks for these drugs to have a complete effect, as if the neurotransmitter and stress hormone "storm" that is raging out of control needs time to be brought back under control.

The SSRIs are the Prozac-like antidepressants. This is the newest and most interesting class of antidepressants available. SSRI (specific serotonin re-uptake inhibitors), inhibit the "cleaning up" at nerve cell junctions of the amine serotonin. The results have been nothing short of amazing. This group, which includes Prozac, Paxil, Wellbutrin, and Zoloft, and a few newer ones in the pipeline, not only has an extremely high success rate at curing most depressions, but results in some very interesting personality changes as well.

A person treated with an SSRI is not only free from depression, but is generally also more positive and, as a result, more successful in human interactions and even career functions. The social and ethical implications of these behavior and attitude changes that go beyond treating depression are beautifully addressed in the book *Listening to Prozac*. In the book, a psychiatrist recounts his experiences with patients on this drug and the dilemma of whether to discontinue treatment when depression is gone, knowing full well that the newly formed positive and productive behavior patterns that his patients have also developed will disappear.

> *SSRIs are also frequently used to treat compulsive eating disorders such as anorexia and bulimia. Apparently, one of the pleasures of binging on foods high in sugar and other carbohydrates involves a release of brain serotonin. This binging might occur less if more serotonin were present as a result of treatment.*
>
> *Anorectics treated with SSRIs generally lose the distorted view of their bodies as being too fat, which is consistent with the findings that the SSRIs produce a more adaptive way of thinking, feeling, and acting.*

Booster: *Antihypertensives*

Certain medications used to treat high blood pressure can cause depression by depleting supplies of the brain neurotransmitters necessary to balance mood. The mechanism of some antihypertensives blocks the effects of norepinephrine and epinephrine on the autonomic system outside the brain and spinal cord.

Unfortunately, some of the drug gets into the brain through the bloodstream and exerts a negative effect there. An example of this is the beta blockers (such as Inderal, Corgard, metoprolol, and atenolol) that can cause depression by blocking the effects of brain norepinephrine. This side effect is unfortunate because these drugs so effectively prevent heart attack in hypertensive people.

Other blood pressure medications, such as Catapress (clonidine), actually prevent the release of norepinephrine from the brainstem, which sends projections out to the body as well as up to the brain. This too can cause depression.

Booster: *Birth-control pills*

Many women who take oral contraceptives (containing varying amounts of compounds similar to estrogen and progesterone) become depressed. Many of the newer pills have mainly progesterone-like substances in them. As we have discussed earlier in this chapter, progesterone is a highly psychoactive substance, and various studies show a wide variety of mood responses, including depression, caused by increases or variations in this hormone.

Booster & Zapper: *Caffeine*

Coffee drinkers tend to rely on their caffeine addiction to maintain normal levels of alertness and good mood. When deprived of their coffee (or chocolate or cola), many people get irritable, depressed, and have difficulty focusing on complex mental tasks (and suffer from a terrible headache).

Booster & Zapper: *Corticosteroids*

Severe depression can occur in patients taking steroids. Steroid medications such as prednisone, which are used to treat chronic inflammatory conditions (such as rheumatoid arthritis, lupus, and severe asthma, for example) initially stimulate mood, but after a few days, exert a depressing effect. This, presumably, is due to the way the drugs simulate cortisol release and its effects on the brain during chronic stress. Even inhaled steroids used to treat asthma (such as Asthmacort and Fluovent) are absorbed into the bloodstream and can have similar dampening effects on mood if used regularly.

Booster & Zapper: *Diet pills*

The stimulants found in diet pills (ephedrine, pseudoephedrine, and fenfluramine) can initially boost mood, but will eventually depress it. All stimulants enhance dopamine and norepinephrine release but eventually exhaust the brain amine system, causing a drop in mood.

Booster & Zapper: *Nicotine*

Like coffee drinkers, cigarette smokers tend to rely on their addiction to maintain normal levels of alertness, good mood, and calm. When deprived of cigarettes, smokers get irritable, depressed, and have difficulty focusing on complex mental tasks. They also tend to eat more sweet foods. This is interesting because the ingestion of sweets causes a release of serotonin to the cortex, giving an extra boost when nicotine has zapped the supply.

Zapper: *Sedatives*

Sedatives may improve mood by reducing the severe anxiety that can produce a stress-like response in the brain. In particular, the drug class of benzodiazepines (Valium, Xanax, Ativan, and Klonopin) act to dampen anxiety and when given at appropriate doses, don't impair performance or memory to any significant degree.

Unfortunately, sedatives are overprescribed by some clinicians as an easy alternative to true antidepressants. This use gets rid of some of the anxiety of depression, but does not treat the underlying cause. The most common reason for this substitution is the fact that we live in a society where fast cures are demanded and all problems should be solved in the 30 to 60 minutes of the average TV sitcom. Sedatives produce an immediate effect on mood, while the antidepressants (discussed earlier) take up to three or four weeks to exert their maximum effect.

The drug lithium is often associated with depression, but this drug does not improve mood per se. It prevents the up and down extremes of manic-depressive illness, also known as bipolar mood disorder. In this disease, which is far less common than major depression and burnout, a person follows a cycle of depressed days or weeks, normal days or weeks, and manic days or weeks.

In the depressive stage, sleep and eating patterns are disturbed, mood is black, and response time is slowed. In the manic phase, people will often react to grandiose delusions about themselves and, for instance, use the family's last dollar to purchase a Mercedes because they are sure they hold the winning lottery ticket. Many creative people tend to suffer from this disorder, and for them, lithium is a lifesaver. Its main effect is probably to block norepinephrine release in the brain. Although you may think this is bad because a balanced mood state needs a healthy supply of norepinephrine, lithium probably prevents the mood elevations that occur in the manic phase, while conserving norepinephrine so it does not become depleted during the depressive phase.

Boosters and Zappers in Foods

Despite the abundance of literature in the popular press on diets that boost mood, raise serotonin in the brain, or fight depression, good scientific data is not available to support a tight relationship between food and depression. Certainly certain vitamin deficiencies (especially folate and B12) can cause depression (see details under "Supplements") but overall, feeding the brain a well-balanced diet that allows it to maintain a healthy balance of the amine neurotransmitters is the best recommendation that can be made.

If you need a quick boost in spirit, you can try increasing your intake of carbohydrates, particularly in the form of sweets. These will raise brain serotonin levels and transiently elevate mood. But then get ready for the crash. The sudden rise in blood sugar levels stimulates the pancreas to overproduce insulin, which lowers glucose, sometimes to levels below where it was before the high sugar load arrived. When that happens, everything slows down and you may feel depressed and sleepy.

There probably are certain diets that improve mood and others that zap it. But at the time of writing this book, none have been shown to have any scientific validity. Beyond recommending a balanced diet high in complex carbohydrates and low in fat, all I can suggest is that if you have the tendency to get tired or depressed after large meals, and/or you get irritable and anxious when hungry, eat more frequently, but eat less at each sitting.

Then you will get your serotonin response with each meal, but not an overwhelming insulin reaction. Also, the time between meals will never be so long as to allow your blood sugar to fall and make you irritable and aggressive.

Boosters and Zappers in Supplements

Because depression is a physical illness, I recommend self-healing with supplements for mild symptoms. The following suggestions are offered to help you reduce the severity of symptoms or to prevent the initial stress overload that can trigger a depressive episode.

Zapper: *DHEA*

DHEA (dihydroepiandosterone) is a supplement that has created controversy in the American press regarding its ability to treat depression. It is a precursor to many of the steroid hormones such as cortisol and the sex hormones. While it is true that when cortisol rises in stress and depression, DHEA falls, this doesn't necessarily mean that raising DHEA levels with supplements will restore the balance. But recent studies are finding encouraging results in the use of DHEA in preventing depression. A suggested dose is 30 to 90mg a day about four times a week.

Zapper: *Folate*

The B vitamin, folate, is necessary to a balanced mood state. When supplies of folate are low, a harmful amino acid called homocysteine accumulates in the brain, preventing normal metabolism of the amine neurotransmitters, thus having a direct effect on mood. There is clear evidence that a deficiency of this vitamin can not only cause depression, but also prevent successful treatment by antidepressants. I recommend taking at least 400mcg of folate a day alone or as part of a multivitamin supplement.

Zapper: *Ginseng*

Ginseng seems to stabilize the levels of brain amine neurotransmitters in the face of stress. Maintaining the delicate balance of serotonin, norepinephrine, and dopamine is important to resisting the depressive effects of long-term stress.

The Chinese believe that the effect of ginseng does not occur without long-term regular use. This is consistent with the response to antidepressants, and I agree that patience is necessary to use this supplement to treat depression. There are several different preparations of ginseng, including Siberian, Korean, and others. I recommend rotating from one type to the next as you complete a bottle of supplements. I recommend 250mg of extract each day.

Zapper: *Kava kava*

Kava kava is a very potent anti-anxiety supplement—but be careful. Although kava kava is widely available in drug stores, it is not to be taken lightly. Research has shown that it works through several brain pathways. In addition to exciting the GABA mechanism like the Valium-like drugs (benzodiazepines), it also works like the tricyclic antidepressants to affect norepinephrine re-uptake.

Because its action so closely duplicates that of antidepressant medications, it should never be taken by anyone taking prescription medication or St. John's wort for depression without a doctor's approval. Kava kava is effective at blocking the stress-inducing effects of anxiety that can trigger depression, but it must be used with caution.

Zapper: *St. John's wort*

St. John's wort (hypercium) seems to act as a mild MAO (monoamine oxidase) inhibitor. MAO is an enzyme in the cortex that breaks down the amine neurotransmitters dopamine and norepinephrine. Several prescription antidepressants act in this manner but require a strict diet to avoid dangerous overload of these substances in the brain. St. John's wort on the other hand has a much milder effect on the enzyme, and thus far, no dietary restrictions have been reported necessary.

The supplement is used widely in Europe to treat depression, and studies have shown generally good results. A purified German extract called LI160 (currently under study and not widely available) has even been found to be superior to tricyclic antidepressants at treating depression. After checking with your physician or therapist, I recommend twice-a-day dosing of 200mg of the extract, which can be purchased at any pharmacy in a tablet or capsule form.

Zapper: *Valerian root*

If anxiety is part of your depression, or if chronic anxiety and worry is setting you up for a dive into depression, valerian root may be of value as a calming agent. Valerian has been used for years to treat anxiety and is found in many herbal anti-anxiety preparations.

One tablet during times of stress is recommended. I would not recommend taking it regularly with the rest of your daily vitamins. It can be sedating and you may develop an artificial chronic fatigue syndrome you didn't bargain for. Take one tablet (without alcohol) when you intend to spend a quiet, relaxing evening at home. I do not recommend using valerian root along with prescription antidepressants or other sedatives without the supervision of a physician.

Zapper: *Vitamin B12*

There is some evidence that a B12 deficiency prevents normal metabolism of amine neurotransmitters, which can trigger depression.

To keep up a healthy supply, some people take a multivitamin that includes B12, but this vitamin is poorly absorbed, particularly in the elderly or those with stomach disorders. I recommend taking one sublingual tablet once every few days. These tablets are placed under the tongue and are absorbed directly into the bloodstream.

Elderly depressed patients may benefit from B12 injections. Although there is little scientific basis for this, I have seen many seniors who swear it perks them up. I recommend sublingual B12 every three days.

Zapper: *Vitamin E*

Vitamin E has an effect on dopamine levels. Because dopamine is involved in mood and buffers the stress response, Vitamin E is able to prevent depression and burnout. Recommended dosage is 1,000 units of vitamin E orally each day.

Boosters and Zappers in Lifestyle

Happiness is not the natural course in a world of uncertainty and challenge. When we are at our limits from the battles and challenges of life, our natural state, the one that takes the least effort, is to ruminate, feel regret and guilt, and want to retreat to a warm bed at home. A brain exhausted from stress that is either repeated or severe or both, tends to somehow lose the normal ability to shift back to the restorative phase and pay attention to the happier aspects of life.

Depression can suddenly take on a life of its own, making it difficult to shift attention to some other less-stressful diversion. Because clinical depression is a very real physical ailment causing changes in brain function, it needs professional medical attention and treatment.

Therefore, lifestyle choices best affect the prevention of depression, rather than the cure. This section will discuss methods of creating happiness, acting in a positive way, and avoiding stress that will help you avoid depression completely or prevent further progression of the disease, assuming you are under the appropriate care.

Zapper: *Accepting your limitations*

Some people are born with the natural ability to get along smoothly in the world, and by either personality, physical appearance, or some combination, seem to sail through life without much stress. Other people seem to walk forever under the clouds of darkness. Knowing this is true, I make a strong recommendation that will make all the self-help gurus cringe: Adapt your life to your natural tendencies.

Trying to act a certain way if you don't have that tendency and repeatedly failing at it can cause more stress than approaching a situation knowing your own personal limitations. If you were 5 foot 2 inches and suffered from very bad vision, would you believe someone who told you that you could play in the NBA if you just wrote this down on a goal list or developed the real desire to do it? In the same way, you shouldn't let some new-age motivational speaker push you into discontinuing your Prozac one month after a suicide attempt because you feel better and have a new life plan.

Accept your limitations and get professional help! Then carefully map out a course that will keep you from trouble while you progress at your own rate towards independence. This is the only way you can "follow your bliss" and adapt your life to a style that matches and compliments your own natural tendencies.

Zapper: *Exercise*

People who exercise regularly sleep better and generally have lower heart rates, indicating more of a balance between the "fight-or-flight" sympathetic and the "rest-and-restore" parasympathetic nervous systems of the body. Exercise also improves bloodflow throughout the body and helps the brain to resist stress and balance its amine levels. All of these physical reactions to exercise equip your body and mind to resist the kind of stress that can lead to depression.

I have recommended regular moderate exercise for 20 minutes at least three times a week. But if this is an unrealistic goal given your state of health, even a daily walk without breathing heavy or raising your pulse has proven benefits.

Zapper: *Healthy relationships*

Depression is not contagious, but who you hang out with will affect the way you view life and the amount of stress you endure each day. These things are directly related to the likelihood of suffering depression.

To avoid the snare of depression, try to spend time with people who are generally upbeat. Avoid those who regularly point out the "flaws of the system" or other "victim" types. Author and radio personality Dennis Prager says in his book *Happiness Is a Serious Problem* that it is impossible to be happy if you consider yourself a victim. Unless you are truly a victim of cancer, trauma, or some other serious condition (where interaction with others of similar plight is actually very therapeutic), avoid making the common ground of a relationship a shared problem, such as your common hate for the boss, the government, and so on.

Monogamy in love relationships is also good for finding happiness and raising spirits. Studies have shown that married people live longer and have a high happiness rating, while those never married are less happy, and those divorced are the least happy. I imagine monogamy in gay relationships is just as healthy.

Zapper: *Posture*

There are clearly feedback mechanisms between each part of the body and the cortex. Did you know that because of this relationship, holding yourself in a certain way can directly affect mood? It's true! If you walk hunched over and step in a shuffling manner it will bring your mood down. On the other hand, if you walk tall and upright, you can actually make yourself feel good. For more information about this amazing body/mind relationship I recommend the book *The Alexander Technique: How to Use Your Body Without Stress* by Wilfred Barlow. You might also try the art of yoga. Yoga is another technique that improves both posture and general blood flow to the brain.

Zapper: *Psychotherapy*

I recommend psychotherapy with a qualified psychologist or psychiatrist for anyone with mood symptoms that get in the way of what you might consider "normal" functioning. There are many schools and styles of psychotherapy that your physician may recommend. Probably on a short-term basis, one that combines a cognitive approach with drug therapy will be most effective. In some cases, however, long-term solutions that combine other types of psychotherapy with maintenance medications may be needed.

Learned Helplessness

Take any animal, such as a monkey or a rat, and expose it to a stressful stimulus, such as a mild electrical shock. (I personally have never done this nor recommend it.) The animal shows a short-lived stress response when the shock occurs and when it searches for a safe area. But if that animal has a way to control or avoid the shock, nothing changes in the way it perceives the world.

Now remove all safe areas and expose the animal to occasional random shocks. Initially, the animal looks for a safe area. But if after multiple shocks, it fails to find a safe area, the stress response (as measured by levels of cortisol and other hormones) fails to turn off, and the animal stops looking for safe areas. Instead it retreats into an immobile position and takes the shock when it comes without much movement. Soon it eats less, shows signs of exhaustion, and is no longer interested in usually novel stimuli (as when a caretaker opens the cage door).

This syndrome is called "learned helplessness" and is physiologically identical to depression or burnout in humans: elevated stress hormones like cortisol and CRH; depleted brain amines norepinephrine, serotonin, and dopamine; depressed immune function and lack of interest in new or interesting stimuli.

The common denominator that seems to be identified in both situations is not just stress, but the lack of control of the stressful stimuli. People who feel they can control their stress or stressful situations physically respond to stress differently than those who feel they have no control. Those who "follow their bliss" vs. those who "do it for the money" are perfect examples. In the former situation, a person chooses to deal with "positive stress" and avoids burnout, while in the latter, a person pulls out of bed in the morning expecting another day of toil and negative, uncontrollable stress. Which person is most likely to suffer the brain changes that will lead to depression?

Should you find yourself experiencing early-morning awakening, tearfulness, extreme mental exhaustion, unending anxiety of unknown cause, sadness, hopelessness, extreme need for isolation from others, obsessive rumination over certain events or worries, or irrational behavior and thoughts, consult a psychiatrist or psychologist immediately, particularly if these symptoms are combined with serious thoughts of suicide.

Booster & Zapper: *Pursuit of wealth*

Multiple studies on depression and on happiness have come to similar conclusions with respect to wealth: Once an individual is above the poverty level and has enough food to eat and a regular roof overhead, there is absolutely no correlation between socioeconomic status and happiness, regardless of the country studied. This knowledge should help us put to rest the notion that drives many to depression: If only I had more money, I would be happy. The fact is that more money isn't the answer to the quest for peace and happiness.

Success, if measured in personal health and happiness, is not found in wealth, despite all our programming to the contrary. When the quest for money becomes a stressful battle and not a blissful pursuit of a passion, you will experience all the physically damaging effects we have discussed caused by the repeated fight-or-flight stress syndrome. Psychologists who study career burnout cite the same symptoms as those found in depression. Burnout and depression are two terms for the same brainstorm.

We would be wise to take the advice of philosopher Joseph Campbell offered in his 1980's PBS series *The Power of Myth* with Bill Moyers, in which he illustrates the value of the theme, "Follow your bliss."

Zapper: *Religion, spirituality, and meditation*

In an increasingly secular society where spirituality frequently amounts to calling a 900 number for "wisdom" on love and money, those who are true devotees to some type of religious faith have been found to have happier lives and to live longer than those without religious faith. If you have some type of religious background, cultivate it further, learn more about it, and pray regularly as a form of meditative practice and contemplation.

The Care and Feeding of Your Brain

If you are atheist, objectivist, or existentialist in your philosophy, regular meditation has similar effects on calling forth the deeper, more rhythmic aspects of your psyche that promote internal peace and happiness. See Chapter 6 for more details about how meditation reduces stress.

Zapper: *Sleep*

To reduce stress in your life and prevent depression, I strongly recommend getting six to eight hours a day of sleep. There is clear evidence that the process of rebalancing the amine neurotransmitters occurs during REM sleep and that people deprived of ample sleep show stress symptoms including mood disorders. For all the details on sleep and its effect on the brain see Chapter 5.

There is an exception to the rule that says that sleep is necessary for balancing mood states. It has been found that once people fall into the full-blown depression syndrome, a supervised program of mild sleep deprivation effectively helps get them out of it. Very new studies still under investigation have found a paradoxical effect: Cycling sleep patterns so that a person gets one hour less sleep each day in a complex cycle of earlier bedtimes until fully deprived of at least one day's worth of sleep over several days somehow helps cure depression. Of course this approach is still under investigation and is not recommended for at-home self-treatment, but it does offer a peak at what's around the bend in the treatment of depression.

Zapper: *Smiling*

Somehow, the simple act of smiling fools the brain into thinking it is happy. You cannot entertain angry, stressful thoughts while smiling. It's an easy lifestyle choice that you can use anytime, anywhere. Smile more often and see if it boosts your mood.

Chapter 9

For Women Only: PMS and Other Mind-zapping States

I am chief of obstetric anesthesia on a labor ward that serves about 4,000 deliveries a year. I also perform acupuncture on and counsel many women with pain problems. Often these problems occur at the time of menopause, are made worse following pregnancy, abortion or miscarriage, or fluctuate with menstrual cycles. These experiences have shown me that clearly women are the stronger sex.

I'm not being patronizing when I say this. Without a doubt, the female mind is most adaptable to stressful circumstances. This is verified in both the psychological and the physiological literature. Although women have a higher rate of depression, more depressed men actually carry out suicide. It seems that while men become aggressive or self-destructive when pushed to their limits, fewer females resort to violence in the same circumstance. In addition, psychobiologists such as Matt Ridley (*The Red Queen*, Penguin 1993) eloquently point out the level of control the female has over the social construct of most animal species, including human.

The fact that the female is the stronger sex is also true from a purely biological standpoint. Women live longer than men and, at the other end of life, premature female infants outsurvive their male counterparts. Even sperm bearing the X chromosome imparting "femaleness" to the egg are heartier and survive chemical assaults better.

So why are women so frequently put down as being "too emotional" to hold important positions? Or "too moody" to be trusted? Or "too scatterbrained" to make intelligent decisions? These negative impressions may be reinforced by the emotional and physical changes women experience during their menstrual cycle, after abortion, miscarriage, or birth, and in menopause. This is not a guess—all women are affected by fluctuations in brain amines and sex hormones. But women who understand these changes and confront and control them are those who can reinforce their position as the "better half."

What Is PMS?

As recently as 1987 there was great reluctance in the medical and psychological community to accept PMS as a clear-cut disorder of mind and body. As a result, the same stigma associated with depression that I described in Chapter 8 became attached to PMS. In fact it was probably worse because the syndrome gained popularity before being officially recognized. General ignorance gave people an unkind way to casually dismiss a woman's range of normal emotions. Even the newly found female assertiveness in the workplace became referred to as "PMS-ing."

A quote from a review of PMS in 1987 in a respectable journal highlights this problem: "A high proportion of women who complain of premenstrual syndrome show evidence of a more general psychiatric problem..." and "No single treatment works better than placebo." These conclusions were reached despite considerable evidence to the contrary, known since 1981.

PMS occurs in 30 to 80 percent of women of reproductive age. It is seen in 88 percent of young women within three to four years after the onset of menses (roughly between ages 16 and 18), just at the time when additional behavioral patterns , common to adolescents and young adults, such as school problems, impulsivity, rebelliousness, and drug use, can become exaggerated. In some women, PMS can ease a bit in their early 20s, and emerge in their mid- to late-20s and early 30s.

The official *Diagnostic and Statistical Manual of Mental Disorders, fourth edition* (or *DSM-IV*), which is the book used by the psychiatric and psychologic community to classify and recognize disorders as "real" based on certain criteria, refers to PMS officially as premenstrual dysphoric disorder.

For accurate diagnosis, this text says that during a one-year period, and during most menstrual cycles except in the week following menstruation, at least five of the following symptoms occur:

1. Depressive symptoms.
2. Anxiety and tension.
3. Emotional fragility.
4. Anger and irritability, including increased conflicts with others.
5. Decreased enjoyment of usual life activities.
6. Distractibility.
7. Fatigue.
8. Craving and (or) binging.
9. Insomnia or hypersomnia.
10. Feeling out of control.
11. Physical symptoms (bloating, weight gain, tender breasts, pain in the head and (or) joints).

These symptoms must meet the following additional conditions: a) interference with life/work/social functioning, b) not merely an exacorbation (worsening) of an underlying psychiatric disorder that is just made worse by the PMS changes, and c) all criteria must be met in two consecutive cycles.

> *Most PMS symptoms can also afflict women at or around menopause and during (but more likely immediately following) pregnancy (including abortion or miscarriage). Symptoms can also be seen when oral contraceptives are discontinued.*

Most scientific papers I have researched don't have such strict requirements for a "real" diagnosis. Many recognize PMS after observing symptoms for two full cycles, but because of its high variability, symptoms might be altogether absent during one particular cycle.

Others have neatly classified symptoms into four major subgroups of sufferers:

1. Tension plus water retention, breast pain, weight gain, and fatigue.
2. Tension plus binging, craving, eating sweets, and physical symptoms of tremor, heart palpitations, fatigue, lightheadedness, and headaches.
3. Tension and full-blown depression (with cases of suicide reported).
4. Tension with overt irritability and anger.

In addition, although less common, positive symptoms can accompany the onset of PMS: increased sex drive, increased cleanliness, accomplishment and focus, creativity, and increased energy. These make the picture all that more confusing for a woman especially if negative and positive symptoms occur together.

All these features can vary widely from month to month. Although treatment is available, many suffer in quiet, guilty embarrassment, risking job loss, divorce, and other life disruptions.

If you suspect PMS, follow your troublesome symptoms on a spreadsheet-like chart daily for two full cycles. Make each row a different symptom you commonly suffer, and each column a different day. This can be done easily on a computer using Microsoft Excel or some other commercially available spreadsheet program. This will be useful information to help you and your doctor diagnose PMS.

PMS and the Big Picture

Estrogen and especially progesterone are key players in the female emotional brainstorm. To understand how these hormones cause the symptoms of PMS, let's look at how they fit into the big picture of the monthly menstrual cycle. In response to the body's circadian (daily) and ultradian (90-minute) rhythms, the hypothalamus at the base of the brain influences the pituitary gland below it (hanging like a pea from a stalk) to release two hormones in a roughly 28-day rhythm: LH (luteinizing hormone) and FSH (follicle-stimulating hormone).

In a complex set of interactions with an egg in one of the ovaries chosen to ovulate during that cycle, the secondary hormones estrogen and progesterone are released and exert their effects on the body, the pituitary, and the rest of the brain.

Estrogen rises early in the cycle, making the uterus ready for a new set of monthly changes. Progesterone rises about mid-cycle, causing the uterus to form an inside coat of thick tissue full of blood vessels that makes a cozy home for a fertilized egg. At the end of the cycle, if no fertilization occurs, both hormones drop off rapidly, causing the new uterine lining to break down and be shed as the blood of menses.

It is between this fall of the hormones and the onset of bleeding that PMS symptoms begin, ranging from mild fatigue and irritability to full-blown depression. (Even rats show increased anxious behavior when they are given progesterone and it is suddenly discontinued.)

During pregnancy, progesterone remains elevated. But after birth, it falls off suddenly, often causing symptoms similar to PMS in some women—the so-called "postpartum blues."

When menopause begins (around the age of 51), both estrogen and protesterone fall and remain depressed. In addition to the traditional "hot flashes" caused by vasodilation in the skin, all the emotional symptoms that occur in PMS can result.

PMS Boosters and Zappers

For the sake of clarity and simplicity, I have divided this section into individual components and causes of PMS. In reality, all of these mechanisms interact in a complex and chaotic manner, each influencing one another. As you read about each booster and zapper, remember that the symptoms of PMS (as well as menopause and similar ones that follow pregnancy and childbirth) are truly brain weather patterns resulting from major hormonal and neurotransmitter disruption. Think of them as the "El Ninos" of the brain.

Boosters and Zappers in Your Own Body

The real action that causes the discomforts of PMS begins in the body on a monthly cycle. Knowing the biological reasons for these symptoms will help you better understand PMS and why the things you eat, drink, and do can change the way you experience this window of time each month.

Booster: *Aldosterone*

The drop in progesterone preceding menses results in an increase in pituitary vasopression release. Vasopression directly raises blood pressure and may be responsible for some elevations in blood pressure experienced during the premenstrual period. It's this vasopression that influences the adrenal glands that sit atop the kidneys to produce the hormone aldosterone. As a result, during the premenstrual period, aldosterone rises.

Aldosterone causes the kidney to retain sodium. The presence of sodium causes retention of water and the edema and bloating common in PMS. Also, aldosterone acts like a male sex steroid. Male sex steroids, when present in women, cause symptoms of depression. The aldosterone-antagonist diuretic (which blocks aldosterone and promotes urination) called Aldactone is often used to treat symptoms of PMS.

Booster: *Blood cells and platelets*

Red blood cells: Through the effect of the so-called "bad" prostaglandins (see the explanation on page 202), red blood cells become stiffer and more swollen and, hence, tend to lodge more easily in clots. This probably happens to aid blood coagulation and to prevent excessive bleeding during menses. Unfortunately, it also results in thicker blood that travels more slowly through the capillaries of the brain, causing negative blood flow changes in the areas that need it. This reduced blood flow to the brain is known to cause symptoms of PMS, including tension and difficulty with mental focus.

Platelets: Platelets are the small fragment-like blood cells that are required for a blood clot to form. In addition to actually becoming part of the clot itself, they manufacture many substances, most notably, thromboxane.

Thromboxane causes blood vessels to constrict, allowing areas of bleeding to narrow, hence, limiting blood loss. This is a necessary function in the uterus during menses, but at the same time, it constricts blood flow in the brain. This reduction in blood supply is generalized throughout the brain, causing decreased flow everywhere, particularly the smaller capillaries known as the microvasculature. This contributes the PMS symptoms such as tension and difficulty with mental focus.

White blood cells: The changes that occur premenstrually call the immune system into action (analogous to the state of readiness of the brain during the early stages of stress). This is probably advantageous in preventing an invasion of bacteria during the bleeding of menses.

One of the effects of this activated immune state is to release substances that call out other immune white blood cells. These active substances are called cytokines. Cytokines have direct effects on the brain, including fatigue. They are probably also responsible for the symptoms of muscle and joint aches common in the flu, and of course, as part of the PMS syndrome.

> *Because the PMS syndrome represents an imbalanced state, the Immune system can also be thrown into imbalance, as during times of stress. That's why infections such as the flu, bronchitis, and vaginal yeast infections are common in the premenstrual period.*

Booster: *Estrogen imbalance*

The symptoms of PMS related to estrogen levels are caused by a state of imbalance. It seems that the fall in estrogen before menses (and after menopause) produces the PMS symptoms. But inappropriate elevations of this hormone before menses also cause similar problems.

Estrogen, made by the ovaries in response to cyclical stimulation by pituitary hormones, has very specific biological effects on the brain. An imbalance in estrogen levels affects blood flow—the most notable example being the "hot flash" symptoms caused by skin vasodilation during menopause.

The right frontal cortex, too, is affected. (As described in Chapter 2, this is the area of the brain primarily responsible for helping us pay attention.) When estrogen levels fall just before menses, the cortex suffers a loss in electrical activity, which impairs the ability to focus and deal effectively with complex life stresses.

Amine neurotransmitters that regulate attention as well as mood are also affected by falling estrogen levels. Like progesterone, estrogen influences the synthesis of "feel good" serotonin. It also regulates the receptors for dopamine (another amine neurotransmitter) and for GABA, a neurotransmitter involved in relaxation of both mood and muscles.

Because estrogen feeds back to the pituitary and, ultimately, to the hypothalamus at the base of the brain, it affects the daily rhythms of the body. During PMS and menopause, this is probably responsible for disruptions in sleep/wake patterns.

It is paradoxical that high estrogen levels in PMS are associated with anger and irritability—the same symptoms associated with low levels of estrogen during menopause. This is one of the interesting properties of the brain: It seems that similar problems can result when specific substances are either in excess or in deficiency; as if the imbalance and not the presence or absence of a transmitter or hormone causes the problem.

Booster: *Neurotransmitters*

The stress of the PMS state has a zapping effect on serotonin, norepinephrine, and dopamine. When depleted, these amine neurotransmitters can cause various negative mood symptoms.

Nicknamed the "godfather" of the amine mood neurotransmitters, serotonin has a major role in PMS. The reduced production of serotonin, regulated by progesterone, estrogen, and other factors in the premenstrual period (including the stress generated by the symptoms themselves), has a direct and negative effect on mood and personal disposition. Its decrease is probably also responsible for the increased craving for sweets and the tendency to binge.

Estrogen has a direct effect on the distribution of dopamine receptors in the cortex and limbic system. This is probably also why an imbalance of estrogen causes mood problems.

Progesterone causes an increase in the enzyme monoamine oxidase, which breaks down the amine neurotransmitters norepinephrine, dopamine, and serotonin in the brain. Although progesterone is low in the phase where PMS occurs, it may be that the breakdown of these neurotransmitters during the peak of progesterone causes a deficiency later in the cycle, matching the point at which progesterone falls. This deficiency is going to depress your mood.

Booster: *Progesterone depletion*

Progesterone, made by the developing follicle of the ovary and by the embryonic tissues in the pregnant state, falls rapidly before menses and after childbirth, miscarriage, pregnancy termination, and menopause. Because progesterone is a psychoactive drug, it is thought that many of the symptoms of PMS represent a "withdrawal state."

So why do the levels of progesterone have to drop? One of the functions of this hormone is to produce a blood vessel-rich uterus lining to allow embryo implantation and pregnancy. When the levels of progesterone fall, that's a signal that causes this lining to break down and induce menses. The PMS symptoms are a side effect of this important process.

Several possible mechanisms are responsible for the effect progesterone has on mood. Its changing levels appear to affect the production of serotonin—low levels of this neurotransmitter are known to produce depression, aggression, and anxiety. (See Chapter 8 for the details on serotonin and depression.) In addition, the signal to breakdown the uterine lining involves blood vessel constriction. This process can affect brain blood flow, as well, causing many of the PMS symptoms, such as anxiety, tension, emotional fragility, anger, irritability, distractibility, and fatigue.

> *Progesterone affects nerve cells as both a powerful local and general anesthetic enhancer. For instance, women who are pregnant—when progesterone levels are at their highest—require about half of the amount of anesthetic to produce a state of unconsciousness. Even isolated lab preparations of nerve tissue are much less responsive to stimuli when treated with progesterone.*

Booster: *Prolactin*

The pituitary gland produces the hormone prolactin in response to a drop in progesterone. This is presumably to stimulate milk production after childbirth. However, it has several unpleasant effects as well. The most prominent of these is the breast pain and swelling common during PMS. When experimentally given to women, prolactin has also been found to increase the emotional symptoms typical of PMS.

Booster: *Prostaglandins*

Progesterone and estrogen are involved in stimulating the production of prostaglandins. These are a group of potent bioactive substances made from fatty acids (the long carbon chains in fats). They are very active in balancing blood circulation. Some prostaglandins slow circulation, and cause vasoconstriction and clotting (these are called the "bad" prostaglandins), while others do the opposite, opening up blood vessels, slowing clotting, and softening blood cells (the "good" prostaglandins).

Before menses, the fall in progesterone stops production of the prostaglandins that keep the blood vessels of the uterus lining open. The uterus lining sheds, causing the bleeding of menses, but the decrease in prostaglandins allows for blood vessel constriction and effective clotting—a built-in mechanism for preventing a woman from bleeding to death when shedding the uterine lining.

Unfortunately, it is thought that these prostaglandins also affect the brain. Because the general consistency of the blood thickens, vessels constrict, and platelets that cause clotting become more active, it is thought that the blood flow through the tiny capillaries of the brain is impaired. Again, an imbalance occurs that restricts free blood flow and causes PMS symptoms, such as anxiety, tension, emotional fragility, anger, irritability, distractibility, and fatigue.

Prostaglandins also cause immune activation, which results in increased pain sensitivity and fatigue. They are also responsible for the painful uterine contractions that can accompany the menstrual flow.

Boosters and Zappers in Drugs

The symptoms of PMS are very sensitive to various drugs. Some will aggravate the discomforts and tension, others will ease them. If you suffer PMS, be sure to ask your doctor about the effects of any medication on these monthly symptoms.

Booster & Zapper: *Amphetamines*

Amphetamine-like stimulants such as Ritalin and Adderal may help with attention-deficit-disorder-like symptoms that can occur as part of PMS, post-childbirth, and menstruation.

Stimulants, however, may also worsen the symptoms by producing added anxiety and sleep problems, and they should be prescribed only in carefully selected patients who have a minimum of anxious symptoms and in whom attention deficit problems are particularly severe.

Booster: *Anabolic steroids*

Testosterone-like drugs, when taken by women (as in their illegal use by Olympic swimmers and gymnasts), cause depression, facial hair growth, and other symptoms of masculinization, and will worsen PMS symptoms. Body builders beware.

Zapper: *Antidepressants*

All of the antidepressants are effective at treating the range of negative emotional symptoms of PMS, postpartum depression, and menopause. The SSRI classes (Paxil, Prozac, and Zoloft) that balance the level of brain serotonin improve mood and have been particularly effective in helping with the binge/food craving problems that occur during PMS.

MAO inhibitors (that inhibit the enzyme monoamine oxidase) raise levels of neurotransmitters and improve mood in both PMS and menopause. Tricyclic antidepressants raise norepinephrine levels and are also effective in improving mood.

Zapper: *Benzodiazepines*

Benzodiazepines such as Valium and Xanax, but particularly the more recently popular drugs Ativan and Klonopin, are very effective at alleviating the anxiety and panic symptoms that accompany PMS. They are also good for alleviating related sleep problems. They work by enhancing the action of the GABA neurotransmitters that inhibit neuron action in the cortex, limbic system, and cerebellum, causing a sense of general relaxation.

Booster & Zapper: *Danazol*

Danazol is prescribed to treat the breast tenderness that occurs premenstrually, especially in women with fibrocystic disease of the breasts. It is also used to treat the gynecologic disease of endometriosis.

Danazol causes the pituitary to release less luteinizing hormone (LH) and follicle-stimulating hormone (FSH). Because these hormones control the menstrual cycle, a reduction in their supply can lessen the intensity of the menstrual hormonal changes. However, danazol can both boost and zap PMS symptoms. Because of its affect on LH and FSH, it can lessen some of the emotional changes experienced during PMS, but it also acts as a weak testosterone-like substance, so it may worsen them.

Zapper: *Estrogen replacement therapy*

Estrogen replacement therapy is especially effective in treating one specific type of PMS: the type characterized by tension without depression. Although estrogen replacement therapy has been shown to raise the risk of uterine cancer and possibly breast cancer, there are proven benefits that are thought to outweigh this risk. The PMS-specific symptoms of depression and confused thinking are effectively treated with estrogen replacement therapy and there are positive side effects that many women find desirable.

Recent evidence shows that estrogen replacement therapy not only improves general performance of difficult thinking tasks, but it also staves off the ravages of Alzheimer's disease. Estrogen replacement therapy lowers the risk of heart disease and probably stroke (a real brain zapper), including multi-infarct dementia, a type of brain degeneration caused by tiny strokes that show few symptoms if any and can only be seen on scans.

Libido improves with mood, and the increased sexual activity further helps with general lifestyle satisfaction. Estrogen replacement therapy has had much more success in treating the emotional changes in menopause and PMS than progesterone replacement therapy (discussed on page 206).

Booster: *Lupron*

Lupron, given as an injection, acts similarly to danazol by shutting down the secretion of estrogen and progesterone. Although it is FDA-approved to treat prostate cancer, it is sometimes used to treat more troublesome symptoms of menses such as endometriosis. I mention it here because reduction of the female sex hormones can produce psychological symptoms similar to those experienced in menopause and in PMS. Like danazol, it also has some testosterone-like effects. This adds to its tendency to produce symptoms such as depression.

Zapper: *Nonsteroidal anti-inflammatory drugs (NSAIDS)*

The nonsteroidal anti-inflammatory drugs (NSAIDS) help relieve the discomfort of PMS by blocking prostaglandin production. This eases uterine cramping and many of the muscle aches, joint aches, and other pain symptoms associated with PMS. NSAIDS also have the added effect of improving many of the psychological symptoms, probably through relief of the immune-related fatigue and the relief of pain. The most popular NSAIDS include Motrin, Anaprox, and Naprosyn.

Booster & Zapper: *Oral contraceptives*

In some patients, oral contraceptives improve PMS symptoms. Those pills take control of the menstrual cycle and moderate some of the extreme changes that may cause PMS distress.

In many women, however, oral contraceptives worsen PMS symptoms. This is not surprising because the main component of most oral contraceptives acts much like progesterone, reducing brain amine levels and causing anxiety and depression.

Zapper: *Parlodel*

Parlodel (bromocryptine) acts like dopamine on the hypothalamus and pituitary and prevents secretion of the breast-stimulating hormone prolactin. This relieves symptoms of breast tenderness associated with PMS. (Prolactin also causes PMS symptoms when given to women experimentally.) Parlodel simulates the effects of dopamine on the hypothalamus, so in addition to stopping the release of prolactin from the pituitary, it has other dopamine-like side effects on the brain that help boost mood.

Booster & Zapper: *Progesterone replacement therapy*

Because a drop in progesterone is responsible for so many PMS symptoms, it would appear to make perfect sense that replacing progesterone by administering it as a drug would alleviate much of the distress caused by this syndrome. But in truth, given the complex nature of this syndrome, only some patients improve with progesterone therapy, which is given as a vaginal suppository or, less commonly, as an injection. Oral contraceptives (specifically those that contain a substance resembling progesterone) have been even less effective at alleviating PMS symptoms.

This unexpected lack of effectiveness of progesterone and progesterone-like substance replacement may be due to the fact that progesterone stimulates monoamine oxidase. This enzyme breaks down amine neurotransmitters in the brain, causing a drop in mood. So even though the premenstrual drop in progesterone is probably the main event in the concert of premenstrual changes, replacing it may even worsen the depressive symptoms experienced by so many women.

Zapper: *Spironolactone*

Spironolactone (Aldactone) combats PMS on two fronts: It is a diuretic that alleviates the sodium and water retention typical of the premenstrual syndrome. It also blocks the testosterone-like effects of the adrenal hormone aldosterone, which is elevated in the premenstrual period and can produce symptoms of depression.

Women with addictive tendencies will more likely return to their habits during the premenstrual period. Problems with drugs, alcohol, cigarettes, and binging will be most apparent at this time. Be aware of this extreme vulnerability by avoiding situations and people that will get you into trouble or tempt you.

Boosters and Zappers in Foods

Premenstrual syndrome is one of the few areas of diet well studied in the scientific literature. This is because sweet cravings and binging are so common to the disorder and make for such fascinating study. Your diet during this time can have a profound effect on the severity of PMS symptoms.

Booster: *Caffeine*

PMS makes many women feel tired and worn out, so they up their coffee intake to get a boost. This is a mistake that can make the symptoms of PMS even worse. Caffeine can actually worsen all PMS symptoms and it increases any breast-tenderness that may be present.

If you are a regular coffee drinker you should drink less (or at least don't drink more) during this time of your menstrual cycle. But don't stop cold turkey. Suddenly stopping regular caffeine consumption causes headaches, fatigue, irritability, and depression, and will worsen many of your PMS symptoms. Taper off gradually.

Zapper: *Carbohydrates*

The recommended diet for PMS is one high in complex carbohydrates (starches, fruit, and wheat). The complex carbohydrates allow for a gradual release of sugar into the bloodstream with digestion (where starches are broken down into simple sugars). A moderate rise in brain serotonin occurs, but not the rapid rise and fall experienced with sweets, soft drinks, and other sources of refined simple sugars.

Booster: *Chocolate*

Many women who crave sweets in the premenstrual period can't resist chocolate. But it's the very thing they crave that worsens the symptoms they're trying to ease. Besides being loaded with simple sugar, the caffeine-like xanthine substances in chocolate cause stimulation and increase tension. These compounds also worsen any breast tenderness you may have and can cause headaches.

Booster: *Dairy products*

Because of their high calcium content, dairy products are not recommended during the premenstrual phase of the menstrual cycle. Calcium causes increased excitability of brain neurons, which, along with the low magnesium that occurs at this time, increases tension and anxiety. At other times in the menstrual cycle, during pregnancy, and after menopause, calcium is absolutely essential to help prevent osteoporosis.

The Care and Feeding of Your Brain

Booster: *Licorice*

Licorice candy contains simple, refined sugar, which is the kind of carbohydrate that increases body tension and the discomforts of PMS. Licorice is also not recommended during the premenstrual period of the menstrual cycle because it contains hormone-like substances that are similar to aldosterone. This is the sodium-retaining hormone that causes water-weight gain and bloating during PMS. Licorice can also increase blood pressure in women with hypertension.

Booster: *NutraSweet*

The artificial sweetener aspartame (NutraSweet) is a brain stimulant and has been reported to cause headaches. Eating and drinking foods containing this sweetener may worsen the headaches and anxiety symptoms of PMS.

Zapper: *Olive oil*

Olive oil, especially the extra-virgin type, has antioxidant properties that promote blood flow. The specific fats in olive oil act to dampen platelets, as well. The combined effect may be to prevent the normal sludging of blood through the brain's microvasculature (capillaries) that occurs during the premenstrual phase, allowing free blood flow, clearer thinking, and less bloating and pain.

Booster: *Refined sugars*

Some women crave refined sugars during PMS. This is because sweets boost your mood and ease tension by causing release of deficient brain serotonin. However, refined sugars quickly let you down because they push the pancreas to rapidly produce insulin, lowering blood sugar levels often beyond where you started and thus lowering brain serotonin and your mood even more.

Booster: *Salt*

The hormone aldosterone from the adrenal glands causes excessive water retention during PMS by holding back sodium. This prompts the kidneys to retain water. Salt aggravates this situation. Avoiding salt (sodium) prevents the fluid retention, water-weight gain, and bloating so common to PMS sufferers.

Zapper: *Water*

It may sound like a contradiction, but the best way to eliminate the excess fluids that cause premenstrual discomfort is to drink six to eight glasses of water daily. This washes the fluids through the system with greater speed and eases the pain and bloating of water retention.

Boosters and Zappers in Supplements and Herbs

There is a lot of good scientific data on various vitamin and mineral supplements and herbal treatments that are purported to alleviate many of the symptoms of hormonal imbalances in women. A few of the important ones follow. The recommended does are suggested for daily use, not just during the period of PMS.

Supplements:

Zapper: *Folic acid or folate*

Folate prevents accumulation of an abnormal and harmful amino acid called homocysteine. This can cause depression, heart disease, and birth defects. I recommend taking 400mcg per day, as was recommended in Chapter 8 for depression.

Zapper: *Magnesium*

Magnesium was not recommended for memory improvement in Chapter 4 because I said it was merely a good laxative and even harmful to patients suffering kidney problems. In the premenstrual period, however, when it is truly depleted, magnesium can be a valuable supplement. A depletion of this mineral may contribute to the increased excitability of nerve cells causing tension and stress. Magnesium has the opposite effect from calcium on nerve cells, and causes a calming of activity.

Magnesium is even used to prevent seizures in toxemia of pregnancy when brain nerve cells are extra-excitable. In addition, magnesium has the effect of decreasing the sludging tendency of blood through the brain microvasculature (capillaries) that occurs during the premenstrual period. It is also required for the conversion of fatty acid carbon chains from fats into "good" prostaglandins that promote blood flow. I suspect that all of these mechanisms are related. If you do not have kidney problems, I recommend taking ½ to 1 gram of magnesium per day during the premenstrual period.

Zapper: *Selenium*

There is some evidence that selenium is depleted during the menopausal period. Selenium is a metal that has antioxidant properties shown to enhance those of vitamin E. Because of this I recommend taking 200mcg per day with vitamin E (see page 211).

Zapper: *Vitamin A as beta carotene*

Because of the potential side effects of taking too much vitamin A, I recommend the safer precursor beta carotene for easing the discomfort of breast pain. (Beta carotene is converted into vitamin A by the body as needed.) Smokers beware, however: Although this vitamin is thought of as an antioxidant and an anticancer agent, there is evidence that, when combined with smoking, it may actually increase the incidence of lung cancer. If you don't smoke and have premenstrual breast tenderness, 15mg per day may help.

Zapper: *Vitamin B6 (pyridoxine)*

Vitamin B6 is actually recommended as part of the medical treatment of PMS in several medical references. It seems to alleviate some of the tension (not the depression) associated with PMS. Several mechanisms by which B6 does this have been proposed, including its involvement in the conversion of fatty acid carbon chains from fat into the so-called "good prostaglandins" discussed earlier. The recommended dosage is 200 to 800mg per day.

Zapper: *Vitamin C (ascorbic acid)*

Levels of vitamin C are often depleted during the premenstrual period. It is important to keep the levels up for several reasons. Vitamin C has an antioxidant effect that keeps the blood flowing, avoiding the thick, "stagnant" blood condition that marks PMS. Vitamin C is also an essential part of the conversion of fats into the "good" prostaglandins, also promoting better blood flow. Vitamin C has also been cited as an effective remedy for some of the tension symptoms of PMS. In Chapter 8, I cited it as at least a partially effective adjunct in the prevention and treatment of depression. I recommend 1000mg per day. (If you have a tendency towards kidney stones, drink plenty of water and reduce the dose to 500mg per day.)

Booster: *Vitamin D*

The use of vitamin D to help ease the discomforts of PMS is controversial. Although levels of this vitamin are depressed in the premenstrual period, vitamin D's ability to raise calcium may make PMS symptoms worse. On the other hand, the use of vitamin D during the menopausal period is recommended. 800IU of vitamin D3 are recommended with 1.2g of calcium per day to prevent bone loss from osteoporosis that occurs when estrogen is permanently depressed.

Zapper: *Vitamin E*

In the medical literature, vitamin E is specifically recommended as part of the first line of treatment for the premenstrual syndrome. In addition to its antioxidant properties, vitamin E has a suppressive effect on the blood platelet thromboxane (discussed earlier in this chapter). This should theoretically improve blood flow through the brain. It has also been shown to be very effective in the treatment of breast pain related to PMS, especially in patients with fibrocystic breast disease. I recommend taking 800 to 1,000IU per day.

Zapper: *Zinc*

Zinc as zinc sulfate is recommended for PMS sufferers, whose levels are depressed in the premenstrual phase. It has been recommended in the scientific literature, based on the fact that it is required in the reaction that turns fatty acid carbon chains from fats into "good prostaglandins" that improve blood flow through the brain. I recommend taking 15mg per day.

Herbs:

Zapper: *Hops*

Hop grains, although bitter, make a tea that is reported to have sedative properties, especially in states of anxiety and restlessness.

Although I am unable to find a mechanism proposed in the literature, it has been used for many years for this purpose. Herbal preparations of hops are available in most health food stores.

Zapper: *Lavender tea*

A preparation of boiling water over 1.5g of lavender extract produces a tea that is reported in folk medicine to calm nervous excitement and relieve smooth muscle (uterine) cramping and spasm.

Zapper: *Peppermint tea*

Peppermint tea is a pleasant-tasting drink that may have some ability to relieve the cramping that is associated with menses and the premenstrual period. Menthol, its active ingredient, has relaxant properties on smooth muscle, the type of muscle in the walls of the uterus and the blood vessels.

Zapper: *St. John's wort*

St. John's wort should help relieve some PMS symptoms, especially if they include mild depression. (See Chapter 8 for a complete discussion of St. John's wort.) This herb acts effectively as a mild MAO inhibitor antidepressant, but without the diet restrictions normally required for full-strength MAO inhibitors.

I recommend taking 500mg total St. John's wort per day if you are not on antidepressants of any kind. Of course, depression that leads to suicidal thoughts or intent to harm yourself or others should be addressed by a competent obstetrician/gynecologist, psychiatrist, or psychologist.

Zapper: *Yeast preparations*

A commercial yeast preparation made from the yeast *saccharomyces cerevisiae* called Sillix Donna, marketed in Italy, has been shown to improve much of the anxiety and emotional lability of the premenstrual syndrome. Yeast is known to contain the B vitamins including B6 and folate, as well as the metal selenium (all PMS zappers). I have been unable to find a distributor of Sillix Donna in the United States at the time of writing. But brewer's yeast is available as a standard tablet in most drug stores in the United States. Two to four tablets a day will probably have the same effect.

Boosters and Zappers in Lifestyle

If you suffer PMS, your lifestyle choice during this time might be to get in bed and pull up the covers. But with life as busy as it is, you may need to find other ways to deal with this monthly "curse." Knowing what to do and what not to do can go a long way to salvaging your sanity and your health.

Booster: *Dieting*

The premenstrual period is not the time to start a weight-loss diet. This is the time when food craving is most severe. Unfortunately, because of the emotional changes brought on by PMS, this is also the time when you are most apt to be dissatisfied with your body and decide to begin a new diet with little chance of success.

Zapper: *Exercise*

Exercise is promoted as the single most effective lifestyle choice for both premenstrual and menopausal mood changes. Moderate exercise (a minimum of 20 minutes of aerobic activity three times a week) not only promotes general cardiovascular health and improved physical appearance, but it raises your own natural painkillers, the endorphins (see Chapter 8 for a discussion). It also helps to buffer brain amines such as norepinephrine and serotonin so that they are neither released too frequently, causing anxiety, nor depleted, causing depression.

Zapper: *Meditation, prayer, and other spiritual practices*

The stress-zapping ability of meditation, prayer, and other spiritual practices has been described at length in Chapter 6. These same principles apply to zapping the stress that aggravates the symptoms of PMS. These exercises make the brain more resistant to the variations and chaos that occur with stressful life events, including abortion, miscarriage, childbirth, or menopause.

Zapper: *Sex and physical contact*

Many women report increased sexual desire during the premenstrual period. Listen to your instinct. The physical contact associated with sexual activity in a satisfying, supportive relationship is a good buffer against the emotional ravages of the hormonal changes that occur in PMS.

In menopause, the decrease in body estrogen causes the lining of the vagina to lose some of its stretch and lubrication ability. It is the discomfort (and sometimes pain) caused by this change that can make sex unappealing. But the desire itself generally doesn't disappear. In fact, libido returns to normal with hormone replacement therapy. If you have the desire, maintaining the ability to have normal, pleasurable intercourse will do wonders for your psyche. See your gynecologist about using an estrogen cream to restore normal lubrication.

Zapper: *Sleep*

Most women report increased fatigue and need for sleep during the premenstrual period. Go with your body on this and make the time for extra sleep. It will help your brain restore the supply of attention-focusing amines such as norepinephrine and serotonin, and it acts as a good buffer for some of the increased worries and anxieties that plague PMS sufferers. If you can allow for it, I strongly suggest a so-called "power nap" of at least 15 to 20 minutes (90 minutes is ideal, as discussed in Chapter 5).

Booster & Zapper: *Working professional vs. at-home mother*

Stereotypes of PMS would suggest that the high-paced professional, rather than the at-home mother, would experience high levels of stress and, therefore, be more susceptible to the ravages of the premenstrual syndrome. Although this is true to some extent, the scientific data available show that the "at-home" mother with no outside source of income is slightly more vulnerable to the psychological effects of premenstrual and menopausal hormonal changes. This may be explained by the relationship between depression and "learned helplessness" (explained in Chapter 8).

It could be possible that the at-home mother without an independent source of income may have less of a sense of control over her life and, hence, perceive fewer outside options when under stress. Any situation where a sense of control over destiny is impaired increases stress and increases the risk of depression.

If you are at home all day, make sure you retain some control and knowledge about family income, finances, and so on, and keep your mind active as much as possible with intellectually demanding hobbies. Even if you do not need an additional source of income, the positive stress and sense of control of a job skill honed on a part-time basis may help battle the psychological blues of PMS and menopause.

Working women should also recognize the relationship between their menstrual cycle and their professional accomplishments. I strongly recommend that PMS sufferers carefully adjust (when realistically possible) professional demands to match their cycle, avoiding major decisions, stressful presentations, and so on, during the premenstrual portion when emotional lability and vulnerability may lead to inaccurate perceptions and reactions.

Our society has attached a stigma to the PMS, post-pregnancy, and menopausal emotional symptoms. But this is a false label. PMS is not the whinings or hysteria of a weak or lazy person, so there is no reason to feel embarrassed or to conceal these symptoms from your doctor. These mood swings are as real and treatable as strep throat or a broken leg.

All the depressive symptoms you experience during PMS, post-pregnancy, or menopause should be addressed by a competent obstetrician/gynecologist. If thoughts of harming yourself and others occur, I strongly recommend seeking the advice of a psychiatrist or psychologist. (The specific symptoms of depression are discussed in detail in Chapter 8.)

Alternative Therapies

Acupuncture: As a trained acupuncturist, I have seen many of the emotional problems from female hormonal changes respond to specific acupuncture treatments.

Hysterectomy: Unless the ovaries are removed with the uterus, hysterectomy will not get rid of the premenstrual syndrome. In fact, because there is no uterine lining being shed with bleeding and menses, it becomes harder to track your menstrual cycles. If the ovaries are removed with the uterus, then one faces the emotional and physical changes of menopause.

Psychotherapy: I strongly recommend psychotherapy for women in whom premenstrual, post-childbirth, or menopausal symptoms reach a point where they interfere with what they would consider "normal" life functioning, interpersonal relations, and decision-making. If thoughts of suicide or other self-destructive thoughts or behaviors permeate your life, it is imperative that you seek help.

Tubal ligation: Despite many rumors, tubal ligation to prevent conception has no effect on PMS because it does nothing to the ovaries, which still cycle regularly and produce estrogen and progesterone until menopause.

Chapter 10

The Aging Brain: Is It Timeless?

In the aging process, the brain is very much like the body—it gets older. It ages, it loses function, it fails. Of course, the questions we'd like answered are: "Is this inevitable?" and "How can the aging process in the brain be slowed or halted?" Some of this information is well-understood; other pieces of the puzzle are still a mystery.

We know for a fact that as we age we gradually lose brain cells, and this loss affects function. For example, 50 percent of neurons in the visual cortex is lost by age 80. There is a similar loss in the auditory cortex from age 25 to 75. Loss in fingertip fine sensory nerve endings can reach 90 percent by age 80. Most changes seem to occur in the newest area of the cortex, called the neocortex (see the illustration on page 218), making up the outer surface of the cerebrum (what has been previously referred to as the frontal, temporal, parietal, and occipital lobes).

Despite these huge losses, brain capacity remains remarkably good in old age in some people (excluding those with degenerative diseases such as Alzheimer's and stroke-related brain damage). It is almost as if we start out with a huge army of neurons that marches into the battle of life at birth. Near the end of the battle, the army that remains consists of the best of our troops, while the other ones have died off. Instead of a weary, worn-out army, think of the aging brain as an elite force of specialized neurons weeded out from an average group of soldiers—some of whom get a consistent supply of reinforcements. This is the most recent and remarkable news to come out of brain research this decade.

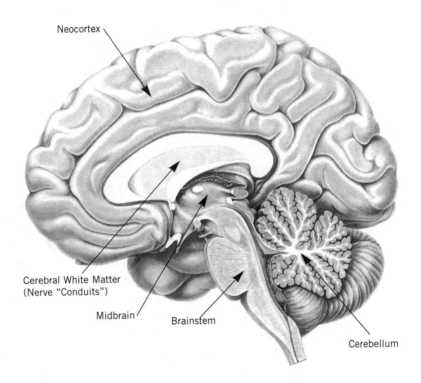

Neocortex

Cerebral White Matter
(Nerve "Conduits")

Midbrain

Brainstem

Cerebellum

Figure 10A

At the time of this writing, it was discovered that the hippocampus (the organ in the middle of the cortex, which is key in memory processing, emotions, and dealing with stress) can regenerate new cells—about 500 each day, even in the brains of the elderly. This is the first bit of evidence that the brain can produce new cells after life in the womb. Perhaps it is in the hippocampus where we have the best chance of taking advantage of the care and feeding of these new cells and, therefore, preserving the functions processed through this area of the brain. (An article in *Science* magazine that presented this study ended with speculation that regeneration might occur in other brain regions, as well, although no evidence exists to that effect at this time.)

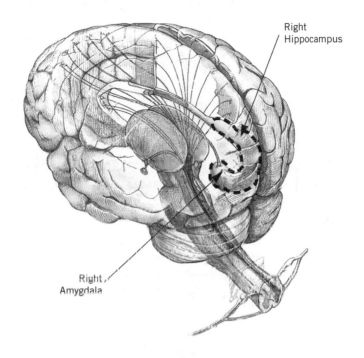

Right
Hippocampus

Right
Amygdala

FIGURE 10B

Despite this exciting news, it is also known that even in the healthiest brain, life and aging are cruel processes that kill off the weak and can leave elite troops too understaffed to function efficiently—causing impaired vision and hearing, memory loss, impaired coordination, and depression. Even with the newly discovered daily gain of 500 neurons in the hippocampus, things are still somewhat grim, from a neuroanatomy perspective, as we age. But all is not hopeless.

Aging Brain Boosters and Zappers

There are many things we do in our daily lives that both zap and boost brain power. Throughout each chapter of this book, you have been cautioned about the role of drugs, foods, supplements, and life-style choices in the maintenance of long-term brain power. Although most brain degeneration is not reversible, the care and feeding of the brain plays a key role in the functioning of remaining elite brain cells.

Late Bloomers

Think you're too old to do something new or interesting? Consider the achievements by these notable "old" people:

Boris Karloff was just an extra in many movies until his mid-40s, when he played Frankenstein in full makeup.

Alexander Fleming discovered penicillin in his 50s.

Jazz great Thelonius Monk did not achieve fame and success as a musician until the 1970s, when he was past 50.

Ian Fleming wrote the first James Bond story at age 45.

Artist Piet Mondrian did not develop his now-famous abstract style until he was almost 60.

Astronaut John Glenn made his second trip into outer space when he was a vigorous 77 years old.

Boosters and Zappers in Your Own Body

Within your own body there are many factors that determine how well your brain will function in old age. Inherited genes and life-long production of free radicals both play an important role in how the brain ages. Also, diseases such as arteriosclerosis, high blood pressure, diabetes, infections, Parkinson's disease, and thyroid dysfunction all affect the health of the brain.

Zapper: *Arteriosclerosis*

Arteriosclerosis is the deterioration of blood vessels over time. When the blood vessel walls become damaged, local inflammation occurs and cholesterol deposits clump together in these areas. All of this keeps the brain from receiving a healthy blood supply. Not only does this lead to an increased risk of stroke, but it also slowly, in step-by-step fashion, affects the brain's ability to think and remember. The elderly person who has trouble concentrating and remembering may be suffering the effects of heart disease that slowly cause brain degeneration.

Zapper: *Free radicals*

Free radicals are waste products released when the body burns its fuel (food) for energy. The nerve cells in the brain are the most differentiated and specialized cells in the body and the most metabolically active, therefore, they produce the highest number of free radicals. Under ideal conditions, these molecules are kept in check by antioxidants released by cells of the immune system or by natural antioxidant substances found in the bloodstream, certain foods you eat, and the liver. A problem occurs when too many free radicals are generated and overload the body's scavenging mechanism, weakening the cells and impairing cell function. (Excessive free radical overload can also be caused by poor nutrition, physical and emotional stress, and environmental pollution.)

Experimental evidence supports the fact that exposure to free radicals speeds the degenerative processes of aging neurons. Once cell function is impaired, brain cell memory functions are among the first to go in a process known as senile degeneration. It's also known that the production of active proteins called enzymes, which neutralize these free radicals, decreases with aging. Free radicals have such a direct effect on the aging brain that The Institute for Brain Aging at the University of California, Irvine, has implicated them as one of the mechanisms by which Alzheimer's disease is hastened.

But the picture isn't completely bleak. There is pretty good evidence that a "well-fed" brain is more resistant to the neuron degeneration and death caused by the accumulation of free radicals. (See "Foods and Supplements" later in this chapter.)

Booster & Zapper: *Genes*

Genetics play an interesting role in determining whose brain will weather the ravages of old age and whose will not. Some people's cells are simply more resistant to aging than others'. In fact, there is mounting evidence that people with Alzheimer's disease have an inherited decreased capacity to fight free radicals because they have brain cells that either produce or accumulate more of them.

Research in this area is in its infancy, but amazing work is already being done that may make genetic factors less important to the aging brain in the future. It is known, for example, that specific genes produce proteins, including enzymes (so necessary to protecting cell health). Those lucky individuals whose genes produce more of these protective enzymes are the ones who remain mentally alert well into old age. Equipped with this knowledge, it is feasible to believe that the artificial production of these enzymes in people whose genes weren't programmed for the job will someday gain the same benefits of brain longevity.

Zapper: *High blood pressure and diabetes*

High blood pressure and diabetes both wreak havoc on blood vessels going in and out of the brain. High blood pressure promotes arteriosclerosis and heart disease. Arteriosclerosis impairs blood flow to the aging brain and increases the risk of stroke. A failing heart from heart disease cannot supply adequate blood flow to the brain for clear thinking.

Diabetes, especially when blood sugar levels are poorly controlled, promotes arteriosclerosis and heart disease. Tiny blood vessels are narrowed more than with nondiabetic atherosclerosis. This promotes earlier cell loss in the brain and even faster brain aging. The effects of these diseases on the brain can be minimized by early diagnosis and treatment.

Zapper: *Infections*

Untreated infections can damage brain cells. These infections cause the body to release cytokines (compounds that are produced by an activated immune system), which directly impair brain function. This is especially important to note in the elderly, who are prone, because of loss in immune system capacity, to infections such as pneumonia. In fact, infection should be considered in any elderly person who suffers from a sudden change in mental status.

Antibiotics are almost always necessary for treating even minor bacterial infections in the elderly because of this decreased immune capacity. Viral infections, which do not respond to antibiotics but can cause similar symptoms of brain compromise, should also be considered as a possible cause for sudden mental dysfunction in the elderly.

> *Systemic diseases stress an elderly brain more than a younger brain. It is as if the remaining members of the specialized "army" of neurons, although competent enough to compensate for a major loss in numbers in healthy elderly patients, lose their ability to resist even slight systemic changes that occur in illness. Even a simple fever can cause disorientation in elderly patients, and general anesthesia produces significant cognitive deficits in the elderly that last for as long as a week.*

Booster & Zapper: *Neurotransmitters*

Adequate and balanced supplies of the neurotransmitter brain chemicals are necessary for a sharp, healthy brain. Projections of nerve cells that release the neurotransmitters acetylcholine, dopamine, histamine, norepinephrine, and serotonin act together to stimulate the higher cortex and produce a sharp and attentive state. An imbalance in the production and/or distribution of any of these chemicals will zap the brain's ability to act alertly.

The brain's supply of neurotransmitters decreases with age. You would think that this would cause a decrease in brain function—but that does not seem to happen. One possible explanation for this is the fact that as the supply of neurotransmitters decreases, so does the number of neurons that need the neurotransmitters to be activated. Also, the functional neurons that remain into old age seem to produce a maximum supply of neurotransmitters until they die. What this means is that the brain is able to maintain an adequate and balanced supply of neurotransmitters throughout its life, even when the levels drop off.

Zapper: *Parkinson's disease*

Part of the symptoms that usually occur in late Parkinson's disease (a disease caused by the loss of dopamine neurons in the nucleus of brain cells below the cortex) is an Alzheimer's-like dementia. This dementia, unlike that of actual Alzheimer's disease, responds positively to treatment with drugs (such as L-dopa and Eldepril) that replace or raise dopamine. (Refer to Chapter 3 for more details on these drugs.) Parkinson's disease patients also seem to benefit from a moderate restriction of protein in their diet.

Zapper: *Thyroid dysfunction*

Low thyroid function is common in the elderly. Surprisingly, it can mimic symptoms of depression and even Alzheimer's disease. This is because the production of the enzymes that neutralize destructive free radical molecules in brain cells is impaired by low thyroid function (called hypothyroidism). Treatment with thyroid hormone can reverse these symptoms of brain dysfunction if caught early. (Thyroid hormone treatment is not effective in treating mental degeneration in persons with normally functioning thyroid glands.)

Boosters and Zappers in Drugs

Certain drugs have a profound effect on brain function in the elderly. Drugs known to improve brain power include acetylcholinesterase inhibitors, antidepressants, aspirin, and L-dopa.

Drugs have also been known to zap brain efficiency in the elderly. The brain-zapping drugs discussed in this section are motion-sickness patches, sedatives, stimulants, and other prescription medications.

Booster: *Acetylcholinesterase inhibitors*

Acetylcholinesterase inhibitors are a class of drugs shown to improve memory in the elderly. There are three drugs available in this class that produce at least moderate improvement of memory in Alzheimer's dementia. These drugs increase acetylcholine in the brain by inhibiting the enzyme that breaks it down. These include tacrine (Cognex), donezepil (Aricept), and metrifonate (now in FDA approval stages). They all require a doctor's prescription.

Zapper: *Alcohol*

Alcohol zaps brain power in the elderly with both long-term and short-term use. Long-term consumption of alcohol impairs brain function in two ways: 1) It directly kills brain cells that cannot be replaced or rejuvenated; and 2) it deprives brain cells of B vitamins, particularly thiamin, which are vital to efficient brain function.

In the short term, alcohol will cause a more immediate and more intense disorientation and impairment in the brain of an elderly person than in a younger person. This is of particular concern in regard to drinking and driving. The legal limit that allows a younger person to drink and drive safely is not appropriate for an older person, who will suffer the effects of "drunkenness" despite having blood levels of alcohol below the legal limit. Essential properties such as reaction time and visual perception become quickly impaired, making alcohol plus advanced age plus automobile a lethal equation.

Booster: *Antidepressants*

Antidepressants can indirectly improve brain function in the elderly. The depression that is almost epidemic among the aging population causes mental problems such as memory loss, disorientation, and confusion. In fact, depression often imitates the symptoms of Alzheimer's disease. When the depression is successfully treated with antidepressant medications, brain function often returns to normal.

Booster: *Aspirin*

A daily dose of 50 to 100mg of baby aspirin or an every-other-day dose of adult-size aspirin will decrease the incidence of stroke and may cut down on arteriosclerosis in the heart and the blood vessels supplying the brain. Aspirin can do this by decreasing the inflammation that encourages the collection of cholesterol and other substances in the damaged areas of vessel walls. Before using aspirin to improve blood flow and brain power, be sure to get the okay from your physician and make sure it is discontinued at least two weeks before any surgery (you need your functioning platelets to clot well to prevent surgical bleeding).

Booster: *L-dopa*

Although the naturally occurring neurotransmitter dopamine is known to enhance memory, it is not given as a drug to improve memory because it does not cross the blood-brain barrier. The drug L-dopa, however, does cross this barrier, convert to dopamine, and deliver memory-boosting elements to the brain. L-dopa has been given to elderly patients with memory problems with impressive results, but it does not enhance memory in brain-healthy individuals.

Zapper: *Motion-sickness patches*

Scopolamine patches for motion sickness are called anticholinergic drugs. Although considered generally safe, they can effect brain function (especially in the elderly), leaving some with significant memory loss.

Anticholinergic drugs compete with the neurotransmitter acetylcholine in the brain. It is well-known that acetylcholine is absolutely necessary for memory function and that in cases of Alzheimer's dementia and Parkinson's disease (where there is extreme memory deprivation), brain acetylcholine is depleted. The scopolamine found in motion-sickness patches directly antagonizes brain acetylcholine. Although it is given only in low doses, the elderly should be forewarned that it has potent antimemory properties.

Zapper: *Sedatives*

The aging brain, because of its limited reserve of brain cells, is affected by sedatives such as Valium and barbiturates much more than the younger brain. The only sedating drugs recommended for the elderly are antidepressants and antipsychotics (Haldol and Thorazine, for example), and both only under close supervision.

Not only do sedatives more intensely affect the elderly brain, they can also result in dangerous falls. Because of loss in neurons mediating muscle position and balance, elderly people are at normal risk of falling. Sedatives increase that risk. This frequently results in fractured hips (the brittle bones of osteoporosis) and can cause a blood clot to form inside the brain when the head hits the ground.

Zapper: *Stimulants (amphetamines, caffeine, and nicotine)*

Stimulants such as amphetamines, caffeine, and nicotine all reduce the neuron "army" population. These stimulants create harmful free radicals, disrupt sleep, and in the long run or with high use, dim memory and mimic the effects of stress. You're not imagining things when you feel these substances surge to the brain and awaken its powers of concentration. At the same time, however, they sabotage any efforts to maintain the health of the brain as it ages. Because of the chronic stress-like effect stimulants have on the brain, it is shown that over time, like stress, they cause a decrease in brain mass. This alone decreases the brain's ability to function as it did years ago.

Zapper: *Other prescription drugs*

The aging brain has limited capacity to tolerate the side effects from any drug. That's why all prescription drugs should be evaluated for potential side effects on the brain in any elderly person suffering mental changes (such as memory loss, disorientation, confusion, and so on.) This can be done by looking at the package insert and by consulting your pharmacist and doctor.

Prescription drugs that commonly zap brain power in the elderly include the heart medicine digoxin, which even if slightly elevated, can produce brain side effects; many drugs used to treat heart rhythm disturbances, such as lidocaine, quinidine, and Mexitil; antihistamines, such as Benadryl and Periactin; and pain medications, including morphine, codeine, and Percocet.

The Halos of Vincent Van Gogh's Later Years

Whether myth or fact (this is debated in artistic medical circles), the story goes that the Dutch painter Vincent Van Gogh, in addition to all his purported mental afflictions later in life, suffered from the edema (swelling from fluid under the skin) of congestive heart failure—or dropsy, as it was known then. To boost his heart function, he was given a drug called digitalis. It was one of the first potent drugs to be purified from a natural source, the foxglove flower (the form used today is called digoxin or Lanoxin). One of the known brain effects of this drug, when used just slightly above therapeutic levels in the elderly, is to cause one to see halos around objects. In many of Van Gogh's later paintings, including a famous self-portrait, the central figures all have prominent halos.

Boosters and Zappers in Foods

Food has a profound effect on the way the brain ages. Carbohydrates, fats, and proteins should be eaten with care. On the other hand, foods containing antioxidants, such as vitamin C and vitamin

E, carotenoids, flavenoids, certain herbs, and vitamin B12, should be frequently included in the diet to boost brain power.

Booster: *Antioxidants*

Under ideal conditions, the free radicals that can damage brain cells are kept in check by antioxidants released by cells of the immune system or by natural antioxidant substances found in the bloodstream. But when conditions are not so ideal (such as when you eat too much fat and protein or are exposed to continuous emotional or environmental stress), you can help your body fight off excessive free radicals by increasing your intake of certain foods with antioxidant properties.

Vitamin C. Vitamin C (ascorbic acid) has potent antioxidant properties and has been proven to promote brain blood flow by enhancing production of nitric oxide, a natural vasodilator, and by blocking the effects of free radicals that can reduce blood flow to the brain. Vitamin C is found in parsley, sprouts, citrus fruits, broccoli, strawberries, potatoes, kiwi, red peppers, cabbage, and leafy greens.

Vitamin E. In researching this chapter, I found more information on the benefits of vitamin E in preventing the effects of aging in the brain than for any other topic researched. Because vitamin E is a fat chain, it fits nicely in between the fat chains of cell membranes, providing strong protection against free radical destruction. Vitamin E also directly absorbs these highly destructive and reactive free radicals by preventing disruption of the membranes around certain cell structures. It also prevents leakage of free radicals to the rest of the nerve cell. Vitamin E is found in nuts and seeds, nut oils, peanut butter, wheat germ, whole wheat, and other grain sprouts.

Carotenoids. Carotenoids consist of long carbon chains that bind particularly well to free-radical molecules and reduce their damage. Carotenoids are found in carrots, sprouts, apricots, sweet potatoes, spinach, celery, squash, red peppers, tomatoes, oranges, and kale.

Flavenoids. Flavenoids are another class of large, high-energy carbon structures that are powerful antioxidants. These are found in onions, broccoli, cabbage, turnips, cauliflower, cantaloupe (and other orange-colored fruits), peppers, bean sprouts, and selected herbs such as peppermint, spearmint, winter mint, and basil. (As an added bonus:

Broccoli, cabbage, turnips, and cauliflower are potent anticancer agents.)

Herbal remedies. Good herbal antioxidant-containing tonics to sip or sniff include green tea, black tea, alfalfa, rosehips, peppermint, nettles, hawthorn, goldenseal, fenugreek, cumin (in curry), capsicum (hot pepper), cinnamon, and basil. Of all of these, green tea has been the most closely studied for its antioxidant properties and has been found to be a potent free radical scavenger.

Booster & Zapper: *Carbohydrates*

Complex carbohydrates (whole grain wheat, rice, and potatoes) are good for the brain. Carbohydrates stimulate serotonin production in the brain, and their metabolism produces fewer destructive free radicals than the metabolism of fats or proteins.

Conversely, simple carbohydrates (sugars, honey, maple syrup, and the high fructose corn syrup in soft drinks) are not good for the brain. Because they go more rapidly from the gut to the blood, they stress the aging pancreas to make lots of insulin, which when secreted, lowers blood sugar levels to below where you started. This causes fatigue, irritability, and further hunger. In addition, your body requires vitamins to metabolize sugars. Sugars don't contain enough vitamins (especially the B vitamins) to support their own metabolism, so they have to be borrowed from your body. This can deprive the brain of the ample supply of B vitamins that are essential to normal brain function.

Zapper: *Excessively low-calorie diets*

While it's true that being overweight is an unhealthy condition, excessively low-calorie diets are also unhealthy—specifically for the brain—for three reasons:

1. Some fat is required for good brain function (see previous discussion of fat).

2. A diet that doesn't allow the body to take in enough protein to maintain current levels causes tissue loss, including in the brain.

3. The brain is fueled only by glucose or ketones (the liver makes these from metabolizing fat when the blood sugar level goes down). When you restrict your diet past a certain level, especially when you take in less than 100g of carbohydrates a day (400 calories of carbohydrates), there isn't enough glucose available for fuel, so your brain runs on ketones. Both the liver process in making ketones and the brain process of using them produces more free radicals than when glucose is used.

Given this evidence, it would seem that a moderate diet that provides adequate protein and does not cause body tissue wasting (negative protein balance) is ideal. The specific number of calories varies, but the best recommendation I have heard is to eat only when you are hungry (as opposed to when you are nervous or bored) and stop eating when you are mildly satisfied, but not full. As a life-long habit, this is definitely a brain saver.

Booster & Zapper: *Fats*

Being "fat free" is not necessarily good for the long-term health of the brain. It has been found that restricting saturated fats in animal models (the kind of fat from lard, steak, butter, and other "unhealthy" foods) actually decreases cognitive performance. Because cell membranes of nerve cells contain a delicate mixture of fats in the form of phospholipids, it is conceivable that a diet totally lacking in saturated fat might deprive the nervous system of good membrane and, hence, electrical function.

In the same way, cholesterol (made by eating saturated fats or "bad" foods directly containing cholesterol) is not always the public enemy of good health. Very low cholesterol levels can actually endanger the health of brain cells. You need a certain amount of cholesterol to keep cell membranes flexible and to protect the cells from free-radical damage.

At the same time, too much saturated fat (and the resulting high cholesterol) can be bad for brain function. A diet high in saturated fats and cholesterol can clog the blood vessels and cause arteriosclerosis, which deprives the brain of needed oxygen and nutrients. It can also lead to stroke (obviously bad for the brain) and can cause increased production of free radicals, which zap brain cells.

To get the most from fats without overdoing it, eat a balanced diet with no more than 30 percent of your calories coming from fat. This doesn't necessarily mean that you should avoid the "bad" fats completely:

Butter, for instance, is recently making a comeback because the unsaturated oils used in margarine may be worse in promoting arteriosclerosis and even cancer.

Olive oil seems to be beneficial and probably worth the expense in cooking. It has antioxidant properties and possibly also decreases blood platelet clotting activity, which reduces the risk of stroke and arteriosclerosis in the brain.

The fats in fish, especially cold-water fish such as salmon, mackerel, sardines, and tuna, seem to be very beneficial in preventing arteriosclerosis and platelet clotting activity.

When you add saturated fats and cholesterol to your diet, make sure you're not overdoing it. And remember that everybody is different—some people have a genetic tendency to make too much cholesterol and usually have a family history of heart attack and stroke at an early age (below age 50 or 60). These people need to be especially careful when adding fat to maintain brain function.

Booster & Zapper: *Protein*

Protein is essential to maintaining the structural integrity of cells in the nervous system. Neurons use a lot of protein to make microtubule structural supports, to make the transport proteins (essential to producing an electrical charge across the membrane), and to make neurotransmitters and their receptors. However, evidence is mounting that, despite the value of protein, animal proteins (found in meat) raise the risk of cancer and arteriosclerosis. (Arteriosclerosis, remember, blocks the blood vessels and reduces the flow of oxygen and nutrients to the brain.)

To get around this problem, it is best to increase your protein supply that comes from plants, instead of animals. Good sources of plant protein are beans, wheat products (pasta, for example,) and soy products (such as tofu).

Aluminum Utensils and the Risk of Alzheimer's?

Because aluminum is found in the protein tangles of dying neurons, people have blamed aluminum pots and cooking utensils for causing Alzheimer's disease. There is no good evidence at the time of writing to make this connection. In fact, it has been found that rats fed diets high in aluminum for 23 months had no increased levels of aluminum in their brains.

Booster: *Vitamin B12*

Vitamin B12 is "brain food." A shortage of vitamin B12 causes a domino effect that, bit by bit, breaks down brain function. In fact, a deficiency of vitamin B12 can lead to irreversible brain dysfunction.

It has been found that anywhere from 7 to 15 percent of older people suffer from B12 deficiency. This probably occurs because the acid content of the stomach decreases with age, so we have more difficulty absorbing B12. The elderly have a particular need to take B12 supplements to maintain full brain function. B12 is found abundantly in animal products such as red meat, eggs, and other dairy products.

Boosters and Zappers in Supplements

Supplements such as antioxidants (vitamins E and C and selenium), vitamin B12, ginkgo biloba, ginseng, melatonin, and multiminerals are all known to help keep the brain sharp as it ages.

Booster: *Antioxidants*

There are a number of antioxidant supplements that will help the body clean out the free radicals that can muddle clear thinking:

1. Vitamin E is the "Mother of all Antioxidants." I recommend 400 to 1000 units of vitamin E per day.
2. Selenium, the partner of vitamin E, is a metal necessary for the production of a free-radical absorbing protein called glutathione. The combination of selenium and vitamin E acts synergistically to decrease free radical damage to neurons. I recommend 200mcg of selenium per day.

---

3. Vitamin C has potent antioxidant properties. I recommend taking 500 to 1,000mg per day, unless you have a tendency towards kidney stones. In that case, take about half that with six to eight glasses of water per day.

Booster: *Ginkgo biloba*

Ginkgo biloba is an herbal supplement extracted from the leaves of the ginkgo tree. A large collection of impressive studies has shown that this natural herb is able to improve alertness and memory. This action is the result of multiple mechanisms:

1. Ginkgo, a free radical scavenger, has antioxidant properties.
2. Ginkgo biloba is a vasodilator, meaning it opens the pathways in the vascular system to improve circulation, allowing blood to flow freely through the body. This increased blood flow enhances brain function by sweeping out free radicals as it flows through, and by bringing in more oxygen and nutrients.
3. Ginkgo biloba inhibits platelet binding. When platelets in the blood bind together, they can cause it to clot and close up small blood vessels. When the blood can't flow freely to the brain because of these clots, the brain can suffer a relentless series of ministrokes (completely unknown to the person), that over time severely affect brain function. This is known as multi-infarct dementia.
4. Long-term use of gingko increases the number of acetylcholine receptors in the brain. This means that when acetylcholine is released in the brain, it becomes more active because there are more molecules that receive it and affect its action. (Remember, acetylcholine is vital to memory function.)

Booster: *Ginseng*

Ginseng is extremely popular for its supposed ability to "balance" brain function. Ginseng does this possibly by modulating chemical activities such as the release of cortisol. Some cortisol is needed to help you deal with stress, but too much can damage brain cells. Ginseng may also regulate serotonin release. Some serotonin is good for keeping your mood up; too much will cause fatigue and lethargy.

Working in this way with many systems of the body, ginseng may enable the brain to maintain an ideal, stable state of arousal.

Booster: *Melatonin*

Because melatonin is a hormone that sets the body's clock to the cycles of night and day, synthetic melatonin is often used to treat sleep problems. More recent studies show that in addition to promoting sleep rhythms in the brain, this hormonal supplement is probably also a potent antioxidant. This makes melatonin another agent in the battle against the long-term brain cell damage and cell loss caused by excessive free radicals. For this purpose, melatonin should be taken at bedtime to avoid daytime drowsiness, in a dose of 3mg (or half that if you have morning grogginess).

Booster: *Multimineral supplements*

Many trace minerals such as zinc, magnesium, copper, and manganese, are required for normal function of many of the protein enzymes necessary for the high level of metabolism in active brain cells. However, unless your diet is extremely varied and well-balanced, you may be missing one or several of these key trace elements. I recommend a daily multivitamin/multimineral supplement tablet to maintain efficient brain function in the elderly.

Booster: *Vitamin B12*

The B vitamins are crucial to normal nerve function—especially vitamin B12. As you age, your capacity to produce a stomach protein called intrinsic factor—necessary for B12 absorption—decreases, so that less B12 from the foods you eat is absorbed by the body. Because B12 is so crucial to normal nerve function, I recommend taking 200 to 400mcg per day in a sublingual form that is directly absorbed into the bloodstream from under the tongue, bypassing the digestive tract completely. Otherwise, a monthly injection of B12 by your physician will do.

Boosters and Zappers in Lifestyle

Although lifestyle is covered last in all chapters, it is in fact the first step before all others in minimizing the effects of aging on your brain. You can take all the supplements you want, but making life-style choices (such as smoking, avoiding exercise, or feeling angry, bored, or passive) puts you at great risk for brain cell loss that cannot be combated with foods or vitamins. You can keep the aging brain alert and sharp through positive lifestyle choices.

Booster: *Attitude*

The way your brain ages is directly related to the way you view life. If you are miserable, unhappy, bored, burnt out, or unchallenged, your brain feels chronically stressed (which is very bad for its health). Studies leave no doubt that negative feelings in both animals and humans cause high levels of stress hormones, such as cortisol and adrenaline, to flood the brain. Over time, these stress hormones definitely reduce brain mass and cognitive ability. The effects can be so drastic that elderly patients suffering depression can develop an Alzheimer's-like syndrome in which they suffer the memory loss and cognitive incapacity or "dementia" of someone with Alzheimer's disease. The symptoms are indistinguishable.

On the other hand, a positive attitude and outlook have been shown to help keep the brain young and healthy. It allows all systems to remain strong and functioning correctly. Blood flows freely, oxygen supplies remain plentiful, free radical production is reduced, and the levels of stress hormones are kept low. All these things contribute to mental sharpness. The lifestyle recommendations in Chapter 6 that include exercise, sleep, social contact, diversion exercises, and relaxation exercises can all help you keep a positive mental outlook that will keep the aging brain from senility.

If you're feeling depressed or trapped in your current lifestyle, it is never too late to seek the help of a trained psychotherapist. It will be good for the quality of your daily life and for the health of your brain.

Booster: *Exercise*

The health benefits of exercise for the elderly are shouted from the mountaintops throughout the country. Exercise strengthens the heart, firms muscles, lowers cholesterol levels, opens clogged arteries, trims the waist, boosts mood, and makes one more resilient to stress. The list of benefits for the elderly derived from exercise is quite long— but it is incomplete without the addition of its brain-boosting powers.

The Care and Feeding of Your Brain

Without a doubt, exercise gives the brain many of the things it needs to function at full power:

1. Exercise is known to raise baseline serotonin levels in the brain. (This alone will decrease depression and improve sleep patterns—automatically improving concentration.)

2. Exercise decreases the amount of hydrocortisone in the brain. (Hydrocortisone is the chemical released during stress, which in excess, can cause depression and eventually shrink brain mass through cell death.)

3. Exercise improves circulation, allowing blood to flow freely through the body. This increased blood flow enhances brain function by sweeping out free radicals and by bringing in more oxygen and nutrients.

4. Exercise has been shown to bring the brain into an aroused, awake state.

Obviously, lack of exercise robs the body of all of these benefits. If you want to keep your brain young and strong, exercise should be on your list of things to do every day. (Exercise only under a physician's supervision, particularly if you suffer from high blood pressure, diabetes, or heart disease.)

Booster: *Medical checkups*

Many diseases and ailments of aging directly affect the brain. Diabetes, high blood pressure, and infections, to name a few (as well as the medications used to treat them), all influence the capabilities of the brain. Regular medical checkups allow you and your doctor to stay on top of problems that, if neglected, can zap brain power.

Booster: *Meditation and prayer*

Meditation and prayer are excellent brain-power boosters because they battle stress. Their ability to promote synchronized brain rhythms and reduce stress hormone levels makes them important tactics for combating the negative effects of long-term stress on the brain. In the elderly these stress-reducing techniques are especially beneficial. Many elderly who lead productive lives well into their eighth and ninth decades report certain daily rituals, such as meditation and prayer, that add regularity and a sense of calm to their lives.

Meditation and prayer both give you some control over the way your brain ages. Give them a try!

Booster: *Mental and social activity*

Just like your body, your brain needs exercise to stay fit. You can't let it sit around doing nothing day after day and then expect it to jump to full capacity when you suddenly want to have an interesting conversation with an old friend. You'll find yourself forgetting, stumbling, and feeling quite senile. It's vital to keep the aging brain active through both mental and social activities.

Mental activities are anything that engages your brain. Crossword puzzles are an excellent brain exercise, as are board and card games, reading, writing, and talking. Hobbies that require active thinking (such as making, building, or repairing anything) are excellent pastimes. Things that challenge you to advance and improve (learning to play the piano or paint, for example) are also brain boosters. Don't spend too much of your time on things that require little brain power (like staring out a window or watching TV).

Social activity is also good for keeping the brain cells active and alive. We are social animals by nature and seem to require a certain amount of positive interaction with other human beings to maintain mental alertness. Studies have shown that social contact can even dampen the hormonal stress response of brain and body in difficult times. All your life you should strive to be socially active. Cultivate friendships. Look outward, not always inward, for mental stimulation. The aging brain needs this kind of interaction to stay sharp.

Booster & Zapper: *Sleep habits*

Your sleep needs and time in REM sleep decrease with age. This means that people older than 60 years of age probably need less than the traditionally recommended seven to eight hours of sleep a night. Less REM time, however, also means less time allowed for the nightly cleanup of amine alertness neurotransmitters, such as serotonin and norepinephrine (so important for wakefulness, alertness, and good mood). It also means less time given to the incorporation of short-term memory traces into long-term storage. Over time, less REM sleep results in less efficient brain function in the elderly.

This situation is compounded by the insomnia that plagues many elderly people and affects brain function. The National Sleep Foundation tells us that those who persistently don't get enough sleep report the following:

♦ Impaired ability to concentrate during the day.

♦ Memory problems.

♦ Difficulty coping with minor irritations.

The sleep syndrome of apnea is also responsible for inadequate sleep in the elderly. Signaled by heavy snoring and moments of what seems like breath holding, this syndrome can deprive the body and brain of oxygen for up to several minutes at a time. The long-term effects of this oxygen deprivation (and release of stress hormones during these periods of apnea), combined with the fatigue and stress it can cause during the day, can trim your "army" of brain neurons much sooner than necessary.

You can boost the aging brain that suffers sleep problems with medical help and daily power naps. There are medical treatment programs that can cure or reduce the occurrence of insomnia and apnea, so it's very important for the elderly to speak to their physicians about any sleeping problems they may have. Not only can these problems affect the way they feel during the day, they can also affect the way the brain holds up over time. In addition, the elderly should not ignore the body's cry for a nap during the day. This nap gives the brain another chance to do the job of cleaning up excess neurotransmitters, of sending memories to long-term storage, and of boosting its capacity for sharp and clear thinking.

Zapper: *Smoking*

The damage done to physical health by smoking is well-known by now. Add to this list the damage it causes to your brain! There are many reasons related to mental health for the elderly to break the smoking habit. These include:

1. Smoking has been proven to promote brain cell loss in the cortex.

2. Smoking has been proven to promote high blood pressure and heart disease. A sick heart will make the blood flow to your brain and body so lousy that your normal activities will be blunted, making you what doctors refer to as a "cardiac cripple." The effects on the cardiovascular system also result in blood vessels clogging in the brain, known as "stroke," a rapid way to permanently lose a few billion nerve cells in a few minutes.

3. If your heart doesn't go and the brain cells hold out, your lungs will degenerate. (All long-time smokers have emphysema.) Losing your breathing capacity can make you what doctors refer to as a "pulmonary cripple," with brain cells deprived of adequate oxygen and prone to damage.

Smoking is a brain zapper. You cannot smoke and expect to be mentally alert in old age. It's as simple as that.

Zapper: *Television*

The amount of time we dedicate to the boob tube is frightening and brain damaging. Some estimates are as high as three and four hours each day for the average person. Imagine how that adds up over 60 years or so! Active use of the body and mind is a proven method of maintaining good brain function. Unfortunately, television involves no active mental processes and no physical activity.

I always found it ironic that when you watch TV, you passively watch someone else actively and productively engage in life. Think how boring a TV show would be if all it depicted were a couch potato watching another TV show for an hour.

Indeed, it's what you don't do because of TV that makes it a brain zapper. You don't read, converse, interact socially, exercise, enjoy nature, or meditate. Every hour spent watching the tube is an hour spent in passive engagement of your mind that could have been otherwise been spent in productive and challenging brain activity. (Even a nap with its restorative powers, is better for your brain than a TV show.) Want to give your brain a boost? Turn off the TV set.

The Care and Feeding of Your Brain

It is a crime by our civilization that we expect our elderly to be forgetful, disorganized, and even senile. It is not inevitable that the brain will fail us in old age. In most cases, senility is a physical event that happens because of the way we have lived, because of the things we have eaten, because of the illnesses and medications that have stressed the brain over the years. How exciting to learn that with proper care and feeding, the brain, like every other body organ, can remain healthy and functioning to the end of our lives.

Bibliography

Algeri, S. "Potential strategies against age-related brain deterioration. Dietary and pharmacological approaches." *Annals of the NY Academy of Science.* 1992:663:376.

Arky, R., et al., eds. *Physicians' Desk Reference, 52nd ed.* Montvale, NJ: Medical Economics Press, 1998.

Baker, L.S. "Smart drugs: a caution to everybody." *American Journal of Psychiatry.* 1998:153:844.

Barinaga, M. "New leads to brain neuron regeneration." *Science.* 1998:282:1018-19.

Baskys, A., and G. Remington, eds. *Brain Mechanisms and Psychotropics.* New York: WW Norton & Co., 1998.

Beauchemin, K.M., and P. Hays. "Prevailing mood, mood changes and dreams in bipolar disorder." *Journal of Affective Disorders.* Oct 9, 1995:35(1-2):41-9.

Bertoni-Freddari, C., et al. "Vitamin E deficiency as a model of precocious brain aging." *Scanning Microscopy.* 1995:9:289.

Betz, J.M., K.D. White, and A.H. der Marderosian. "Gas chromatographic determination of yohimbine in commercial yohimbe products." *Journal of AOAC International.* Sep-Oct 1995:78(5):1189-94.

Bisset, N.G., ed. *Herbal Drugs.* Boca Raton, FL: CRC Press, 1994.

Bisset, N.G., ed. *Herbal Drugs and Phyctopharmaceuticals: A handbook for practice on a scientific basis.* Boca Raton, FL: CRC Press, 1989.

Bloom, F.E., and A. Lazerson, eds. *Brain Mind and Behavior 2nd Ed.* New York: WH Freeman & Co., 1988.

Budeiri, D., et al. "Is evening primrose oil of value in the treatment of premenstrual syndrome?" *Control Clinical Trials.* 1996:17(1):60.

Butterfield, D.A., et al. "Free radical oxidation of brain proteins in accelerated senescence." *Procedures of the National Academy of Science.* 1997:94:647.

Carlisle, E.M., et al. "Effect of dietary silicon and aluminum on silicon and aluminum levels in rat brain." *Alzheimer's Disease and Associated Disorders.* 1987:1:83.

Cassileth, B.R. *Alternative Medicine Handbook.* New York: WW Norton & Co., 1998.

Chevallier, A. *The Encyclopedia of Medicinal Plants.* New York: DK Publishing, 1996.

Chun, J.C., et al. "Neurotoxicity of free-radical-mediated serotonin neurotoxin in cultured embryonic chick brain neurons." *European Journal of Pharmacology.* 1996:303:109.

Cooper, J.R., F.E. Bloom, and R.H. Roth. *The Biochemical Basis of Neuropharmacology, 7th ed.* New York: Oxford University Press, 1996.

Couzin, J. "Low-calorie diets may slow monkeys' aging." *Science.* 1998:282:1018.

Davison, J.K., ed. *Clinical Anesthesia Procedures of the Massachusetts General Hospital, 4th ed.* Boston: Little Brown, 1993.

"Deaths associated with a purported aphrodisiac—New York City, February 1993–May 1995." *MMWR Morbidity Mortality Weekly Report.* Nov 24, 1995:44(46):853-5.

Delmonte, M.M. "Case reports on the use of meditative relaxation as an intervention strategy with retarded ejaculation." *Biofeedback and Self Regulation.* June 1984:9(2):209-14.

DiGeronimo, Theresa. *Insomnia.* New York: Penguin Books, 1997.

Electronic Gourmet Guide, Inc., The. "Did You Know...?" Available at: http://www.foodwine.com/food/egg/egg0298/didyouknow.html. Date accessed: September 29, 1998.

Eskeland, B., E. Thom, and K.O. Svendsen. "Sexual desire in men: Effects of oral ingestion of a product derived from fertilized eggs." *Journal of Internal Medical Research.* March-April 1997:25(2):62-70.

Gabbita, S.P., et al. "Aging and caloric restriction." *Free Radical Biology and Medicine.* 1997:23:191.

Gautier-Smith, P.C. "Cerebral dysfunction and disorders of sexual behavior." *Review Neurologica* (Paris). 1980:136(4):311-9.

Ghadirian, A.M., L. Annable, and M.C. B'elanger. "Lithium, benzodiazepines, and sexual function in bipolar patients." *American Journal of Psychiatry.* June 1992:149(6):801-5.

Gill, Brendan. *Late Bloomers.* New York: Artisan, 1996.

Gurney, W. "10 ways to sharpen your memory." *McCall's.* Nov 1996:124(2)92.

Hardman, J.G., and L.E. Limbird, Editors. *Goodman and Gilman's: The pharmacological basis of therapeutics, 9th ed.* New York: McGraw Hill, 1996.

Harman, D., et al. "Free radical theory of aging: effect of dietary fat on central nervous system function." *Journal of the American Geriatric Society.* 1976:24:301.

Hassmen, P., et al. "Mood, physical working capacity and cognitive performance in the elderly as related to physical activity." *Aging.* Feb-April 1997:9(1-2):136-42.

Hobson, A. *Sleep.* New York: WH Freeman & Co., 1989 (rev. 1995).

Horvitz, Leslie Alan. "Forgetful seniors may thank smart drugs for their memories." *Insight on the News.* 20 Jan:40: 1997.

Howard, P.J. *The Owner's Manual for the Brain.* Austin, TX: Leornian Press Bard Productions, 1994.

Huerta, R., et al. "Symptoms of perimenopausal period: its association with attitudes toward sexuality, life-style, family function, and FSH levels." *Psychoneuroendocrinology.* 1995:20(2):135.

Joseph, J.A., et al. "Cholesterol: A two-edged sword in brain aging." *Free Radical Biology and Medicine.* 1997:22:455.

Kalgutar, A.S., et al. "Aspirin-like molecules that covalently inactivate cyclooxygenase-2." *Science.* 1998:280:1268.

Kandel, E.R., J.H. Schwartz, and T.M. Jessel, eds. *Essentials of Neural Science and Behavior.* Stamford, CT: Appelton and Lange, 1995.

Kandel, E.R., J.H. Schwartz, and T.M. Jessel. *Principles of Neural Science 3rd Ed.* New York: Simon & Schuster, 1991.

Kelley, K., and D. Musialowski. "Repeated exposure to sexually explicit stimuli: novelty, sex, and sexual attitudes." *Archives of Sexual Behavior.* Dec 1986:15(6):487-98.

Khachaturian, Z.S. "The role of calcium regulation in brain aging." *Aging.* 1989:1:17.

Khalsa, Dharma Singh, et al. *Brain Longevity.* New York: Warner Books, 1997.

Koch, M.E., et al. "The sedative and analgesic sparing effect of music." *Anesthesiology.* 1998:89:300.

Li, et al. "Clinical course of gamma-hydroxybutyrate overdose." *Annals of Emergency Medicine.* 1998:31:716.

Llinas, R.R., ed. *Readings from Scientific American/The Workings of the Brain: Development, Memory, and Perception.* New York: WH Freeman & Co., 1990.

Mano, T., et al. "Changes in lipid peroxidation and free radical scavengers in the brain of hyper- and hypothyroid aged rats." *Journal of Endocrinology.* 1995:147.

Marksbery, W.R. "Oxidative stress hypothesis in Alzheimer's Disease." *Free Radical Biology and Medicine.* 1997:23:134.

Meng, I.D., et al. "An analgesia circuit activated by cannabinoids." *Nature.* 1998:395:381.

Menken, B.Z., et al. "Organic solvent soluble lipofuscin pigments and glutathione peroxidase in mouse brain and heart: effects of age and vitamin." *Journal of Nutrition.* 1986:116:350.

Mo, J.Q., et al. "Decreases in protective enzymes correlates with increased oxidative damage in the aging mouse brain." *Mechanisms of Aging and Development.* 1995:81:73.

Morriss, R., M. Sharpe, et al. "Abnormalities of sleep in patients with chronic fatigue syndrome." *British Medical Journal.* May 1, 1993:1161-4.

Murray, J.B. "Psychopharmacological therapy of deviant sexual behavior." *Journal of General Psychology.* Jan 1988:115(1):101-110.

Nagy, I.Z. "Semiconduction of proteins as an attribute of the living state: the ideas of Albert Azent-Gyorgyi revisited in light of the recent knowledge regarding oxygen free radicals." *Experimental Gerontology.* 1995:30:327.

National Sleep Foundation. *The Nature of Sleep.* Washington, DC: The National Sleep Foundation, 1995.

National Sleep Foundation. *When You Can't Sleep.* Washington, DC: The National Sleep Foundation, 1994.

Natural Medicine Collective. *The Natural Way of Healing Chronic Pain.* NY: Dell Publishing, 1995.

Nicholls, J.G., A.R. Martin, and B.G. Wallace. *From Neuron to Brain, 3rd ed.* Sunderland, Massachusetts: Sinauer Associates, 1992.

Panser, L.A., T. Rhodes, C.J. Girman, et al. "Sexual function of men ages 40 to 79 years: The Olmsted County study of urinary symptoms and health status among men." *Journal of the American Geriatric Society.* Oct 1995:43(10):1107-11.

Ramirez-Exposito, M.J., et al. "The molecular basis of neurodegenerative processes in the central nervous system." *Review of Neurology.* 1998:26:91.

Reiter, R.J. "Oxidative processes and antioxidative defense mechanisms in the aging brain." *FASEB Journal.* 1995:9:526.

Reiter, R.J., et al. "Prophylactic actions of melatonin in oxidative neurotoxicity." *Annals of the NY Academy of Science.* 1997:825:70.

Ridley, M. *The Red Queen: Sex and the Evolution of Human Nature.* New York: Penguin Books, 1993.

Rowe, J., and Robert Kahn. *Successful Aging.* New York: Pantheon Books, 1998.

Sadow, T.F., et al. "Effects of hypothalamic peptides on the aging brain." *Psychoneuroendocrinology*. 1992:17:293.

Sapolsky, R.M. *Why Zebras Don't Get Ulcers*. New York: WH Freeman & Co., 1994.

Sastre, J., et al. "A ginkgo biloba extract prevents mitochondrial aging by protecting against oxidative stress." *Free Radical Biology and Medicine*. 1998:24:298.

Satoh, T., et al. "Walking exercise and improved neurophysiological functioning in elderly patients with cardiac disease." *Journal of Internal Medicine*. 1995:238:423.

Schardt, D., and S. Schmidt. "Fear of forgetting." *Nutrition Action Healthletter*. May 1997:24(4):3.

Schardt, D., and S. Schmidt. "Matching memories." *Nutrition Action Healthletter*. May 1997:24 (4)3.

Schardt, D., and S. Schmidt. "Who ya gonna call?" *Nutrition Action Healthletter*. May 1997:24(4)3.

Schwartz, G. *In Bad Taste: The MSG Syndrome*. Santa Fe, NM: Health Press, 1989.

Segarra, A.C., and F.L. Strand. "Perinatal administration of nicotine alters subsequent sexual behavior and testosterone levels of male rats." *Brain Research*. Feb 20, 1989:480(1-2):151.

Selye, H. *The Stress of Life*. New York: McGraw-Hill, 1984.

Soininen, H., et al. "Diabetes and brain atrophy: a CT study in an elderly population." *Neurobiology of Aging*. 1992:13:717.

"Stress can cause—um I forget." *Forbes*. Nov. 18, 1996:158(12)S105.

Swabb, D.F., L.J. Gooren, and M.A. Hofman. "Brain research, gender and sexual orientation." *Journal of Homosexuality*. 1995:28:283-301.

Tanaka, M., et al. "Aging of the brain and vitamin E." *Journal of Nutritional Science and Vitaminology*. 1992:240.

Task Force on DSM-IV. *Diagnostic and Statistical Manual of Mental Disorders, 4th ed*. Washington, DC: American Psychiatric Association, 1994.

Trichopoulou, A. "Diet and overall survival in elderly people." *British Medical Journal.* 1995:311:1457.

Trichopoulou, A., et al. "Diet and survival of elderly Greeks: a link to the past." *American Journal of Clinical Nutrition.* 1995:61:1346S.

Tytgat, J., and P. Daenens. "Solvent-free sample preparation by headspace solid-phase microextraction applied to the tracing of n-butyl nitrite abuse." *International Journal of Legal Medicine.* 1996:109(3):150-4.

Walker, D., et al. "The relationship of loneliness, social isolation, and physical health to dietary adequacy of elderly." *Journal of the American Dietary Association.* 1991:91:300.

Wermuth, L., and E. Stenager. "Sexual problems in young patients with Parkinson's disease." *Acta Neurologica Scandinavica.* June 1995:91(6):453-5.

White, J.R., D.A. Case, et al. "Enhanced sexual behavior in exercising men." *Archives of Sexual Behavior.* June 1990:19(3):193-209.

Wurtman, J., and S. Suffes. *The Serotonin Solution.* Columbine, New York: Foset, 1997.

Zhou, Y., et al. "Free radical formation in autopsy samples of Alzheimer and control cortex." *Neuroscience Letters.* 1995:195:89.

Zimmerberg, B., and J.M. Reuter. "Sexually dimorphic behavioral and brain asymmetries in neonatal rats: effects of prenatal alcohol exposure." *Brain Research Development. Brain Research.* April 1, 1989:46(2):281-90.

About the Author

Kenneth Giuffré, M.D., received his degree from Johns Hopkins University School of Medicine, then went on to train in Anesthesiology at Harvard Medical School/Massachusetts General Hospital. During medical school he worked in the area of stress research with the National Institutes of Health, for which he received the Lamport Prize for excellence in biomedical research. He went on to train in medical acupuncture at UCLA and currently practices clinical anesthesiology, pain management, and acupuncture. He has received NIH grant funding for recent physiology monitoring research, which now centers on the areas of brain and body state monitoring, stress responses to labor pain, and using artificial intelligence to predict outcomes in patients.

Index